HELMETS, HANDCU
HOSES

The Story of The Wallasey Police
Part One

de

THE WALLASEY POLICE

by
Noel E Smith

Published by the Author:
"Sandheys" 164 Rake Lane,
Wallasey CH45 1JP
Tel: 0151 639 6923

Design and Origination:
Ian Boumphrey
Tel/Fax: 0151 608 7611
e-mail: ian@yesterdayswirral.co.uk

Printed by:
Printfine Ltd Gibraltar Row Liverpool L3 7HJ
Tel: 0151 242 0000 Website: www.printfine.co.uk

ISBN 0-9517762-3-1

Price
£6.95

Dedication

These two volumes are dedicated to all the members of the
Old Wallasey Borough Police
and
Wallasey Borough Fire Brigade.

Author's Note

This is not an official history of Policing in Wallasey, nor that of the Fire Service. Rather, it is a look into those services from an outside observation, based on research and stories given to me. I apologise beforehand, should some of the facts and events be not quite accurate. I also apologise for all those Police Officers and Firemen whom I have failed to mention. There have been many faithful Officers who have served the town over the years and I am sure they, or their families, have stories to tell. I am always happy to hear from readers, should they care to write to me. I hope you all enjoy these two volumes.

Noel E Smith

By the same author:

Nonfiction
Almost an Island
Sandstone and Mortar

Fiction
Stories of a Wallasey Detective

Annual Inspection in the grounds of the Navy League, Withens Lane 1939

Law and Order
Early Days

Some form of Policing in this country has existed since the time of Alfred the Great.

The ancient Courts from Anglo-Saxon times were responsible for seeing that law and order was maintained in the land. The adults of each settlement were expected to see that their families and others in the settlement abided by the laws. Those that offended were brought before the community. A chief settler, known as a Tythingman, would be in charge of about ten or twelve families. We then had what was known as the Hundred - an area of land that contained approximately one hundred families. Wallasey was a part of the Wirral Hundred. The Wirral Hundred became larger than other hundreds in that it reached 405. This number stands for heads of families and the population would have been well over 2,000, including 12 foreigners and 23 Radmen (or Riding Men - who did some sort of service on the road).

In pre-Norman times the Tythingman was under the Hundredman. Those who broke the law were brought before the Shire-reeve (Sheriff). In cases where a community did not comply, they were faced with a fine that each settler had to contribute to. Punishment included fightwitt, frithbrec and grithbrec.

The nearest equivalent to our present day Constable is the Tythingman who was the Borsholder or Headborough.

As time went on the King stated that if they obeyed the laws of the kingdom he would establish a state of peace throughout the land, known as the King's Peace, hence the wording, 'causing a breach of the Peace.' The Justices of the Peace were appointed.

Everyone over twelve years of age was expected to chase anyone who committed a serious crime (a felon). It had been King Canute who had made tything compulsory.

The Normans improved the laws by introducing the *Frankpledge* to the system. It required certain people, through their townships, to promise to be of good behaviour or they could end up in trouble if the promise was broken. It was a forerunner of the present bail system.

The Normans had Constables as an office in the Royal Courts; in castles and as High Constable in charge of the Hundred and lesser Constables whose responsibility was that of a village, Manor or to take charge of tything.

The name 'Constable' was used in Norman times and refers to a master of the stable (from the Latin *comes stabuli*). These Officers eventually took the duty of the ancient Tythingman, though they had little in common. They had to report any unusual happenings that were going on in their neighbourhood to the Sheriff.

A law was passed in 1166 that forced villages to report to the sheriff's tourns (Courts) any suspicious acts of their numbers and those who were lingering around after dark. Also those who did not seem to be working for their living.

The Manorial Courts replaced the Sheriff's Courts which elected Constables to keep the King's Peace.

As early as 1195, it was expected that every able-bodied man should join in the 'Hue and Cry' in pursuit of offenders or get into trouble if they failed to do so.

The Magna Carta (AD 1215) used the word 'Constable' to describe a man who exercised judicial powers over those who sheltered in his castle. We still have the Constable of the Tower of London.

In 1233 the citizens and burgesses, free tenants, villeins and others between the ages of 16 and 60 had to take their turn of 'Watch and Ward' in every city, borough and township.

Men were later elected to act as a sort of guard to perform police duties on behalf of their fellow citizens. This was voluntary at first but they later received payment.

One of the early prisons in England was that of Chester which had been established in 1237.

In 1252, a statute was passed that gave the Norman Constable similar powers to that of a Mayor or Bailiff. Later, the office became more important being the annually elected representative of the Parish or Manor and was recognised by the Crown.

Boundaries often caused problems in early days as they were not clearly defined and resulted in law suits. On 1 June 1260 William Sansum sued Hamon de Mascy and other persons over pasture land in Kirkeby (Wallasey). De Mascy denied that the land was in Kirkeby and said it was in Budeston (Bidston) in his land. The Court agreed and gave him the verdict.

Others also brought claims before the Court concerning land in Lisecark (Liscard) and Pulton (Poulton). One Robert de Pulle was awarded 6d damages. Another case in 1260 saw the same man win an action against Henry de Becheton and others for taking the crop of heath and broom from his field, known as Heiefeld, in Lisecark. He was awarded 6d damages.

Jurors date from early times. A property qualification was first established in 1285.

The Statute of Winchester of 1285 with its object 'to abate the powers of felons' and the cities that had walls adopted a system of Watch and Ward. Watchmen were appointed from the citizen but if they failed to act, they could be placed in the stocks along side the law-breakers. The Hue and Cry system was introduced again in which everyone was responsible for chasing the fugitive. Male adults were expected to keep arms in their houses, whether it be the humble bow and arrow of the peasant or elegant sword, helmet and other weapon of the richer man who had a horse.

The High Constable of the Hundred could order the use of them and would pay a visit every six months to inspect the weapons. The Shires for the County and the Hundred for the Hundred, the latter being under the Wakentake Court.

As regards the Moreton and Saughall Massie areas, one sees that in 1323 Lucy, wife of Robert, son of Henry de Salghal, obtained by fine from Richard the Earl, a tenement in Salghal Masey (Saughall Massie).

This half timbered cottage which stood on what is now the corner of Saughall Massie Road and Saughall Road was rebuilt in 1690. In 1953 Mr Robert Blackburn Hill decided to rebuild the cottage, using some of the sandstone from the old white-washed two storey cottage in the new construction.

There has been several disputes over lands owned by the de Mascy and the de Moreton families over the years. Indeed, the township of Moreton was fined in 1359 for failing to be properly represented at the Judge's Eyre Court in Wirral.

In 1402 a special Hundred Jury were called to deal with letters patent issued by the Prince of Wales concerning a number of men who had driven cattle out of Wales into the Hundred of Wirral.

They commissioned Sir John Mascy of Puddington, Hamon de Mascy and Richard de Morton to arrest the offenders and bring them to Chester Castle for judgement.

Taken from the County jail
By a set of curious chances;
Liberated then on bail,
On my own recognizances.

WS Gilbert

William, the son of Thomas de Poulton and Thomas de Saynesbury, was in office at the Wakentake Courts in the 1380s. There was even a Coroner's Court as early as 1309 in Wirral.

It is recorded that one Thomas from Poulton was killed by Henry de Walley in self defence. The wounded Henry was taken to Chester Castle and was later released on payment of 40 pence fine as he had acted in self defence.

On 29 September 1350 William, the son of William Alcock, stole 22 ells of linen from William Morley at Seacombe and sold it. The same person got into further trouble when he and his wife, Margery and his servant, John Poole, assaulted William, son of Roger of Seacombe on Sunday 26 May 1353 at Seacombe. They were brought before the Court but denied the charge. The Jury found William guilty of both crimes; his wife of the second. The servant was not guilty of the second charge. He and his wife were fined 6/8d. Pledges: Richard Hough and Robert Poole on pain £5 to be on good behaviour.

There were also three separate cases brought before Court.

Thomas Wallasey, monk at Birkenhead, for assaulting Richard Jolibrid on 6 May 1353 at Moreton, against the Earl's Peace; William Goss faced a charge of forcibly entering John Lasselles's mill at Seacombe and taking away a bushell of corn; and Richard Cook (both of Puddington), faced a charge of assaulting Adam Fillcock. All admitted their guilt. Thomas was fined five shillings (pledge Henry Chirleton); William, one shilling and sixpence (pledge John Lasselles and John Danyan) and Richard two shillings (pledge Richard Hough).

The Jurors of Wirral were presented with the case of Matthew Wallasey who assaulted William Bechyngton with a stick on about 31 May 1349 at Wallasey. He was also charged with assaulting William Porter at Seacombe on about 29 September 1347. He pleaded not guilty. He was found guilty of the assault of Porter but not of Bechyngton. He was fined 6/6d. Pledges: Hamo Massy and Thomas Wheelock.

Thomas, son of William Seacombe was deprived of land in the Township of Poulton by William, son Thomas Poulton, tenant of Richard Hough. Thomas went to see Richard at Thornton Hough on 14 June 1350 and begged him to engineer the recovery of the lands. Richard refused unless Thomas agreed to give him a third of the land in question. It was agreed that Richard would go to the Court on Thomas' behalf on the understanding he receive his third part then.

They prosecuted William so fiercely that he stood in fear of death and gave them a portion of the land. Regarding the rest of the land in Poulton, Thomas took William to Court whereupon Richard then acquired the same lands. All pleaded not guilty.

The Jury found that

A) John Domville (who faced another charge), Richard Hough and Robert Poole guilty of taking £13.6/6d from Henry Samson's goods.

B) John Domville guilty of concealing treasure trove; Richard Hough not guilty.

C) Richard Hough guilty of champerty.

Domville was fined five pounds (Pledges: Hamo Massy and another). Richard Hough, twenty pounds (Pledges:` Sir Hugh Venables and Robert Poole).

On 9 June 1348, John Lasselles, took a boat from Seacombe Pool belonging to William Coyde and William, son of William Alcock, to carry turves. He damaged the boat and lost an anchor and another boat's tackle. The two Williams went to Lascelles for compensation bur he threatened them and they were afraid to prosecute him.

Lasselles assaulted John Tyross at Liscard on Tuesday 27 July 1350, tying him to a post then compelling him to become his servant. On Monday 10 May 1350 he assaulted John the Miller, Henry Litherland's servant at Poulton and forced him to leave Henry's service and work at his own mill instead.

On 15 August 1352 he went to Matthew Wallasey in Wallasey and struck his servant.

He was also charged with assaulting Richard Sampson at Poulton for firing arrows at him, forcing him to leave the country, not daring to return home.

This was not the end of the matter. For his misdeeds he was charged with compelling his brother, Robert Lasselles to assault Adam Gray, a boatman at Birkenhead on Monday 9 April 1352.

John Lasselles admitted he had damaged the boat belonging to the two Williams but denied all the other charges.

The Jury found him guilty of striking Matthew Wallasey's servant and causing his brother to assault Gray but not guilty of assaulting John Tyross, John the Miller nor the case concerning Richard Sampson.

He was fined one pound. Pledges were given by Thomas Hockenhull and William Stanley, on pain of twenty pounds to be on good behaviour.

William, son of Roger Seacombe, complained that William, son of William Seacombe forcibly entered his ship on the banks of the Mersey at Seacombe on Monday 6 November 1340 and took 22 ells of woollen cloth which was worth £2 and made off with it.

He was found guilty, had to pay damages of 6/8d and was committed to gaol.

William Seacombe complained that William and Margery Seacombe and John Poole assaulted him at Seacombe on 18 August 1353 and threw him down a hill. The Jury found them guilty and they were sent to gaol.

Also before the Court was Roger Newbolt who had assaulted Richard Jolybrid. He admitted the offence and was fined 3/4d (Pledges: William Gregory and John Warwick, on pain of two pounds to keep the Peace)

The Justice of Peace Act in 1361 brought powers for law enforcement with the Constables and Watchmen ensuring that the laws were obeyed.

John Litherland and John de Meoles, both of Wallasey, were among the 'Conservators of the Peace' appointed by the Prince of Wales in 1399. They were similar to Magistrates and set up when there was trouble between King Richard II and Henry of Lancaster. There were also the risings in Wales which affected Cheshire.

In 1400, six Wallasey men were fined for stealing cattle from Richard Molyneux, who in turn had captured them from rebels in Wales. There was also fear that Owen Glendower and his followers would invade Wirral and again Litherland and de Meoles were recalled in 1403 to be Convervators.

In 1408 a Wallasey man, John le Barker, was acting as Court Bedell. He had told the Court that he and a friend had come from Wrexham to Chester in 1404 to avoid contact with certain rebels but nevertheless he and his friend had to do fealty to the Earl and to find a security.

In 1463 Alice Dodde and her second husband David obtained by fine from John and Henry Chauntrell, *inter alia*, 'a moiety of 60 bovates of land 20 acres of meadow and 100 of pasture in Pulton in Waley, Secum, Bebynton and Neuton in Wirehal; a moiety of half the Manor of Pulton in Waley; and a 4th of the Manor of

Sketch of the old Cheshire Cheese, Wallasey Village

Liscark.'

Edmund and Henry Litherland were Sheriff's Approvers in 1467 and 1468.

It appears that Edmund Litherland kept the revenue as in 1467 the Sheriff had not received any revenue from the Wakentake Court as he records 'Edmund Litherland the Bailiff of Wirral took it himself'.

In 1516, Robert and Margery Dod levied a fine in the favour of one John Porte and passed over to him lands in Kirkby, Pulton, Luscart, and a '4th part of the passage of Secum'.

The first Magistrates were appointed in the 14th century.

Licensing laws date back many years. In the Wirral Licensing Sessions in the time of Elizabeth I's reign we have in 1561 'The NAMES of all p'sons which keps Alehouses within this Hundred of Weroll, beynge bunden by obligac' the xxvii daie of June, iij Eliz.'

Wallasey had four, viz:-

Robert Stanney, Harry Yonge, Margaret Wylson and Robert Tassey.

Eleyne Ensdall is also listed as having an alehouse in Seacombe. These inns were, no doubt, the *Boot Inn*, the *Old Cheshire Cheese*, the *Pool Inn*, the *Seacombe Boathouse* and possibly one by the river.

In the Moreton area, for the same year, we have the names of Thomas Smyth and William Rathbon de Murton as keepers of ale houses.

Some towns had the Bellmen who would walk around ringing their bells and calling out the time and state of the weather. They were equipped with a staff and large lantern. Their dress consisted of a long gown or coat over a doublet. The hat had a turned-up brim. The Bellmen had the power to arrest strangers who were loitering about during the night.

Law and Order was kept by the Palatine Officer, known as 'Sargeant of the Peace', who was under the Central Grand Sargeant. These

The original Boot Inn , Liscard, was one of four alehouses named in Wallasey in 1561

Sargeants patrolled the Hundred on foot and had the help of assistants called Bedells (Beadles). Wirral had twelve Sargeants. Writs were issued in the name of the Earl.

An 'Eyre' was held every year for the particular Hundred in Cheshire run by a Circuit Judge. Such cases that were brought before the Court were for selling bad ale, theft of livestock, forest offences, boundary disputes, false rumours and other minor crimes.

Other communities had Parish Constables, Beadles or Night Watchmen and some of these could be dishonest.

The 'Watchmen' carried a large lantern and were known as 'Charleys' after their King Charles II.

They were similar to the Bellmen, carried a stout staff, were dressed in a long heavy greatcoat, with a cape and wore breeches. The coat had the Watchman's number on the back. They wore a small woollen cap under their wide-brimmed hat for extra warmth and also carried a bell. Some would have a 'clapper', which was a kind of rattle, in place of the bell. This could be attached to his coat so that hands were free to carry the lantern and staff.

Many of these Watchmen were old and considered to be incapable of keeping Law and Order.

The Watchmen were still patrolling the streets in this country up to the Nineteenth Century.

On the more humorous side we find that 1592, George Pemberton of Moreton was accused of 'sitting uppon the crosse at service time and would not come at the Churchwarden's request'.

Little attempt was made to see that there were sufficient numbers of Justices appointed for the seven Cheshire Hundreds.

In 1605 we see that there were ten Justices of the Peace living in Bucklow Hundred and eight in Macclesfiled and Nantwich. Edisbury had seven with five in Broxton and Wirral. The Northwich Hundred had only four.

After 1634, the Constables had the assistance of a 'Beadle' or 'Marshall'who were paid a stipend as suggested by the Authorities and were also paid for whipping rogues. Beadles wore a buttoned overcoat that was faced in yellow. They also wore a hat, carried a whip and had an official staff with a gilded knob.

Certain powers of the Vestry of the parish dealt with local issues. The Parish Constable could be chosen at the Vestry meeting (or sometimes at Court Leet). He was responsible for the peace and goodwill of the parish. Having been elected by his fellows, he could turn to them for support when dealing with crime.

The Parish Constable took an oath similar to the following:-

"You shall swear that you should keep the Peace of our Lord the King well and lawfully according to your power and shall arrest all those who shall make any contest, riot, debate, or affray, in breaking of the said peace, and shall take them into the house or Compter of one of the Sheriffs. And you shall withstand by strength of such misdoers, you shall upon them hue and cry and follow them from street to street and from ward to ward until they are arrested . . . . . . So God help you and the Saints."

Young Thomas Meoles, who on the death of his father had inherited lands in 1639 when he was a minor having Richard Yonge as guardian. Soon after on coming of age in 1649 there arose a dispute between him and his late guardian concerning Thomas it was alleged had mismanaged the estates. Yonge had taken Thomas to London leaving the estates in the care of Richaerd Coventry. An inquiry was held in 1659 and it was stated that the hall buildings were in a dilapidated condition, the two bays of the barn in ruins and the gates decayed. William, Thomas's younger brother, had also not been brought up to any trade whereby he could make a living. Coventry said that the wars had caused the lands to be set at a low rate.

The Constable said "during which time neither the Hall of Wallasey nor any lands of Thomas Meoles Esquire, the plaintiff's brother, in Wallasey aforesaid, were charged for the quartering of any soldiers, nor with any of the contributions towards the quartering of any soldiers, and whereas the Township of Wallasey did that year pay taxes to the garrison then kept at Birkett, nothing was paid for the Hall at Wallasey, nor was anything paid towards the horses which were charged upon the township for the Parliament service, under the command either of Sir William Brerton or of Col. Moore."

No one knows the outcome of the action.

The idea of imposing an Hearth Tax dates way back to the Anglo-Saxons. In 1662 it was reintroduced and in 1663 there were 84 for Wallasey, Liscard and Poulton-cum-Seacombe.

There is no evidence that Court Rolls of Manors were ever held in Wallasey but in 1689 Margaret Wilson Junior was fined three shillings and four pence for a pound breach at one of these Courts in Wirral.

One of the old families in Wallasey was that of the Houghs of Leighton who held land here in the fourteenth century.

Charles Hough, Lord of the Manor, was succeeded by his son, John, in 1752. He lived in a house near where Liscard Road and Westminster Road are. He wrote a Journal (which was destroyed when the Picton Library in Liverpool was bombed during Second World War) in a simple paper-backed notebook in which he recorded everyday life in the town. He served as Church Warden at St Hilary's Church and was appointed Constable in 1754 and in the October of 1755 he served as High Constable at the Sessions at Nether Knutsford for the lower division of the county.

He was responsible for the collection of taxes from Oxgangs and also the land and window taxes. He died and was buried at St Hilary's Church Yard on the south side of the old church on 18 June 1797.

William Willson, yeoman, had been Constable of Wallasey during the year 1653/4.

Part of the job of the early Constables was to arrest all felons and persons 'making Riots, Debates or Frays, or breaking the Peace' and to enforce the statutes concerning 'Watch, Hue and Cry, Sturdy Beggars, Vagabonds, Rogues and other Idle Persons'. They were also told to arrest such persons who played unlawful games. Under their jurisdiction was the control of beggars and they had to see that the poor found some sort of lodgings. Poor children had to be found apprenticeships.

Some offences carried the Death Penalty as late as 1819.

Parliament first used the word 'Police' in its modern sense in 1786. It is from the Latin word *Politia*, Civil Government.

Henry Fielding (1707-54), the novelist, was called to the Bar in 1740 and in 1748 was appointed Justice of the Peace for Middlesex and Westminster. In 1750 he introduced the first organised Police Force in England known as the Bow Street Runners. He set himself two tasks, to Stamp out crime and Prevent crime.

He was a great believer in having a strong Police Force that would involve public participation which in turn would help in removing the cause of the crime.

There were the Horse and Foot Patroles who were not given an official uniform until 1805 when the Horse Patrole was reintroduced having blue coats and red waistcoats. Some years later the Foot Patrole were given a uniform consisting of a blue coat and trousers. The Horse Patroles were nicknamed 'Robin Redbreasts'. These men were armed with a pistol and cutlass as well as a truncheon. Other parts of the country had individual Constables and Watchmen to carry out Constabulary duties. These were appointed by their local area.

For a peaceful society where everybody can live without fear, there have to be rules - rules for the common good, hence why we have a Police Force.

Two advantages of our Police that are different from that of other countries, namely, A) they are based on the tradition of common law and B) the Officers are drawn from the community who perform their duties on our behalf. The Police have the job to uphold our own self-imposed rules.

Bobbies

The Police, as we know it today, dates back to 1829 when the Home Secretary, Sir Robert Peel, established the Metropolitan Police Force.

The first 1,000 Policemen left their Stations and went on their 'beats' at 6pm on the evening of 29 September 1829. They were often called 'Peelers'. A more popular nickname used for a Policeman was a 'Bobby' as he was known as Bobby Peel. The latter was, and still is, used with affection.

However, there was one Children's Rhyme at the time that went:-

There goes the Bobby in his black shiny hat
And his belly full of fat.

They wore a dark blue uniform and a large oilskin top-hat that was reinforced with stays of cane. The tunic had pewter buttons which fastened to the neck and carried the Policeman's number and letter of the Division to which he was attached. They later wore a leather belt. They were also issued with an oilskin cape. When the weather was fine, the cape would be rolled up and strapped to the belt. Sometimes they wore white trousers with a strap that went under the instep. The Berlin gloves were sometimes white. The blue and white armlet was introduced to enable the public to distinguish which men were on duty. This was worn on the left arm and it 1855, Sergeants wore one on the right arm. They were issued with two pair of boots annually but at a later date the men received a cash allowance instead. During the winter months they wore a warm brown overcoat.

The wooden staff, which they carried, measured about twenty inches in length. It carried the Royal Coat of Arms and Divisional

A 'Peeler' or 'Bobby' was named after Sir Robert Peel, founder of the first police force in 1829

letter and number. The staff was carried in a pocket in the swallow tails of his frock coat. The rattle was carried in the hours of darkness so that he was able to summon the assistance of other Constables that were on patrol in the area.

The Lighting and Watching Act of 1833 permitted any town with a population over 5,000 to appoint Watchmen. The Municipal Corporations Act of 1835 laid down that each of the 178 Boroughs was required to set up a Watch Committee who would appoint Constables. The Committee was to include not more than a third of the Town Council plus the Mayor. Regular Police Forces were set under this Act.

The early Force were not liked by the general public and their work was met with resistance. It was a long time before they were accepted. People had their own names for them, such as 'Blue Devils' and the like. The first two Commissioners were Colonel Sir Charles Rowan, KCB and Sir Richard Mayne, KCB.

The Metropolis became under the control of the Home Secretary. Their object was the prevention of crime. The Constable had to be civil and obliging to all people of every class and rank. Not to interfere with matters in order to display his authority. When the occasion arose, he was expected to act boldly and be able to control his temper and not be moved by threats of any kind. He was to carry out his duties in a quiet and determined manner.

Mr. Mayne summed up the principles of the new Force as follows:- "The primary object of an efficient Police Force is the prevention of crime; next the detection and punishment of offenders, if crime is committed. To these ends all the efforts of Police must be directed. The protection of life and property, the preservation of public tranquillity and the absence of crime will alone prove if these efforts have been successful and whether the objects for which the Police were appointed had been attained."

These words are still the basic objects of the modern Force.

The County Police Act of 1839 enabled the Justices to set a paid County Police Force. A Further Act authorised the amalgamation of Borough and County Forces where it was thought to be desirable.

The County Boroughs Police Act 1856 required the Justices to set up a Force for any parts of the County not covered.

The historian, Mortimer, writes that prior to 1843 'much inconvenience had long been experienced from the want of a lock-up or prison, there being none nearer than Birkenhead, a distance from some parts of the parish of five or six miles, and prisoners were frequently confined in the houses of the Justices until their final commitment.'

A meeting was held on 21 September 1833. Present were J Feilden, Secretary, Joseph H Lyon and Richard Nile Feilden.

The Magistrates were of the opinion that it was more desirable to rent the Lock-Up House and premises already erected at Birkenhead than to make a new building that could be taken on moderate terms and adapted at a small expense and Mr Potts was ordered to ascertain from Mr Price whether he would let the premises to the County and if so on what terms and that Mr Cole make a plan and estimate for adapting the Lock-up House to the purpose. The meetings was adjourned.

The Wirral Magistrates met on the following Saturday regarding the matter and resolved that application made to the Inhabitants of Birkenhead to ascertain what annual sum the town would be willing to pay for the use of the room attached to the premises of their Towns Meeting and of the House for the residence of their Constable. The meeting was adjourned to Neston on the following Friday 21 October. Mr Price was willing to sell the property for £30 or grant a lease for 21 years at £30 per annum and the cost of repairs not to exceed £100.

As some day it may happen that a victim must be found
I've got a little list - I've got a little list.
WS Gilbert

John Aspinall lived in Birkenhead for the last twelve years and was acquainted with the surrounding country and stated that the population on the north side of the Wallasey Pool had immensely increased and that 'numbers of people of the lowest class constantly came over from Liverpool to the shore on that side for riotous amusement'.

The Commission of the Peace refused to act unless supported by an efficient Police Force with a Lock-Up House for securing offenders and that a lock-up House at Birkenhead would not answer the purpose without communication across the Wallasey Pool as the distance to go around by road from Seacombe was nine miles.

Mr. Aspinall had been informed that 'a most indecent outrage' the previous week had been committed by four men upon some females on the shore near Egremont. The men went off in a boat and were pursued - one man was taken, the other three escaped by jumping overboard. The prisoner was conveyed to the Constable's House at Liscard but escaped for want of being properly secured.

John Aspinall wrote about the matter on 15 October 1833.

John Greene, who lived in Liscard, near Egremont Ferry, wrote to the Marquis of Westminster about the problem and was told the matter lay with Rt Hon Earl of Stamford. In turn he put pen to paper and wrote to the Earl on 13 November 1833. "Permit me", he wrote, "most humbly to represent to you the very depraved state of this part of the country, entirely owing no acting Magistrate residing no nearer than Bebington, Seven miles off; and in consequence of this many very atrocious Crimes are committed, offenders knowing how difficult it is, and how very few have it in their powers, (indeed) to devote a whole day in obtaining a one shilling summons; thence the very many Delinquents go unpunished.

Mr Maddock of Sea Bank, Magazines, and Mr Wilson of Wallasea, I have heard, are appointed Magistrates, but these Gentlemen refuse to act, because there is no place of confinement here or at Seacombe, Magazines or Wallasea, the nearest place of this sort in Cheshire being Birkenhead - five miles distant. I trust your Lordship will cause an enquiry into the matter, and that our Houses may in consequence made secure. At present", he continued, "Murders and Robberies are becoming common, and I assure Lordship, call for loudly for interence."

He ended his letter with a sort of enticement in a way of saying that many a monument had been erected to an individual who had done a most meritorious act should he put down this profligate behaviour.

He received a reply from Dunham Massey a few days later. He was assured for the last three months, there had been much correspondence with the 'Gentlemen of Wirrall' to act as Magistrates and the Earl regretted to say that his applications

Seabank, later Liscard Manor House

had been unavailing.

He had written to the Lord Chancellor two years previously and was told that Mr Wilson and Mr Maddock had been in the Commission of the Peace for the Cheshire County since that time and was sorry to add, they could not be prevailed to act.

There had been correspondence in the December, 1833 between Mr JN Wilson of Heath Bank in Wallasey and Mr Henry Potts of Chester.

In his reply to Mr Potts, Mr Wilson wrote regarding the escape of offenders for the want of proper assistance to apprehend and secure them.

It had been resolved to call the attention of the Magistrates at the next Sessions to the propriety of establishing a lock-up house in an eligible situation to the north of the Wallasey Pool. Mr Wilson pointed out that he had no knowledge of the report made to the Magistrates and that his house was a distance of two miles from the Ferries and that he had no personal knowledge of the disgraceful scenes of riot and brutality which occurred on the shore of the river, particularly in the Township of Liscard on Sundays but admitted that such scenes were quite notorious to the serious annoyance of many respectful families who lived in the immediate vicinity of the river.

He agreed that there should be a place of confinement in the Parish and the difficulty of taking them to Birkenhead which enabled many offenders to escape. He regretted that it was not in his power to furnish the Magistrates any particular instances thereof. He pointed out that the population of the Parish exceeded 2,400 and that the establishment of the two Ferries with steam packets crossing the river every half hour that the intercourse with Liverpool had been greatly increased and that a great number 'low dissolute characters' came over the river particularly on Sundays and that scenes of drunkenness, riot and confusion took place on those days at a frequent occurrence and called loudly for remedy. He was of the opinion that the Township of Liscard was in a central position and most exposed to riots from the vicinity of the Ferries and was considered to be most proper place for a lock-up house. He also pointed out that there was a quarry close at hand where the building materials could be easily procured.

Mr J Dennil Maddocks replied to the letter which he had received from Mr Henry Potts on 26 December 1833.

He stated that his was the only intimation that he had received concerning the outrage at Liscard and admitted that there were calls for a more efficient police force and lock up-house. He told Mr Potts that offenders were usually detained in the public house until they were taken before a Magistrate. If the offender had committed a serious crime they would have to be taken away at an early hour, or on account of no proper place of security, they would have to be held in custody overnight at the public house or set at liberty.

Mr. Maddocks went on to say there was difficulty of crossing the Wallasey Pool as it made Birkenhead almost inaccessible to the town as Neston. There was extra ordinary trouble in the loss of time and expense which deterred many individuals from noticing offenders of minor importance. What was needed was a Lock-Up House at Liscard, as it was the centre of the township and an experienced person paid exclusively for the purpose as a Constable, in addition to the Township Constable.

Mr. Maddocks made the suggestion that may be considered by the Magistrates was to establish bridge or ferry across the Wallasey Pool. If the neighbourhood had not received any benefit, he wrote, from the County Rates, they might consider the suggestion. The proprietors would gladly join in defraying a part of the expense.

I do not know what the Magistrates thought of his suggestion but there was a small ferry of sorts across the Wallasey Pool at the foot of Limekiln Lane which is shown on the very early maps. Mr. Vyner had built an embankment across the Pool in 1809 but it was later taken down. At all events, Wallasey had to wait some twelve years before a proper Lock-Up House was built.

Policing in Wallasey
Mr Mullins

Bertram Furniss, the local historian of yesteryear, tells the story of a local Policeman named Mullins who lived in Seabank Road at the foot of Trafalgar Road in the 1840s. One evening he was in shirt sleeves and was about to sit down to his tea when someone started knocking at his front door. On opening it he found a woman who cried, "Mr Mullins, come at once, there's two men fighting like anything at the bottom of Tobin Street."

"I'll be there", said Mullins. He closed the door and sat down at the table to eat his meal.

A few minutes later another person knocked at his door and again he promised to go to see what it was all about. A third knock on the door and the caller said "You better come quickly. Two mad men are fighting like demons."

"Do you take me to be a damn fool?", said Mullins, "Am I going to stop two mad men who want to fight? No! Let them have another ten minutes and the very name of Mullins will be enough."

Mr Furniss reckons Mullins must have been one of the Watchmen who acted as Police in the town. There are no records regarding these Officers in Wallasey. We can assume that there would only be a small number and maybe with a Sergeant in charge.

******

The English Policeman
Paul Prendergast writing in 1840 says:-

"The Policeman is essentially necessary to the well being of the State; he it is who keeps in order the truculent and bloodthirsty mob, who, but for him, would at once rise upon their betters, deprive them of their lives and property, overthrow the Church, subvert the Government and dethrone the Queen. Thus he is esteemed by one class of politicians."

He goes on to say, "The English Policeman, whose vocation practically consists of keeping an eye on swindlers, pickpockets, and all manner of vagabonds; in maintaining order and decency; and preventing riot, robbery and violence."

County Police

The County Police Act was passed in 1839 which gave powers to Justices to create Police Forces for each county. At this date there were six paid Constables in the Wirral Hundred. (The Liverpool City Police were established in 1836, being the third authority in the country to do so. Michael James Whitty was appointed Head Constable).

A further Act of Parliament was passed in 1856, making it compulsory to set up Police Forces in town or county in England and Wales. Four years later there were over 200 Forces in the country.

A detective department was established at Scotland Yard in the 1800s and soon they were using fingerprints as a method of tracking down criminals.

The name 'Scotland Yard' comes from the fact that the land near Whitehall, where the Commissioners and their staff have been since 1890, was known as Scotland. The Scottish Kings and Queens used to stay in building when visiting the English Kings at the Palace of Westminster. A sort of court was called Scotland Yard.

Four Whitehall Place was used as Police Headquarters in the 1800s which backed onto Scotland Yard and the Police Station took the name that became known all over the world as the Headquarters of the Britain's Police Force.

Today, there are two Police Forces in the Capital - the Metro and New Scotland Yard and the City of London. There are over 26,500 members in the Metro. The County have a Chief Constable, but in London the position is known as Commissioner.

When Police Forces were set up, most of the men who applied for the position of Chief Constable had been military men and the various Forces were inclined to adopt a military-type uniform of sorts for their Inspectors. The Chief Constables opted for a similar uniform to that of an Army Officer and one could see a likeness in the frog-type coat of the Hussars or the 1904 Rifle Brigade with no buttons visible. The old Robin Hood Rifle Volunteers had a similar long coat.

Borough Watch Committees had been set in other parts of the country and Borough Police Forces were formed. The Chief Constable in each case was responsible to the Watch Committee and he in return held his second in command responsible for the duties and discipline of the force. The second in command, through his Inspectors, held the Sergeants responsible in their sections and they in turn held the Constables responsible for their beats. The first policeman to lose his life in the course of duty on Merseyside was that of PC. William Ross, of the Liverpool City Police, who was bludgeoned to death whilst trying to break up an angry crowd in Lodge Lane.

Two of the first Police Officers to be shot dead whilst on duty in this part of the country was a Constable at Oxton who was killed by a lunatic named W Knowles on 4 September 1854 and Sergeant Jonah Sewell of the Lancashire Constabulary on 1 November 1878. He had stopped a man in St Helens for questioning when the man drew out a gun and fired.

From the mid 1800s until the outbreak of the Second World War, 20 Liverpool Police Officers were killed whilst on duty.

Wreckers and Smugglers

My object all sublime
I shall achieve in time
To let the punishment fit the crime -
The punishment fit the crime.

WS Gilbert

Wallasey and the Cheshire coast were known for ship wrecking. They called themselves fishermen or small farmers, but their main occupation was luring vessels onto the sand banks and causing wrecks. There was also a great deal of smuggling going on in these parts of Britain. No one knows when it first started in Wirral as the practice had been going on for many years.

A smugglers' Act of 1735 carried the Death Penalty for killing or wounding or using arms against an Excise Officer.

Salt was smuggled in and landed on the shores of Cheshire and Lancashire. Large profits were made through this illegal trade. Salt Officers were appointed. Christopher Bibby of Seacombe held the appointment. His burial is recorded in the parish register in 1753. Francis Stuart, also of Seacombe, and Edmund Hayworth were Custom Officers in these parts in the 1760s.

In a report of the Royal Commission of 1839, Cheshire and Cornwall were said to be the worst in the Kingdom for wrecking. It stated "that on the Cheshire coast not far from Liverpool, they will rob those who have escaped the perils of the sea and come safe on shore and will mutilate dead bodies, for the sake of rings and personal ornaments."

They would hurry down to the beach, dragging carts, wheelbarrows and anything that would hold the loot. Horses and even oxen would be brought down to pull the heavier goods away.

If a sailor was trying to get out of the water, they would hit him over the head and rob him of what little he had on his person. Fishermen would use their nets to gather in floating casks of brandy. They seemed to adopt the slogan 'Seeking's finding and finding's keeping'.

Goods were taken into the cottages and the rest hidden in a sort of pit that was under what is now the New Palace Amusement Park. Some was hidden in the sandhills and collected later when the coast was clear. All manner of goods could be washed ashore, such as oranges, sugar, sides of bacon, tobacco and cases of silk. These wreckers would marry into similar families and so the practice continued.

On one occasion, a ship was wrecked on the sandbank and her captain's body was washed ashore. They took the clothes from the body and even cut off a finger in order to get the ring before the corpse could be taken away for the inquest. A woman even bit off the ears of a drowning woman in order to get the earrings.

The old caves, known as 'The Worm Holes' were used by smugglers and wreckers. These caves ran well inland and once a smuggler or wrecker went in the tunnels it was a very difficult job to catch him. The situation became serious as the Coastguards and others were unable to bring the offenders to justice.

In the January of the year 1839, the gales wrecked many ships on the North-West coasts and little was done by the Constables. The Liverpool Police decided to take action. Superintendent Quick and a band of about 20 men came over to try to save life and property. They were able to catch 25 villains as they went about their ugly business of plundering. These folk were brought before the Cheshire Magistrates who were very annoyed that the Liverpool Police should interfere in matters in Cheshire. Superintendent Quick reminded the Magistrates that as Constables of Liverpool, they had authority in Chester as it was within seven miles of the Borough. The Magistrates were not happy with this view of the law and they appealed to the Clerk of the Court, who upheld them. However, Quick knew that he was right and he asked that the prisoners should be held in custody. This was granted and the following day, the Superintendent got the Town Clerk of Liverpool to send an extract from the Act to the Cheshire Magistrates. They had no alternative but to send the prisoners for trial. By 1860, the Liverpool Police Force had 982 men.

Captain T Wylie was in command of the 242 ton brig *Elizabeth Buckham* when she was caught in a gale as she approached Liverpool and was wrecked on the Wallasey beach on 26 November 1866. The high winds drove the vessel ashore and the waves soon broke the boat up before any assistance could be rendered. Her cargo of coconuts and caskets of rum were washed overboard and the waves washed them ashore where the local inhabitants were waiting. The caskets were broken open and it was poured

Wreckers are helping themselves to the spoils of oranges from a Spanish ship off Leasowe Bay in 1906

into jugs and buckets or anything that came to hand. It was quickly carried away and hidden in their houses; others just drank it on the spot which resulted in fights. Five men of the Wallasey Police Force (there were only about a dozen or so members in all) were called to the scene but they were greatly outnumbered and could do very little. Drunks had fallen asleep on the sands through drinking too much rum and as the tide came in, the Policemen were kept busy dragging the culprits to a safe place above the high-water to prevent them being drowned. There were at least two deaths, one being 'The Boots' at the Victoria Hotel at New Brighton. The ship's log was washed ashore. At the inquest, Coroner Churton passed comment about the Rector at St Hilary's Church, who asked his congregation to wait till after the collection so that all could start fair, as the parishioners, having heard of the wreck, were heading for the door!

He also referred to the old Wallasey Prayer, "God bless feyther, and muther, and God send us a wreck afore morning".

None of the crew of the brig were washed ashore and it was several weeks before any of her timbers were seen on the sands. There is mention of a Policeman by the name of Barlow at this period.

Clerks of the Peace date from 1380; Coroners from 1194.

******

In towns I make improvements great
which go to swell the County Rate.

WS Gilbert

The first Wallasey Improvement Act was passed in 1845 which gave powers to improve the Street Lighting, Watching, Cleansing and the establishment of a Police Force. It also included the erection of a Public Market and Weighing Machine.

Licensed houses were to remain closed until one o'clock on Sundays, Christmas and Good Friday. Dogs were not to be used for drawing carts and street musicians were to leave 'when desired'!

The Act authorised the appointment of 22 Commissioners who had to be residents in the parish and rated therein toward the relief of the poor in the annual sum of not less than £30 or to enjoy the property of the value of £1,000 or upwards in the parish.

They were empowered to construct sewers to drain land but house owners had to pay to be joined up to the common sewer. However, every house had to have a private privy and ashpit for the purpose. Health was a problem with scares of cholera and typhus.

The Commissioners held their meetings in a room above the stables that were attached to the Queen's Arms Hotel in Liscard Village.

Court House

And make each prisoner pent
Unwillingly represent
A source of innocent merriment!
Of innocent merriment!

WS Gilbert

The nearest Prison or Lock-Up was at Birkenhead being about five or six miles from some parts of the parish and it was most inconvenient that prisoners had to be kept in the homes of the Police Constables or the Magistrates so at the summer General Sessions of 1843 the authorities allocated a grant of £30 towards the erection of a Prison and Court House in Wallasey which was completed by private subscription.

A local Act received Royal Assent on 8 May 1845 and shortly after this date the Court House and Police Station was built in

Court House built in Liscard Road

Liscard and Wallasey Road (now Liscard Road) at the cost of over £1,000. It was a two-storey stone building with steps leading up to the front entrance with a stout stone wall made up of pillars in front. The upper windows were of large rectangular design whilst the lower ones had an arched top. There was also a raised area from the pavement level and as the years went on, the building became darkened with grime. There were cells beneath with stout studded doors and the only natural light coming in was through the high-level barred windows. These windows could be seen at the side of the Court House at ground level. The prisoners were able to be brought up to the Court Room from below.

In the latter part of the 1800s, the Magistrates held sittings every Wednesday at 10am for the Wallasey Division. Petty Sessions for the Western Division were also held at the Court House every Monday, covering the neighbouring townships. In the 1860s, Mr. EJ Kent was the Clerk of the Courts.

In the 1850s the Wakentake Court was held at Tranmere Hotel in Birkenhead. They sat quarterly.

On 3 September 1855 an action for damages was heard before Robert Grace, the steward, for false imprisonment that was brought against Elliott Hodson, a Birkenhead Police Detective, by a schoolmaster named James McMahon who lived in Liscard.

The average intelligence of a Policeman in Victorian times was far from being high and they were usually recruited for their physical strength. Most of them came from working class families and their pay was low. To some degree, Victorian Policemen would turn a blind eye to certain cases of lawbreaking, often or not with their superior's approval. Those counties without a professional Force were asked to form one. The first Wallasey Local Board was elected on 28 April 1853

Cheshire Constabulary

The Cheshire Police Committee called a meeting at the *Crewe Arms Hotel* on 3 February 1857 to set up the Cheshire Constabulary. The Force came into being on 28 April 1857 and Captain Thomas J Smith, who had served with the Bedfordshire Militia, was appointed Chief Constable. He rented a private house in Chester for his Headquarters and had a horse and trap or cart for transport. Two years later he set up a Detective Force, albeit that it consisted of just one Constable named Burgess who was attached to HQ but was also available for duty in other parts of the county.

Captain Smith died in 1877 and was succeeded by Captain John William Arrowsmith. In his previous military career, he had served in Africa, Ceylon and the Crimea. Before coming to Cheshire, he had been Chief Constable of the Bedford Force. He brought with him a great deal of military-style attitudes which resulted in a strict discipline in the ranks (there was another Captain JD Arrowsmith who was Chief Constable of Bootle County Borough Police between 1887 - 1888).

On the death of Arrowsmith in 1879 another military man, Col

John Henry Hamersley, became Chief Constable. He had little experience of Police duties and remained with the Cheshire Constabulary for almost thirty years. During this period, he introduced transport in the form of the bicycle; He thought a lot of his men and he put in their first pay claim for 20 years.

With the coming of the motorcar, he devised a method of catching drivers exceeding the 20 mph speed limit by checking the registration numbers of passing cars at a certain point along a measured length of main road and again further along where Constables were watching. The time covered by the vehicle over the distance enabled them to work out the speed the driver had been travelling.

Colonel Hamersley retired in 1910 and became one of the first Officers in the Police to receive the King's Police Medal in the New Year's List. He was succeeded by Lt Col Pulteney Malcolm CBE, DSO, MVO.

Those men who joined the Cheshire Constabulary were issued with uniforms, consisting of two frock coats, two pair of trousers, a top hat and stock. In accordance with Lord Normandy's rules, which were introduced in 1856, the recruit had to be able to read and write, be intelligent, active, certified to be free from bodily complaints, of a strong constitution and be of irreproachable character. The reinforced tall hat was strong enough to allow the Constable to stand upon it in order to see over walls or hedges.

In 1873 a Borough Bench was set up for Birkenhead; prior to that date, the Wirral Hundred came under the jurisdiction of the County Magistrates. A Stipendiary had been appointed in 1867. Sittings were held daily for the Borough.

Some Constables in the Force in the 1860s that patrolled Wallasey included the following:-

PC 94 (111)	Patrick Keenan	PC 117 (89)	WJ Samuel Horne
PC 96	Samuel Heaps	PC 121 (158)	George Parker
PC 99 (98)	John Hindley	PC 123 (25)	James Bowden
PC 103 (95)	Thomas Hindley	PC 126 (160)	Thomas Percival
PC 103	Anthony Ibbotson	PC 129	Samuel Threadgold
PC 104 (7)	Thomas Duffy	PC 138 (54)	William Duffy
PC 112	Joseph Millington	PC Albert Sudlow	

PC Henry Doyle PC Robert Lea PC Joseph Wragg
Sgt. Thomas Gosling Det. Sgt. William Hoole Sgt. Robert Jackson
The numerals in brackets indicate the renumbering of Constables that took place from time to time.

Officers wore a badge consisting of the Prince of Wales' feathers. There was a Policeman living in New Brighton in 1861, ten years later there were three Constables residing in the area.

With the development of New Brighton as a resort, it became necessary to have a Police Station in that part of town.

A brick two storey building was duly erected in about 1860 in Hope Street, which was of adequate size and was equipped with five cells.

It is quite likely there was living quarters on the first floor for a Sergeant but at all events the Inspector resided next door at No.3.

New Brighton Police Station

The rental for this house was £24 per annum.

Joseph Millington joined the Cheshire Constabulary on 25 April 1861 to the Reserve Division where he remained for two months before being posted to Seacombe which was in the Wirral Division. The Police Station was in the Court House in Liscard Road. His pay was increased by a shilling, making it twenty-one shillings a week. The ferry was an important part of the life at Seacombe but in those days, the actual village of Seacombe consisted of one main street (Victoria Road, later Borough Road) and a number of smaller streets with very poor housing and much squalor.

It was in contrast to Antrobus, his native village in Cheshire where he had been brought up. He had several brothers and sisters. His father, Thomas, a cordwainer (a worker in leather), was unable to read nor write but nevertheless a good father to his children. Young Joseph was lucky enough to attend the newly opened National School in the village in 1844 at the age of six where he learnt to read and write. The young Constable made it his business to uphold the law in the village and was for ever dealing with drunkenness, which was paramount in the district. He was a Constable at Seacombe between 1861 and 1895 and eventually became an Inspector at New Ferry.

PC James Bowden came from Hatfield in Derbyshire and joined the Force in April 1857 and PC Samuel Threadgold joined the Police on 4 February 1860. Scotsman Patrick Keenan hailed from Glasgow and joined the Police in January 1864 moving to Wirral in the March of the same year. Thomas Percival joined the Police in March 1857 and was a native of Bowness in the Lake District. He began his career at Preston, serving for five years and was transferred to Wirral on 15 May 1861. Another Constable active in Wallasey at the same period was PC Mealor. PC George Parker was a native of Hartford in Cheshire. He joined the Police on 22 May 1858 and was in the Force for about eight years, beginning with the Manchester Borough Police where he served for two years and nine months. He seems to have left the Force due to a domestic argument. PC. Duffy was a native of Bath who became a Policeman on 14 March 1857.

PC Samuel Horne who came from Reading in Berkshire had joined the West Riding Police serving for two years before coming to Wirral in the autumn of 1861. It seems that he had served as a Sergeant. On 8 December 1863 he was posted to Nantwich.

The name Hindley crops up several times in the early records. Thomas Hindley was born in Stretton and joined the Police on 20 May 1857 and another Hindley, John, joined eight days later. Although he was a native of Leeds, he could have been brother of Thomas. Both of these Constables were discharged from the Force through drinking in a public-house whilst on duty. Thomas received a pension. There was also a Sergeant at New Brighton Police Station named John Hindley who was born in 1830 and married Rebecca Cole. Her family lived in a house in Hope Street called 'Summer Hill'. Her father, John, had served in the Navy and been a Coast Guard before taking a position in management on the New Brighton Pier. It appears that the Sergeant was also known by the name of Edward and later became an Inspector. I do not know whether he was related to the other two Hindleys or not. Mr. Hindley was later promoted to Chief Superintendent of the Cheshire County Constabulary.

Samuel Heaps, a 29 year-old Policeman, went to Cheshire in September 1861 and was posted to Wirral the following month remaining for four years.

PC Anthony Ibbotson, who came from Skipton in Yorkshire joined the force in September, 1865 but was fond of his drink and was found drunk on duty in 1867.

Another man who joined the Police on 25 April 1857 was William Egerton. He was posted to Wirral and served with the Birkenhead Borough Police.

The Superintendent William Watson of the Division and Inspector Rowbottom made regular appearances in the Liscard Court House. Mr. Watson was born in April 1814, joining the force at the age of 33 he served five and a half years with the Liverpool Borough Police and four years three months with the Cheshire Police. He was an Acting Inspector from 8 June 1864 and promoted to full Inspector on 1 March 1864. He was posted to Wirral on Christmas Day 1864 but four years later in May 1868 he was demoted to Sergeant for taking a partridge's nest. Constable Joseph Wragg lived at *Wirral Villas* in Wallasey Village and one can assume that he was the Local Policeman. In 1898 there were three police officers living in Charlotte Road, Egremont – Det. Sgt. William Hoole, Sgt. Robert Jackson and Cons. Albert Sudlow. James Walker was the keeper of the Court House in the 1880s.

Drunkenness

Drunkenness had always been a problem in Seacombe. Men who were found drunk and fighting were fined between four shillings and sixpence and a pound. A fine of five shillings or seven or fourteen days in prison was often given. A 34 year-old Michael Quinn was found drunk and disorderly in Seacombe January 1863 and had to pay a fine of ten shillings and sixpence (including costs). If he had not paid his fine he would have had to serve 21 days imprisonment.

Drunkenness and fighting in Seacombe often landed men in the cells at the old Court House in Liscard Road.

The present day still has its drink problems. Offences caused by late night revellers who leave the clubs in New Brighton in the early hours of the morning doing damage to property. Measures are being taken to ban the drinking of alcohol in certain areas of the resort.

Although our dark career
Sometimes involves the crime of stealing
We rather think that we're
Not altogether void of feeling.

WS Gilbert

In 1865, Edwin and Alfred Edwards were sent to prison for 14 days' hard labour for stealing apples from William Byerley's garden at 5.45am.

It cost Edward Walmsley of Seacombe three shillings and six pence fine for allowing his chimney to catch fire in 1862. Other people doing the same were fined a half a crown.

In 1863 the Police were called in to look into the matter of obnoxious smoke and fumes that were coming from the chimney of a mill in Liscard. Many people had complained. The owner of the mill, Mr. Ellis Davis, was fined five pounds under the Smoke Act of 1853. Richard Jones was sent to Chester Castle for a month with hard labour for stealing at Seacombe in 1865.

There was also the odd case of a man stealing a horse. The Chief Constable received a complaint against the Sergeant in 1868 who had placed the dead body of a person in one of the stables that was behind the *Royal Ferry Hotel* in New Brighton instead of having it taken to the Dead House at the Magazines. The compliant hoped that the practice would not be repeated as there were several dwellings in the vicinity. The Chief Constable looked into the matter and said that the Sergeant had taken him there in the hope that the victim might be resuscitated by a medical man whom had been sent for. It would not have been appropriate to have taken him to the Dead House.

The Dead House at the Magazines was set up in the Old Lifeboat House in 1865. As for bodies taken from the Wallasey Beach, there was a small Dead House in an old cottage at the far end of the *Black Horse Inn* yard which had been established at an earlier date.

It has been said that the villages of Seacombe, Poulton and Wallasey Village were patrolled by one Constable on horseback in the early days and as previously mentioned, there were only about a dozen in number. The Police Force in Wirral was under the Cheshire Constabulary. John Newton was given charge of Wallasey, Liscard, Poulton and Seacombe in 1850. He was followed by Superintendant John McHale, who was in charge of the North Wirral section which covered Wallasey. He was assisted by Inspector Edward Hindley who had been at Wallasey since the 1860s.

On the other side of the river, Liverpool Borough Council set up a Force in 1836 which had 390 men and the Lancashire Constabulary was formed in 1839. They were responsible for the County with the exception of Liverpool and Manchester. The Southport Force was formed in 1870, albeit with a total of seven men. St Helens set up a local force in 1884, with a Chief Constable, eight Sergeants and 53 men. Bootle established their own Force in 1887, with a Chief Constable, two Inspectors, six Sergeants and 38 Constables. Birkenhead Borough Police was formed in 1877. Mr. Walter C Davies was Birkenhead's Chief Constable in the early 1900s.

The Local Government Act 1888 abolished Police Forces that were run by Boroughs with less than 10,000 population.

Uniforms

The early uniforms worn by the Constables were made of dark navy blue material; the collared tunic having six or seven bright metal buttons that fastened in the middle and right up to the neck which meant they did not need to wear a collar and tie. The tunic collar carried the Officer's number. The 'Shako' helmet was a tall hard hat with a flat top and chin-strap, similar to that worn by the postmen of the same period. It had a bright plate (badge) at the front. The 'Shako' military-type helmet was a note of individualism to the Cheshire Constabulary who continued with this helmet until 1935 when it was replaced with a lighter flat peak cap. The Police first introduced the helmets in 1864, which replaced the top-hat, and the music-hall of the day were quick to seize upon it with a song that included the verse:-

Instead of the old flower pot tile
the helmet is a better style.
It has more room and cap-ac-i-tye
To hold cold mutton or rabbit pie.

Tunics also replaced the swallow tail coat and the Sergeants had chevrons on the arm and the duty armlet was worn on the left arm. In 1839 Constables carried a rattle and in addition, a truncheon, night stick and a lamp. They wore white gloves. The leather belt was to hold the truncheon case and lantern.

Whistles

Some Forces, such as the Lancashire Force, had a whistle as early as 1859. By 1884 all Police Constables throughout the land were issued with a whistle.

Prior to the old seventeen inch truncheon, the Police carried a twenty inch stave. The early capes were made of oilskin.

Police whistles were manufactured by J Hudson and Co of Barr Street in Birmingham which was a small business was set up by Joseph Hudson. Someone told him that the Police were looking for something to replace the wooden rattle and he got in touch with them and suggested a whistle. But they wanted one to have a special tone. He thought about it for some while and a little later on decided to pick up his violin and play, hoping to hit on a note or two. However, he somehow let the instrument fall from his grip onto the tiled floor of his little cottage. The strings gave a peculiar vibrating discordant sound. He stood listening and knew that he

Policemen wearing Shako hats on Coronation Day 1911 pictured in Claremount Road, Wallasey

had discovered what he had been seeking. Joseph set about making a whistle with a similar tone and he duly let the Police have one. The Commissioner of Scotland was interested in it and decided to test it himself on Hampstead Heath. It was heard a mile away and the Commissioner was so impressed that he ordered 21,000. Poor Joseph Hudson was very short of finance to set up a proper business, so the Police advanced £20.

'The Metropolitan Whistle' was so popular, that in a short period of time Hudsons were making Police whistles for forces all over the Empire. Before the year was out, he was employing 50 people. Hudsons made the Mates Whistles that were used on the liners and also the famous 'Acme Thunderer', which was used by the football referees which was so powerful that it could be heard above the noise of the crowd when it was first used at Nottingham Forest's ground Up to 1878, the official used a white handkerchief to control the play. Before the whistles left the factory, they were personally tested by Joseph Hudson.

******

Uniforms and Equipment

The wooden plain staff or truncheon as used by the Police was introduced in 1887. It was later carried in a suitable pocket in the greatcoat or trousers. Black gloves were issued in 1910 and a year later, white cotton gloves.

The Constables were issued with a paraffin oil lantern when on night duty. This clipped onto the wide leather belt. After leaving the Sergeant, they would often blow it out to save oil. The bobby received 3d a fortnight for the paraffin. Apart from its uses as a lamp, the lantern provided warmth for the hands and would be used to warm his enamel cup of tea or cocoa by placing it on top. When Wallasey took over, it was the intention to let the men have battery torches but they found difficulty in getting them.

The belt had a buckle and may have once been a snake-type fastener. Many a youngster felt the sting of the leather belt if they were caught misbehaving. Often a clip behind the ear was sufficient to ensure that they did not cause trouble again.

The new helmets that were used by other British Police Forces were modelled on that worn by the soldiers, such as those of the 1908 Glamorganshire Royal Garrison Artillery or the Army Veterinary Corps of the same period. Other Army helmets of similar design were that of an Army Captain in the 107th Regiment, who wore the 1878 pattern, or the 2nd Battalion Connaught Rangers of 1881.

When the Police became under local control in Wallasey, the new Force opted for a change of style of helmet. Only a small number were ordered at first. Previously, while in the Cheshire Constabulary, the Constables had worn the 'Shako' helmet with a flat top. The pattern chosen for the new Force was the new Army-type. This was a taller navy blue hard top helmet with a blunt spike that was screwed in at the top. The helmet carried the metal Wallasey Borough Police Plate (badge) on the front. All the Police helmets had a small fastened strap that was attached around the lower part of the helmet, the same as the present day helmets. The chin-strap was the norm. Some Constables wore a lighter helmet in the summer months which was similar in design but made out of brown and black compressed straw which they called 'A Donkey's Dinner'. It was light and cool to wear but could be quite humiliating when it rained as it would become soft and lose its shape. Some of the Liverpool Police also wore them. These summer helmets were supplied by Mr. J Anderson of Luton at the cost of five shillings and six pence each and the caps four shillings and six pence. The normal Inspectors' caps cost fifteen shillings and six pence each, Sergeant and Constable helmets were eight shillings and ten pence each.

Tunics and trousers were made of navy blue cloth for the winter whilst in the summer it was a serge jacket and trousers. The jacket had seven silver buttons, which fastened in the middle up to the collar which carried his number. Some tunics had epaulettes. The duty overcoat and cape were of cloth. There was no such thing as 'short sleeve order' in those days. If they were still in the winter weight on a warm day while on duty on the promenade, it could be most uncomfortable. They wore white gloves in the day time and navy blue at night.

The cape was of high quality and was ideal as one had free use of their hands beneath. It had a bronze buckle and a lion's head on a chain enabling it to be fastened at the neck. Capes kept their woollen gloves dry and if the Constable held his hands out in front of him under the cape, the rain would fall to the ground and away from the trousers.

When these became shabby, they were sold off to the general public for as little as four pence each. Cyclists would try to get them as they covered the handlebars and were ideal in wet weather. These Police capes may have been responsible for the introduction of the light waterproof cyclists' capes that one could purchase at a later date. The cape was an invaluable piece of equipment as it would take eight hours' rain without letting in, albeit very heavy and stiff in the process. Capes were folded in fine weather and carried over the shoulder.

Rubberised mackintoshes, supplied by Messrs Fenton Bros of Liverpool at the cost of twenty-three shillings and six pence each, were issued but these caused the Constable to sweat on warm days. The cost of capes rose in 1918 to 47 shillings and six pence; great coats were 75 shillings each; patrol jackets 63 shillings; serge trousers 37 shillings a pair; riding breeches 45 shillings a pair; Sergeants' chevrons amounted to nine shillings for a set of three. The Firebobbies' mackintoshes cost 70 shillings each and their tunics 95 shillings.

******

The Music Hall Songs

The Village bobby was a popular figure of the times and there were many good-humoured skits and sketches about them. On the music hall there was a well-known song. It was called:

The Bobbies of the Queen
You've sang about the Navy and our brave and bold Jack Tars
You've sang of Tommy Aktins and our gallant sons of Mars
But what about the "Boys in Blue" who promenade the street?
They're worthy of a song of praise, who is there can beat.

Chorus:

Bold Policemen keep the peace
Men oh, don't the cookies love us
They think no men above us,
We take the cake and biscuit too
When we come on the scene,
Not the soldiers or the sailors,
But the "Bobbies of the Queen".

Who is it guards you every day from our country's foes?
Who is it on the night duty smokes a pipe or has a doze?
Who is it thinks that telling lies is such an awful sin?
And who are running poor un-muzzled bow-wows in?

Chorus

Who sees that all the pretty girls get safely o'er the street?
Who is it holds you gently up when overcome with heat?
And who are they when rows are on and shrieking fills the air?
Who, just an hour afterwards- are certain to be there?

Words by Eardley Turner.

The music was composed by Maud Santley who also sang the song. She would dress in a blue tunic with tights and a Policeman's helmet.

Another well-known music hall artiste was Charles Austin, who had success with his character 'Parker'. He would dress as a bobby in a sketch entitled 'Parker, PC'. Austin, who was born in 1878, wrote most of his own sketches and was known as 'The King of Cockney Humour', but it was Charles Penrose who was known the world over as 'The Laughing Policeman'. It was claimed that the person is yet to be born who could not hear this great laughter-maker and not join in laughing. He needed no antics and he would open his act by laughing and the audiences would do the rest for him. He made a recording of 'The Laughing Policeman' and when the wireless became popular, children from all over the country would write to Uncle Mac of the BBC to have the record played over the air. Penrose also had other laughter-raisers, including 'The Laughing Major', 'The Laughing Sneezing Man' and 'The Cornet Player'.

However, he is best remembered as 'The Laughing Policeman' and we can still enjoy his recording of the song from the sketch. Another popular song that older readers will recall was 'Ask A Policeman'. It was sung on the music halls up and down the country.

"Ask A Policeman"

The P'lice Force is a noble band that safely guard our streets
Their valour is unquestioned and they're noted for their feats.
If anything you wish to know they'll tell you with a grin;
In fact each one of them's a complete 'enquire within'.

Chorus: If you want to know the time ask a P'liceman
Every member of the Force, has a watch and chain of course
If you want to know the time ask a P'liceman, if you P'iceman!

And if you stay out late at night and pass through regions queer
Thanks to those noble guardians, of foes you have no fear.
If drinks you want and 'pubs' are shut, go to the man in blue.
Say you are thirsty and good natured and he'll show you what to do.

Chorus: If you want to get a drink, ask a P'liceman!
He'll manage it, I think, will a P'liceman

He'll produce a flowing pot, if the pubs are shut or not,
He could open all the lot; ask a P'liceman.

If your servant suddenly, should leave her cosy place
Don't get out an advertisement, her whereabouts to trace.
You're told it was a soldier who removed her box of clothes;
Don't take the information in, but ask the man who knows.

Chorus: If you don't know where she is, ask a P'liceman!
For he's in 'the know' he is, ask a P'liceman
Though they say with 'red' she flew, yet it's ten to one on blue
For he mashes just a few, ask a P'liceman!

And if you're getting very stout and your friends say in a trice
"Consult a good physician and he'll give you this advice:-
Go in for running all you can, no matter when or how
And if you'd have a trainer, watch a Bobby in a row?

Chorus: If you want to learn to run, ask a P'liceman!
How to fly, though twenty 'stun'! ask a P'liceman!
Watch a Bobby in a fight, in a tick he's out of sight.
For advice on rapid flight, ask a P'liceman!

Or if you're called away from home and leave your wife behind;
You say "Oh! that I had a friend to guard the house, could find
And keep my love in safety". But let all your troubles cease;
You'll find the longed-for keeper in the member of the P'lice.

Chorus: If your wife should want a friend, ask a P'liceman
Who a watchful eye will lend, ask a P'liceman.
Truth and honour you can trace, written on his manly face
When you've gone he'll mind your place, ask a P'liceman!

(I am unable to find out who wrote the words).
******

"When A Felon's Not Engaged In Employment
Or Maturing His Felonious Little Plans."
WS Gilbert

Sheep Stealing

Sheep stealing was a common practice in most parts of the country. In the 1870s there was such a case in Wallasey. In those days, the town had only a small Police Force. Police Constable No.7 Duffy lived in Poulton whose beat was around Somerville, Mill Lane, Wallasey Road and down to Wallasey Village. One night he was patrolling along Breck Road at about midnight when he spotted a man coming up the footpath from the direction of Bidston carrying a sack over his shoulder. The Constable watched him and when the fellow got to the top and turned into Breck Road, he went across and tapped him on the shoulder and asked him what he had in the sack. The fellow said that he would show him and dropped the sack to the ground and taking PC Duffy unawares, he threw himself at the Constable before he could draw out his truncheon. The assailant was none other than the licensee of the *Ship Inn*. This fellow also looked after some horses that belonged to John Leicester who was a butcher in Liscard Village. The beer-house keeper was a rough character and a known fighter. Sheep had been reported stolen from the Moss. They had been killed and skinned and the carcases taken. A struggle resulted and the fellow gripped the Constable by the throat and it could have had serious consequences had it not been for Major William Chambres who was returning home in a cab. He lived at 'Mosslands', close to the footpath where the two men were fighting. Being a Liverpool Alderman, he had been to a banquet at the Town Hall. The

Constable was crying out for help so the cabman and the major rushed to his assistance but they were unable to break the ruffian's grip. "Hit him on the head with the butt of your whip !" shouted the Major. The cabman responded with the whip, which felled the assailant. Once handcuffed, he was bundled into the cab and driven to the Court House in Liscard Road where he was locked in the cell. Next morning, PC Duffy, took the prisoner his breakfast but was unable to open the cell door. With the help of another Constable, they managed to force the door open only to find that the prisoner had hung himself with his braces that were attached to a hook behind the door.

The shame of the consequences was too great for the man. He was well-known in the town and was, to some degree, popular, despite his bad temper. Major Chambres, who was a JP, was a kind and well-respected gentleman in Wallasey, who would have done all he could to have helped him from the results of his folly.

******

"Mosslands" the home of Major William Chambres

Local Scene

One of the early Police Officers in Wallasey was 24 year old James Hunt. Born in 1857, he came here in late 1870s, finding lodgings with Frances McKie. He became a Sergeant, married Agnes Mary Halliday of 9 Wallasey Village and they had three children, Elizabeth, Edward Frances and George. James died in 1924.

Another Officer in Wallasey was Sergeant WG Skiff who served in the Force in the 1890s. PC Robert J Pearson was transferred to Wallasey in 1902. He went on to become a Chief Constable.

Charles Herbert Emsley was in the Force in about 1903. He was a Yorkshireman who had served in the 2rd Battalion Scots Guards and become a Sergeant. Soon after joining the Police, it seems that he came to New Brighton and later transferred to Helsby in 1909. From there he went on to Buxton, then Hoylake and finally to New Ferry, where he retired as Sergeant.

The Police Station had a Police Dog. The black Labrador was named Blackie and accompanied him around the town.

District Council

As the town population increased the Urban District Council came into being under the Local Government Act of 1894. Mr. Richard Steel of Zig Zag Hall was its first Chairman and the town was divided into eight wards.

Council Offices were built at the bottom of Church Street.

No Lamp

In the days before batteries, cyclists used an oil lamp. Amy Gawith was caught cycling without a lamp one day in Wallasey. A Constable spotted her and called for her to stop. However, she continued on and when she eventually came to a halt, she refused to give her name and address. She appeared before the Liverpool Police Court on 4 April 1896 where she said:

"It was a windy night and the lamp blew out. I gave my surname, but I thought it undesirable to give my Christian name with such a crowd of ruffians about. As to what the Officer said about not alighting immediately, he should remember that a lady cannot alight until she reaches a kerbstone." She was fined one shilling.

New Police Station

Manor Road Police Station was opened in 1900 at the cost of £11,000 which was provided by the Cheshire County Council. Also housed in the building were the various Courts.

On 21 February 1906 the Court opened having been transferred from the Old Court House in Liscard Road which had been in use since the reign of William IV and Queen Adelaide. The Old Court House eventually became redundant and later housed the Weights and Measures Department for a while. William James Holland was Inspector. When the building that was no longer needed it was converted into a 400 seat picture house under the management of Mr. James Burt and opened as such on 31 January 1914 when they screened a programme of films, including 'Her Majesty the Little Queen'.

The Higher Courts were the Quarter Sessions and Assizes at Chester and North Wales, with Higher Courts in Liverpool.

The new Police Station had a number of cells with a wooden bench in each. There were various offices and a Parade Room.

The Growing Force

In about 1908 the Inspector of Taxes Office was looked after by Inspector John Lees of 19 Virginia Road, New Brighton, assisted by Robert Richardson and Constable Thomas Woodward of 24 Balfour Road. The Inspector took over at Hope Street Police Station.

One of the early Policemen patrolling the town in the days of the Cheshire Constabulary was George Kingham of 5 Liscard Grove. Seacombe had a Constable as did Wallasey Village. The latter was Edward Dodd who lived in a stone-built, thatched cottage that stood near foot of what is now St Johns Road and was later converted into a garage.

There was no Sub-Station in Wallasey Village, however, Sergeant Lockley was in charge of four men who paraded from their houses. If they were short of a man, one of the other men who was off duty would come in.

The Police Forces (Weekly Rest Day) Act was passed in 1910.

The new Police Force went through elementary drill instruction.

Manor Road Police Station, Liscard, opened 1900

Liverpool General Transport Strike

The Liverpool General Transport Strike of 1911 developed almost into a revolution. Some 66,000 workers came out on strike. Liverpool came to a standstill as seamen, dockers, carters, railwaymen, tramcar workers, power workers and Corporation employees were all involved. Tom Mann was elected Chairman of the Strike Committee and the situation became worse. 80,000 people attended a demonstration at St George's Plateau. The Police re-enforcements from Birmingham and Leeds came out of the Hall and cleared the crowd with the use of batons. The Warwickshire Regiment was called in. Food rotted at stations and there were ugly scenes in the streets as workers threw bricks and stones at the Police and troops.

The Cheshire Police were not involved.

******

WALLASEY BOROUGH POLICE

AUDEMUS DUM CAVEMUS

Mr Percy L Barry – Chief Constable

Towards a man of rank so high-
We shall know better by and by.

WS Gilbert

When Wallasey became a County Borough, the town had its own Watch Committee under the Chairmanship of Alderman Edwin Peace, who held the position until 1924, and Police Force with Superintendent John McHale of the North Wirral Division in charge until a Chief Constable was appointed.

An advertisement was placed in the *Police Review* on 23 September 1912 for the position Chief Constable. From the short-list of six, Superintendent and Assistant Chief Constable Percy Linnel Barry of the Central Division of Stoke-on-Trent was selected by 14 votes to 8. A native of London, he was 34 and six feet two inches tall. He joined the Army and was a mounted Infantry Volunteer throughout the African Campaign, being awarded the SA and five clasps. He was selected to serve in the British South African Police duties in the Transvaal. Mr. Barry started his Police career in the Hauley Borough Police in 1901 where he joined as a Patrol Constable and was appointed Assistant Chief Clerk five months later. In June 1906, he was promoted to Sergeant and was also made Chief Clerk. Two years later he was promoted to Inspector and the following year he became Detective Inspector. When the six Pottery Towns were amalgamated, he was appointed Chief Inspector.

As Chief Constable of Wallasey he was provided with a horse. Being an expert horseman, this dark-haired, moustached gentleman with a long dark navy blue frog (braided) frock coat (not unlike that of an Army Officer), white gloves and belt with silver buckle,

Mr Percy L Barry – Chief Constable

looked very smart as he rode about town. The collar carried the town's new Coat of Arms on either side as did his cap badge with the peak having silver braid around the brim. For ceremonial occasions, he would have a sword attached to his belt.

Mr. Barry was a tall, fine figure of a man and when he walked into the Court, the Magistrates would stand, unlike the practice today. Known as 'PLB', Mr. Barry was respected by the men and he became one of most popular Chief Constables in the country.

Mr. Barry and his wife, Emily, lived at 46 Grosvenor Street and had two sons. One of them, named Eddie, became a river pilot in 1933 and on 10 August 1940, aged 34, became the first person to be killed in the town as the result of a bomb falling on 'Stroude's Corner' at the junction of Magazine Lane and Rake Lane [this is where Mr Benjamin James Stroude had his drapery business]. He was rushed to the Victoria Central Hospital in Liscard where he later died. His widow was Irene Mary, at the family home with his mother.

******

It's a Bobby's Job

The Watch Committee held a meeting on 21 November 1912. They decided to raise the Policeman's salary by a shilling a week. The men now bought their own boots so an allowance of six pence was granted. One of the suppliers was the firm of J Lloyd and Son. A Constable paid seven shillings and eleven pence for a pair of boots.

They would last him about sixteen weeks as there were over 65 miles of streets to be patrolled in the Borough (Police Forces had first introduced the cash boot allowance in 1897).

I believe that at a later date some of the Birkenhead Policemen used to cut up the tread of a rubber motorcar tyre and nail strips across the soles and heels of their boots in order to save leather. This had another advantage wherein they could creep upon a suspect without him hearing them approaching.

The Committee also decided to give an allowance of half a crown a week for those men who used their own bicycles while on duty. The County Borough of Wallasey Police Force came into being at

10pm on 31 March 1913 when control was transferred from the County to Wallasey with the officials gathering on that night at the Town Hall (then in Church Street). The occasion was marked by a symbolic handing over of the keys of Manor Road Police by Superintendent McHale of the Cheshire Constabulary to Alderman Edwin Peace, Chairman of the Watch Committee, at 12.01am 1 April, 1913 thus setting up the new Police Authority. A cameraman was at hand taking a photograph with a plate camera and flash-powder. The local dignities present included:- Mr Barry, the new Chief Constable; Alderman Sydney Dawson; JP, Mr James Chester; Alderman John Oldershaw; Alderman Walter Eastwood; Alderman John Farley; and Mr C Hewetson Nelson, FSAA.

A crowd had gathered outside the Police Station in Manor Road hoping to witness some sort of triumphant entry into the building. A member of the public shouted "Hurry up there, let's be seeing something". A face appeared at a window. The crowd looked up. The man made a joking "Bow Wow" sound and closed the window and disappeared. There was little else in the way of activity and after a while the crowd quietly dispersed.

Some of the men that joined had not been in the Police before. William Seldon came on duty at 10pm with others from the south of England

The new Force was officially welcomed by the Magistrates the following morning. Alderman Bulley thanked Mr. McHale for all he had done as Superintendent and then welcomed Mr. Barry as Chief Constable.

Seacombe and New Brighton Police Stations came under their control with Inspector Thomas Morris in charge of the former and Inspector Phillips, the latter. The Chairman reported that he had the furnishing of the Police Station in Manor Road from Lt. Col. Malcolm, Chief Constable of the County.

Superintendent McHale refused to resign and was eventually forced into retirement at the age of 56 with a pension of £173.6s.8d. per annum (in 1928, he was allowed half pay for a further six months).

Officers and Conditions

The Police Force in Wallasey, prior to the town becoming a County Borough on 1 April 1913 (the town achieved Borough status in 1910), was under the North Wirral Division of the Cheshire Constabulary.

In 1913 the area of the new County Borough was 3,408 acres including 65 miles of streets. This meant that each Constable had 37.86 acres to Police and with the population at 78,514, there was one Constable to 872 inhabitants.

Wallasey's new Force had 90 men of all ranks, which were made up of members from other Forces. The Cheshire Constabulary contributed 53 men. By September, 1913 there were 91 men in all

Alderman Edwin Peace, Chairman of the Watch Committee, receiving the keys to Manor Road Police Station from Supertindent McHale of the Cheshire Constabulary

ranks of the Wallasey Borough Force, of which 72 had an Ambulance Arts Certificate and 17 men had a Life Saving Certificate.

The Police Constables from the Cheshire Constabulary who obtained appointments with the Wallasey Borough Police in 1913 were:-

PC. 2	J Davies.	PC. 293	WGG Short.
= 7	W Nelson.	= 297	M Leigh.
= 10	RJ Thompson.	= 299	J Molyneux
= 11	J Hesketh.	= 309	J Wainwright.
= 19	J Latham.	= 322	(Acting Sgt) G Sawage.
= 22	WA Lidgett.	= 323	E Pearse.
= 24	FA Robinson.	= 328	EF Scott.
= 36	L Kenny (Acting Sergeant).	=329	M.Brenman
= 62	FE Jones.	= 351	WC Hallam.
= 67	W Nutt.	= 371	JB Lockley.
= 72	E.G.Burgess.	= 382	D Tweadle.
Sgt. 74	A Sandland.	Sgt.396	A Phillips.
PC. 180	W Griffiths.	PC. 418	J Bebbington.
= 186	W Jackson	Sgt.419	RJ Pearson.
= 188	J Wedge.	PC. 437	WC Wood.
= 189	T W Roberts.	= 444	C Farran.
= 215	L Currell	= 448	T Shore.
= 201	J Smith (Acting Sergeant).	= 457	GB Fairhurst.
= 221	T Latham.	= 458	EA Fradley.
= 226	DP Swetman.	= 462	W Thomlinson
= 227	JW Marshall.	= 465	G Taylor.
= 242	T Shore	= 469	J Pickford.
=	K Cartwright (No. missing)	= 473	D Dawson.
= 248	J Winstanley.	= 485	W Barber.
= 255	WF Newbrook.	= 486	W Webb.
= 275	C Bland.	= 499	Walter Smith Price
PC. 507	WJ Batty.		

There were 53 in number with additional men being made up from recruits and members of other Forces from the Midlands and the South of England who had seen the advertisement for the Wallasey Borough Police.

Inspector Thomas J Morris three Sergeants and three Acting Sergeants.

There was one Superintendent, four Inspectors, eight Sergeants and 60 Constables - a total of 73 when Mr. Barry became Chief Constable. Of the 73 men, 54 of the Cheshire Constabulary had sought permission to join the Wallasey Borough Police. This left 19 'County' men to be reallocated.

Walter Price was in the Police for several years. He lived in Walmsley Street as did PC. John Hughes. Walter Barke lived at 190 Wallasey Village. William Sheldon was a member of the Halifax Police who saw the advertisement the Wallasey News in December 1912, decided to apply and was accepted. He was paid twenty-seven shillings per week in Halifax so he was a shilling better off by joining Wallasey. In 1926, he went into the CID.

The rest of the men patrolled on foot, working on beats and would meet the Sergeant every half hour.

In March, 1928 a Morris Oxford motorcar (Registration Number WL 4546) was added at the cost of £225.

I was told of one mischievous little lad who lived in Magazine Brow who used to try to drop an object onto the Chief Constable's hat as passed under his bedroom window. I do not know whether he was successful or if Mr. Barry was aware of the fact.

Two Constables, Edward Gilbert Burgess and James Steel resigned in December 1913.

Headquarters were established in Manor Road with Sub-Stations at New Brighton and Seacombe. Repairs to Hope Street Police Station were carried out by WH Roberts in 1914 at the cost of £18.10s.0. Alterations were also carried out by Henry Dodd amounting to £35. When New Brighton wanted re-enforcements, a Policeman would be sent down on his bicycle. The same applied to Wallasey Village.

Seacombe Police Station was in Church Road opposite Russell and Robinson's business. It was a fine two storey building of red brick with iron railings in front and two entrances, one having a porch. It was often known as the Seacombe Bridewell. The building had leaded windows and there were living quarters above with an Officer in residence. The term 'Bridewell' means a place where there is a lockup or prison. Originally the name of a London Prison (Fr.Taken from a prison near St Bride's or Bridget's Well, London). Applicants for a Police Constable had to be under the age of 27 and not less than five feet ten inches in height and they should have a chest measurement not less than 36 inches. He had to produce satisfactory proof of good character and had to pass an entrance examination in arithmetic, composition, dictation, reading and general knowledge. His birth certificate and, if married, marriage certificate had to be presented. They were not permitted to have other employment, nor any of his family whom he was living with, have any interest in licensed or entertainment premises within his district. His wife was not allowed to run a shop.

A Constable was not allowed to have a lodger in his home without permission of the Chief Constable.

> *"The Law is the true embodiment*
> *Of everything that's excellent.*
> *It has no kind of fault or flaw,*
> *And I, my Lords, embody the Law."*
>
> **WS Gilbert**

Each new recruit had to make a declaration of office before a Justice of the Peace.

The Constable's Declaration was:-

"I, ————, do solemnly and sincerely declare and affirm that I will well and truly serve our Sovereign Lord the King in the office of Constable for the County Borough of Wallasey without favour or affection, malice or ill will, and that I will to the best of my power cause the peace to be kept and preserved, and prevent all offences against the persons and property of His Majesty's subjects; and that while I continue to hold the said office I will to the best of my skill and knowledge discharge all the duties thereof faithfully according to law."

The Conditions of Service

1. Every Constable must devote his whole time to the Police Service. He must attend at any time to any matter which arises within the scope of his duty as a Constable, and must promptly obey all lawful orders of persons in authority over him.

2. A Constable is on probation for at least one year.

3. A Constable must serve wherever he is ordered, and his place of residence is subject to the approval the Chief Constable of Police.

4. A Constable must not marry without the previous consent of the Chief Officer of Police.

5. (a) A Constable must not engage directly or indirectly in any trade for hire or gain.

(b) Neither he nor his wife nor any member of his family living with him hold or have any interest in any licence under the Liquor Licensing Laws or in respect of any place of public entertainment within his Police district.

6. A Constable shall not upon any occasion or under any pretence whatever receive money or anything in the shape of a fee, present, or reward without reporting it immediately, nor shall he retain any such gratuity without consent of the Chief Constable. He shall on no account ask for even hint ar remuneration for any services rendered. He is strictly prohibited from soliciting Christmas or New Year gifts, or contributions for any purpose whatsoever; or from selling tickets for any object unless permission is given by the Chief Constable or Watch Committee.

7. A Constable shall promptly pay all his lawful debts as they become due.....

8. A Constable must avoid whether on duty or in private life, any conduct of behaviour likely to bring discredit on the Service to which he belongs........he must not take any active part in party politics.

9. A Constable becomes on appointment a member of the Police Federation, instituted under the Police Act 1919.......and must not be a member of any Trade Union.

10. A Constable must not resign or withdraw himself from duty except after giving one month's notice in writing or such shorter notice as the Police Authority may accept.

11. Each Constable shall learn to swim if unable to do so and during period of probation will be required to attend lectures in his own time, also to obtain the First Aid Certificate of the St John Ambulance Association.

12. Each Constable must be willing to serve as a Fireman if the Chief Officer of the Police desires him to do so.

A Constable was expected to prevent crime and to preserve the peace and good order of the community and acquaint himself to the conditions of his office and have respect and obedience shown to his superiors. The two essentials necessary in carrying out his many duties were honesty and truthfulness. A Constable could be likened to that of a football referee who has to decide if a player has broken a rule and take the necessary action.

Each member of the Force was expected to have at least one 'respectable suit of clothes'.

In most Police Forces, a recruit was on probation for two years and if he did not reach the grade required he would have to leave. Constables were not allowed to wear spectacles nor beard. In some cases a moustache was not allowed.

Discipline

The men were instilled to 'tell the truth like a man' at all times and next to truthfulness was fairness. Everybody, good or bad, were entitled to the benefit of the law. Drunkenness and drinking while on duty was punishable under Police Regulations and a Constable guilty of such behaviour could face heavy punishment. Good temper and civility were absolutely necessary at all times and they were expected to treat the humblest and poorest person with the same courtesy as one would to the highest in the land.

Cleanliness and smartness of appearance was insisted upon. A Constable was to do his duty in such a manner that the public could see that he was out to help and not to oppress. Observation, memory and description were essential in their duty. Good health

Seacombe Police Station

was necessary for a Policeman and this could be enjoyed by a man who leads a sober clean life. Participating in games and healthy forms of recreation was encouraged. These and other principles are still expected of a Policeman today.

The first Borough Magistrates were appointed 27 October 1915.

******

Police Constables

Constable Victor Alexander lived 2 Ivy Bank in Cresent Road. PC Latham lived at 17 Windsor Street, New Brighton with PC Evans at No.28. Also in the same street was Sergeant Hugh Kenny who lived at No.15 was as a Patrol Sergeant and a native of Co. Mayo. He had enrolled in the Cheshire County Police as a Constable before joining the Wallasey Borough Police at its formation in 1913. He kept turkeys on a piece of land in Waterloo Road close by and next to the Billiards Hall. No doubt he had a lot of neighbours asking for a bird at Christmas time. He later left the Police in order to set up his own debt collecting agency. He went to live in Bromley Road where, at the time of writing, his sister, Mary, still lives. She used to be employed by Lunt's in Victoria Road. He died in 1952, aged 82 years, leaving four sons and two daughters.

It is interesting to note that juveniles were responsible for committing 100 of the 240 crimes in 1913.

******

"Of society offenders who might well be underground, And who would never be missed - who would never be missed!."

———

"He's got her on the list - he's got her on the list; And I don't think she'll be missed - I'm sure she'll not be missed!"

WS Gilbert

Prostitution in New Brighton

There was also the problem of prostitution in New Brighton. The old 'Ham and Egg Parade' was well known for that sort of thing. The Council was well aware of the fact and this together with the poor draining system from the building resulted in the Council taking the decision to have it demolished. Victoria Gardens and the Floral Pavilion were created on the site, resulting in the prostitution trade moving to the Marine Hotel. This was a large hotel with several bars attracting up to 1,400 customers on Saturdays and 2,000 on Bank Holidays. The prostitutes took their clients to the sandhills by the Red Noses. The licensee applied for the license to be transferred to the brewery in 1915 but was refused. A number of witnesses against the licensee were impressive. The Chief Constable refused to give evidence but a plain-clothed Sergeant did, stating that prostitutes had been seen leaving the hotel with clients in the summer of 1913 and at Easter and Whit the following year he had arrested seven women. There were also cases of drunkenness. The licensee stated that he did not serve known prostitutes and looked to the Police for advise as a lot of women came from Liverpool. There was an Appeal against the refusal.

More trouble followed in the April when five women gave evidence, one having been in prison. Counsel for the licensee stated it was hardly orthodox that nine Police witnesses from Wallasey's very small Force, or to assemble the unfortunate women to prevent a transfer of a licence. He also pointed out that it was not an offence to serve prostitutes.

Permitting drunkenness was an offence, several licensees were convicted from time to time. Prostitutes were also convicted. The

A policeman looks on as the Mayor bids farewell to the King and Queen after their visit to Wallasey 25 March 1914 when they layed the foundation stone for the new Town Hall

Police did their best to control the situation by shows of strength to curb the unworkable law.

Royal Visit

King George V and Queen Mary came to Wallasey to lay the Foundation Stone of the new Town Hall on 25 March 1914. The ceremony was carried out from Central Park by means of electricity. The Chief Constable had already been authorised to engage extra Police to deal with the crowds that had assembled in the Central Park and along the streets of the town and at Seacombe Ferry. The Royal couple were entertained by the singing of a choir of 9,000 school children in the park.

Liverpool sent 200 Constables to help on the day. The Royal Route in Wallasey started after the King and Queen had completed their visit to Birkenhead, by crossing the Poulton Bridge, up Mill Lane, along Liscard Road to Central Park. After Leaving the park, they went down Liscard Road, Church Street and turned into Brighton Street, then Church Road to Victoria Place and so to Seacombe Ferry where the Ferryboat was waiting to take them to Liverpool.

Reward

On 9 April 1914 the Chief Constable recommended that one John Owens, who was manager of a pawnbroker's shop at 82 Great Crosshall Street, Liverpool, should be rewarded with ten shillings for helping the Police in securing the prosecution of a man named Ivan Lewis Croxton for stealing a gold watch at Liscard.

Rescue

In June, 1914, Constables John Latham and George Taylor were each given thirty shillings in recognition of their prompt action in rescuing eight children that were in danger of drowning whilst playing in the water near New Brighton Lighthouse on Whit Monday. Their names were reported to the Royal Liverpool Shipwreck and Humane Society and the Royal Humane Society.

******

The First World War Years

For when threatened with emeutes, And your heart is in your boots, There is nothing brings it round Like the trumpet's martial sound.

WS Gilbert

After the First World War started on 4 August 1914, some of the younger men in the force joined the Army so their places had to be filled by reservists who were older men. In August 1914 it was reported that eight members of the Police Force and two members of the Fire Brigade who were in the Reserves had been called up. Five new members were needed and two Firemen in lieu of the two Police Firemen.

PC Alfred Bebbington went into the Military Foot Police. He was allowed eight shillings a week for his mother. Constables James Warner and John Hesketh were allowed two shillings each (for father).

PC Mann received an extra four shillings a week under the Police Reservists Allowance.

Some of the Constables found lodgings at Miss Surrel's home at 79 Wheatland Lane. She cared for her lodgers well and when she died in June 1927 four Policemen acted as coffin bearers at her funeral. They were Det Sgt Keith, PC Prescot, PC Bland and ex-PC Clay.

The Chief Constable released PC Fred Scott to join the Gordon Highlanders for three years as a Recruiting Officer in September, 1914.

Eight members of the Wallasey Force were called up and five new members had to be appointed. PC Edward Ferris Jones went into the Army Veterinary Corps; PC John Leslie Reade enlisted into the Royal Field Artillery. PC William George Cripps joined the King's Liverpool Own Regiment; PC John William Marshall chose the Royal Field Artillery and PC William Bert Clague went to serve as a driver with the Army Transport Service. PC John Henry Mann entered service with the King's Liverpool Regiment and PC Jonathan Thorley enrolled as a member of the Manchester Dock Police for a spell before returning to Wallasey. Lance-Corporal Samuel Brown with the 20th Service Battalion Kings Liverpool Regiment applied for pay allowance under the Police Reservists.

As many as 48 members of the Wallasey Force saw active service in the First World War, with five losing their lives, including an Inspector. They were RK Drakeley, GB Fairhurst, JW Marshall, R McDonough and A Phillips.

From October 1914, the Constables worked a six-day week and seven days holiday. This was later altered to a seven-day week and one day a month off.

Whilst performing plainclothes duty, a Constable received six pence a day extra pay. War Bonus amounted to two shillings extra pay. This was later increased to five shillings.

The Wallasey Force was increased to 101 in 1914, when the average age was 32 and the average length of service was 5 years, 235 days.

The war brought extra duties, such as keeping an eye out for spies, the blackout and the occasional deserter. Constables had to deal with riots against Jewish shopkeepers. They were required to arrest every alien, guard vulnerable points, enforce lighting restrictions and to deal with air-raids. Lighting was forbidden and any lights that could be seen from the sea were not allowed.

It was estimated that there were some 500 German residents living in Wallasey with 52 of them were deemed to be enemies for internment to the Isle of Man or deportation, although most of these families posed no threat.

A number of German people were taken away from Wallasey and there were restrictions on the movement of aliens. In August, an Austrian, who had lived here for 23 years, was fined £5 under the Aliens Restrictions Order for travelling more than five miles when he had been to Manchester to see his wife.

A German engineer, who had refused to join the German Army in 1913, had managed to leave his country and was living here, was fined for going on a day out in a char-a-banc to Llangollen.

In August 1914 a young German was seen with a telegram form in the Post Office at New Brighton. This caused concern and he was followed down Victoria Road by a large crowd which a Policeman managed to control. The telegram was taken from him and when translated by a local German-speaking shopkeeper, it was found to be innocuous.

Constables were asked to keep an eye open in October 1914 for a reported German Spy who was travelling around the country on a motorcycle. He was five feet ten and a half inches tall, a fair complexion, clean shaven with a scar over his right eye. However, he was not seen in Wallasey.

One young fellow was taken in for acting suspiciously. He was thought to be a spy of sorts and was taken away by the local soldiers and presented to their Commander and after questioning was handed over to the Police. They interrogated him and discovered that he was a salesman for a Liverpool firm and was released.

A youth was found guilty to be selling secret information to the Germans.

Those men who were not attached to the permanent staff of the Fire Brigade received extra pay for attending fires and drills, beginning in May 1914. For each attendance at drill they received a shilling (but not allowed to exceed twice that amount). For attending fires they received two shillings and sixpence for the first hour and one shilling for the succeeding hour.

Mr. JC Bate was the District Coroner.

Inspector Sandland at New Brighton was loaned to the army authorities as Instructor at Chester. The Army paid his salary together with an allowance of fourteen shillings a week. Sergeant Leigh, who took over as Drill Instructor at Wallasey in his absence, received fifteen shillings extra pay.

Farming at night was difficult without lamps. Ploughing at night was not uncommon and restrictions were lifted to some degree, allowing a form of lighting to enable them to plough.

This fine photograph was taken of the full assembly of Police Officers at the rear of the Manor Road Police Station. Wallasey

The public were not allowed to keep or shoot carrier pigeons as the Admiralty were using them.

When the *Lusitania* was sunk off Ireland on Friday 7 May 1915 by a torpedo from a German submarine there were anti-German riots in Seacombe, Birkenhead and Liverpool as many local seamen had lost their lives in the liner. A crowd gathered outside a German's pork butcher in Seacombe and became rowdy and a German ship in dock in the West Float was seized. A local German had his motorcar confiscated. Claims under the Riot Act were made to the Council in September 1915. Ten properties were damaged in Poulton Road; one in Seaview Road; one in Demesne Street; one in Chapel Street; one in Somerville and three in Tobin Street. Shops in Wallasey and Birkenhead had their windows smashed by some members of the public thinking the owners were of German extraction.

Although the public were not allowed to take photographs of ships in the river from the ferryboats, one lady quite openly did so and the Captain spotted her, left his bridge immediately and demanded her camera, removed the photographic plate and handed the camera back. No doubt she was not aware of the restrictions. The Policemen's one day leave was discontinued and one day a month off was introduced. This arrangement was altered to one day off a fortnight then it returned to one day in eight.

Mr. Barry, the Chief Constable, attended a conference that was called for dealing with the air-raids and how precautions could be taken. Street lamps were switched off by use of a long walking stick when an enemy plane was reported to be heading in direction of the town.

Some of the bombs that were dropped did not explode and the men had to be told how to deal with the situation should it occur. An ammunition depot was set up in Gorsey Lane.

Setting off fireworks was banned and only small fireworks were allowed on 5 November.

There were also new licensing hours to be adhered to. These came into being August 1915 when the public-houses in Wallasey had to close at 9pm (altered to 9.30pm the following March). It was an offence for a person to pay for another person's drinks. Men were not allowed to pay for their wives' drinks and this caused a lot of trouble. These changes had been brought about by the Temperance Movement. By the September, the first offenders were brought before the Courts and those found guilty were fined.

Two Wallasey ferryboats, *Daffodil* and *Iris*, were taken over by the Admiralty and used in the raid at Zeebrugge on St George's Day, 1918.

Runaway Horses

One of the first Policemen to receive a medal for meritorious service in the Borough was that of PC Robinson. Whilst on patrol with Sergeant Whiteside one Monday evening at 6pm near the Cemetery in Rake Lane, he encountered a runaway horse and float running towards them at speed. Constable Robinson acted promptly and rushed into the road and gathered up the loose reins and was dragged a considerable distance along the road before getting the horse to a standstill near Liscard Village. In his efforts one rein had broken.

The float belonged to Messrs Comberbach, the wine merchants (who had four branches, including Victoria Place, Seacombe, and Victoria Road, New Brighton). Mr H Little of Duke Street, New Brighton had been delivering goods to a house in Zig Zag Road when the horse became frightened at a passing motor-van and bolted down the road into Rake Lane. For his bravery, Constable Robinson received the Bronze General Medal with Silver Bar on 9 February 1914.

Almost two years later a similar thing happened when a horse bolted in Wallasey Village. Constable Robinson again rushed to the scene and brought the horse to a standstill. For his swift action, he received his second Silver Bar.

Chief Constable

In 1916, the Wallasey Superintendent, SF Butler was appointed Chief Constable of Ramsgate and three years later in 1919, Superintendent RJ Pearson became Chief Constable of Cambridge. These two gentlemen served for many years in their respective forces.

Fire-Bobbies

The Fire Station was in Manor Road with Horse-Drawn engines. The Chief Constable reported that several members of the Force had had Fire Brigade experience and he suggested that the services of the Auxiliary Firemen could be dispensed with in the near future and their places taken by members of the Police Force. Those selected as Firemen would received an extra two shillings and six pence when acting as Firemen.

The Police Strike

I think you ought to recollect
You cannot show too much respect
Towards the highly titled few;
But nobody does, and why should you?

WS Gilbert

The working conditions for the Policemen dropped to a lower level and caused concern. Pay was not good. The first trouble started in 1909. One of the young Inspectors in the Metropolitan Police, by the name of Syme, differed with his superiors. He accused them of injustice and oppression. He brought Parliament and the press into the matter which led to his dismissal from the force. He attacked the Commissioner, Sir Edward Henry, by having libellous handbills printed. In 1913, Syme started a secret Police Union and he was often in prison for libel and for trying to cause disaffection among the Police in wartime. While in prison he refused food and eventually was sent to Broadmoor. In 1931 he was let out and received compensation. By now it had affected his mind and he went down to the Home Office and threw stones through the windows. He died in 1955.

The Policemen were made up from the working class and were subject to certain controls which did not apply to other men in other employment. They were out for better wages. It was expected that a Policeman was respectable in his private life.

In Wallasey, a Policeman worked a six-day week and got a seven day annual holiday. From the October of 1914, he had to work a seven-day week and got a day off a month. They worked a split shift of a twelve hour day with a four hour break. Other Forces made their men work longer hours.

As the war progressed the Police pay was not increased with the cost of living and by 1918 their families were suffering hardships. A meeting was held in the Home Counties in 1918 to discuss Police pay. The Union were of the opinion that the men would not get a decent wage. Certain politicians had brought the matter up in the House but the Government did not wish to hear of it as they had the war to think about. In 1918, the Metropolitan Police had pay and pensions under review. On 27 August 1918 the Police Union sent letters to the Prime Minister and the Home Secretary, calling for a rise in pay, recognition of their Union and the reinstatement of the Constable who had been dismissed and if they had not been accepted by midnight the following day, they would take strike action.

By midnight on 30 August 1918, over 6,000 Officers of the Metropolitan Force were on strike. General Smuts was asked to meet with the Superintendents but a small number of Union men arrived and he would not discuss the matter with them so the London City Police came out on strike. A Police Bill was passed on 8 July 1919 that made it quite clear that any Police Officer going on strike would be dismissed from the force.

The Police strike came into effect 1 August 1919 in London with a total of 2,364 men from seven forces. These included 1,056 from the Metropolitan , 57 from the City of London and Birmingham had 119 men out on strike. On Merseyside, Liverpool had 954 on strike, followed by 114 in Birkenhead with 63 from Bootle and Wallasey had only one Constable.

The situation grew worse in Liverpool where riots broke out and troops and tanks had to be brought in. Some of the Constables in Wallasey were not happy about the way they had come to know about the strike through the press after receiving a telegram from London saying that the strike had been cancelled on the day that it was to start so they decided not to strike. On 31 March a Police Sergeant came over from Liverpool with a number of strikers to talk to the Wallasey Constables to get them to come out on strike, but Mr. Barry refused to allow him to speak to the men but he said that he could come over next day, which was a Sunday, and address the whole force in the Court Room and see if they were agreeable to go on strike or otherwise, on condition that he (the Chief Constable) would be able to address the men first. This was agreed and they returned next morning. Mr. Barry addressed the men. He told them that the strike was illegal and they could be dismissed from the force which would result in their wives and children suffering hardship.

Mr. Barry was not bitter about the situation. The men knew that they would be breaking the law if they went on strike and their livelihood would be in jeopardy. After speaking he left the Court Room. The Liverpool Sergeant then spoke to the men and a vote was taken. The Wallasey Policemen voted overwhelmingly against going out on strike with the exception of one man.

A band of strikers from Liverpool came over and confronted the Birkenhead Police. Sixty members of the Birkenhead Force joined in and others followed suit soon after. Wallasey was left as the only working force in these parts. A group of strikers gathered on the landing stage at Liverpool and came over on the ferry to Seacombe and caused trouble. Constable Nichols was on duty at Seacombe. He was attacked, kicked and tormented with a stick. Three women who witnessed the action, came to his rescue.

The Constables in Wallasey had the backing of the Chief Constable. He suggested that they went home and changed into plain clothes – It was the only time that Wallasey was without a uniformed Police Force.

The bobbies (in plain clothes) stood by the bank at the bottom of Borough Road and saw the Liverpool Policemen looking in every side street and around every corner, hoping to see a Wallasey Policeman.

"Where's all the so and so Policemen in Wallasey?" asked one fellow to a colleague.

Nearly 400 strikers from other parts of Merseyside set about looking for Wallasey uniformed Constables on their beat but they were unable to find any, so they reverted to picketing. They broke up into groups and they tried to find out where the Policemen lived so that they could picket outside their homes. Again, this was not successful.

The strike began on the 1 August and two days later the Army were called in. Armoured vehicles were brought into Liverpool and placed on St George's Plateau. The strike began to fail and on

4 August the troops had control. Rioters were arrested and tried. Those Constables who did not report for duty as soon as the strike was over were dismissed. 2300 Policemen lost their status, of which 955 were from Liverpool. Some of these had been in the force for 25 years.

Constable Edward F Jones was dismissed on 14 August 1919 for having Union activities and joining the strike. The rest of the force received a week's special leave as a reward for not striking. The strike had, however, brought to the fore the general working conditions. Standardisation came into being and the Police Federation was set up. Soon, the Policemen were looked upon as Officers and paid accordingly. From 11 April 1918 the Police received a war bonus. Inspectors were given 16 shillings a week, Sergeants and Constables ten shillings and eight pence a week with an additional two shillings a week in respect of each dependant child under fifteen years of age. There was also the Tramway Strike that started on 12 September 1917.

In 1919 there were 120 men in all ranks. In that year there were ten house break-ins compared with 26 in the previous year.

The old horse prison van was disposed of for £5 in 1918 and a second-hand vehicle was sought to replace the Austin motor van.

Dr Charles Wilson, the Deputy Police Surgeon, acted as Police Surgeon with the same salary as Dr Napier.

The Chief Constable's salary was increased to £600 on 1 April 1918. DC John Wedge was taken Prisoner of War in Germany and £25 was granted in gratuity.

Constable Richard Aldridge decided to resign from the Wallasey Force and enlisted in the Royal Marines. He took poart at Zeebrugge and received fatal wounds. Constable James Molyneux died in the Victoria Central Hospital.

On a brighter note, Alderman Edwin Peace received the OBE.

******

Alderman Edwin Peace OBE

Minstrels

A wandering minstrel I -
A thing of shreds and patches
Of ballads, songs and snatches,
And dreamy lullaby!

WS Gilbert

There were a number of talented bobbies in the Wallasey Force who could sing and dance who were encouraged to form a group. After a while they decided to put a stage show at one of the local theatres. They hired the *La Scala Theatre* in Seacombe (the old Irving Theatre) for a One Night Show in the early part of 1919. The Wallasey Police Minstrels advertised it as a 'Unique Entertainment'. They sang songs and danced. There were also musical interludes included and an original comedy sketch called 'The Twin Assistants' completed the bill. This show was the last show staged at the theatre under the name of *La Scala*.

On Tuesday 13 April 1920 the Police Minstrels gave a concert in aid of St Paul's Church New Building Fund which was well supported.

The Church was to build St Peter's Church in Brentwood Street, Poulton.

******

Changes

Women were admitted to the Police Forces in 1919/20 and motorcycle patrols were introduced in 1921. Patrol cars were fitted with two-way radios in 1927 and it was not until 1960s that the Policemen had a beat radio (these are switched on at all times).

It was Captain Popkess, the Chief Constable of Nottingham, who was among the first to pioneer the two-way radio units and Brighton Force worked on a pocket set.

In the days before the Second World War the sight of an Officer in uniform was enough in itself to frighten misbehaving youths and older ruffians that were up to no good. The tunic had only two breast pockets and the collar carried the plated Shield from the Wallasey Coat of Arms and Constable's number. At a later date, the Shield was removed from the collar.

Police Constables still wore the striped armlet. This practice was later discontinued.

Those who had qualified in First Aid wore an Ambulance Badge on the left arm placed at a certain number of inches from the cuff or chevrons. The same applied to the Royal Fire Saving Society Badge.

Not long after another change to the helmet was made. The next issue had a coxcomb on top with a small chromium-plated badge at the end. This design replaced the helmet with the spike and is still the standard issue of the present day Merseyside Police. Some Police Forces, such as the Yorkshire Force still have the helmet with the spike on top. The new issue was slowly phased in and some Constables would be seen wearing the older type.

There are people who think that the present helmet was modelled on the style of the brass helmet that was worn by the Fire Brigade. The double-breasted greatcoat was warm as there were two layers of cloth across the chest and it fastened right up to the shoulder with the tunic underneath fastening to the neck. The garment was greatly appreciated on a bitter winter's night.

When they were on night duty, they wore a matt-black painted helmet plate and comb badge. Only the Constable's number was in bright metal. The tunic also had black buttons, but the greatcoat carried the bright metal buttons.

Most Police Forces made their men wear the greatcoat from October until May. They were also issued with a battery-operated torch, replacing the old oil lantern. These proved to be rather inadequate. Thick woollen gloves were also issued but these were not suitable in wet weather. The early tunics did not have pockets. Then top breast pockets were introduced and followed by pockets on either side (four in all). The side pockets were later discontinued and it was not until a later date that they were reintroduced. The Constables liked the tunics that fastened to the neck as they could just wear a vest in the summer in order to keep cool.

Sergeants wore three stripes on either arm. The Home Office suggested standardisation of uniforms in 1934.

In 1924, the Wallasey Borough Police had 100 Constables, with Mr. Barry as Chief Constable, and Arthur Sandland Chief Inspector. He lived at 2 Queens Street which was part of the Police Station.

In addition to the Chief Constable and Chief Inspector, there were six Inspectors, 13 Sergeants and 100 Police Constables.

Inspector William Crook Whiteside was in charge of New Brighton Police Station. He lived next door at 3 Hope Street. Arthur Sandland, before being promoted, had been the previous Inspector at New Brighton.

Inspector John Bebbington was responsible for the Seacombe Division at the Police Station in Church Road. He resided on the premises with his wife, Ada.

Mr. Arthur Sandland –Superintendent

Mr. Sandland joined the Cheshire County Constabulary in August 1899 and was first stationed at Seacombe. He had served in the Cheshire Regiment at the outbreak of the South African war. He was called up with the Reserves with whom he served until 1902 receiving the Queen's and King's South African Medals with five bars. After joining the Cheshire Constabulary he was transferred to HQ at Chester as a Detective Constable where he remained for five years and was picked for promotion. He made several smart captures and his general ability brought him promotion from Police

Superintendant Arthur Sandland

Constable to Acting Sergeant to full rank in one week. As Sergeant No.74 he was stationed at Hoole near Chester. The small Police Station was at 18 Hewitt Street. Mr. Sandland was Drill Instructor under the County Constabulary for seven years at Chester and came to Wallasey twelve months after the foundation of the Force in 1913, being promoted to Inspector. The family moved to Wallasey and lived in Hope Street before moving to Queens Street. Mr. Sandland had been Chief Inspector since about 1920 and became Superintendent. He wore a frog-type coat with the Silver Imperial Crown on either side of the collar and a belt with a metal clasp. The peak cap had a decorated brim and a Crown badge. He had to retire due to ill-health and died in 1925 at the age of 49.

Pay and Conditions

The Police Constable's pay was as follows:-
Twenty-eight shillings a week on appointment.
Twenty-nine shillings after one year.
Thirty shillings after two years.
Thirty-one shillings after three years.
Thirty-three shillings after five years.
Thirty-four shillings after eight years.
Thirty-six shillings after twelve years.
Thirty-seven shillings after fifteen years.
The Sergeants received:-
Thirty-nine shillings on commencement.
Forty-one shillings after two years.
Forty-three shillings after four years.
Forty-five shillings after five years.
In 1915 a Constable got thirty shillings and six pence a week and after eight years it went up to thirty-seven shillings and six pence a week. A Sergeant got forty-two shillings and six pence a week rising to fifty shillings and sixpence after eight years. An Inspector received fifty-two shillings a week on appointment. This would rise to fifty-eight shillings and six pence after eight years.
Total wages for five weeks ending in September, 1914 was £861.10s.7d.
The wages per week for October, 1914 was £185.
A Constable Clerk received thirty-one shillings a week.
Men paid thirteen shillings a week for 'digs' for full board. This was paid out of the twenty-eight shillings weekly wage. A man could purchase a good pair of shoes in those days for seven shillings and eleven pence and a suit of clothes for £2.5s.0.
At a later date, the Police pay rose to £3.10s.0. a week with ten shillings rent allowance. In those days a suit of clothes cost fifty shillings and an overcoat £2.5s.0. Uniforms: Constable £7, Sergeant. £8, Inspector £9. Out of pocket, £3, £4, £5 respectively. In 1918 the Superintendent received £200 per annum, rising to £210. The Asst. Superintendent was paid £2.18s.6d a week rising to £3.1s.0. The rate for Chief Inspector was £210 for the first year, £215 for the second and £220 for the third. Inspectors received £180 for the first two years, then an increase of £5 each year up to £200 at year six. The Plain Clothed Inspectors had an allowance of 16 shillings and Sergeants 13 shillings. Constables had a reduction in their pay for pensions ranging from 10.5d to 1s.2d Sergeants had from 1s.0.5d to 1s.4.5d deducted. Inspectors had a reduction of 1s.8.5d to 1s.11d and Chief Inspectors 2s.0.5d.
The Policemen later worked a six day week. If they started on the Monday, the next week it would be a Tuesday and so on. This meant the men could get a weekend off occasionally. The day off altered week by week, starting on a Monday meant that the Saturday and Sunday as the weekend off, followed by a week without a day off.
Annual leave was allocated and could be any time from April to October for 'Summer Leave' and one was very lucky to change the rota.

Manor Road Police Station on the left and Concert Hall on the right

The Police were allowed on the public transport free of charge while going to their beat, provided that they stood on the conductor's platform Bus passes were issued.

Clifton Hall

I seem to remember the Policemen walking down Urmson Road to receive their pay packets from the old Clifton Hall in the Navy League grounds. The large house had the look of a temple, having been built in the mid 1830s. Among the people to have lived there was Peter Wright, Clerk of the Peace of Liverpool and Samuel Smith, MP. It was demolished in the 1950s.

Fancy Dress Ball

The Police held a Fancy Dress Ball at the New Brighton Tower Ballroom on 12 February 1920 in aid of the Widows, Orphans and Benevolent Fund. Constable W Williams was MC. In those days Thomas Rimmer Orchestra provided the music at the Tower.
The Council had purchased the Concert Hall, Manor Road in June 1920 for the sum of £20,000 (*see picture above*).
Five boys were rescued from a boat that had been in the river opposite the Mariners' Home in 1920. After the alarm had been raised, Det. Constable Cartwright and a stage hand, had jumped into a boat at Egremont Ferry and came to the boys' aid.
By 31 December 1920 the Chief Constable reported that the Wallasey Police Force had 120 men in all ranks including the Fire Brigade with 105 holding certificates in St John's Ambulance Brigade and 26 members had certificates of proficiency in swimming, rescue and resuscitation. The Police cost 3.5d in the pound on the Rates. The Chief Constable reported that there had been 184 offences in 1919 compared with 244 in 1918.
During the General Strike in May 1926 a few volunteers manned the trams and buses. A body of men were at Seacombe with an Inspector in command to control the violent scenes as men tried to stop transport running with Policemen having to hang on to the outside of the buses to protect the crew from the strikers. Wire mesh was placed over the windows to deter strikers from throwing stones at the windscreens of the vehicles.
In 1927 all the aeroplanes had to carry markings painted once on the lower surface and once on the upper surface for identification purposes.
In July 1927 the Chief Constable of Cheshire recommended Superintendent Thomas Ennion, who was in charge of the Wirral Division, for grant of His Majesty's Police Medal.

*When constabulary duty's to be done.
Ah, take one consideration with another,
A Policeman's lot is not a happy one.*

WS Gilbert

Day-to-day

In the early days, the lawbreakers consisted of men being drunk and disorderly, minor thefts, cases of cruelty to animals and children, touting and people trying to travel across the river on the ferryboats without paying. There were also the pickpockets, people attempting to commit suicide and fellows stealing live poultry. The savage dog that had no collar or muzzle which had to be caught and brought in to the Police Station.

There is a story told about two men who were quarrelling outside Seacombe Police Station. Their wives were with them and they also joined in and started to attack the men. Soon the women were pulling each other's hair. Sergeant Collins appeared on the scene and tried his best to stop the women from fighting. They did not care for his intrusion so they turned on him and grabbing hold of him, they pulled him one way then the other. The Sergeant was very annoyed and the whole thing ended when the two men walked off to the public-house.

'Boys will be boys' as the old saying goes and football is a great game. All the lads needed was to throw a few coats on the ground, and 'hi bingo', they had a couple of goal posts. All that was necessary was the ball. Some would play on the promenade and were told that it was not allowed. After the bobby had gone they would start playing again. Five youths were later spotted by the bobby playing football on promenade at Seacombe. They duly appeared before the Magistrates and were fined six pence each! There was a fellow by the name of John Avory who would often sleep rough. The bobby would be always telling him to move on. He ended up appearing before the Bench and was sent to prison for sleeping out at Seacombe. I don't suppose he minded as he was sure of a bed for the next fortnight!

On another occasion a woman was causing a disturbance by throwing stones and all kinds of rubbish in the road. A huge crowd of children gathered to watch the proceedings. The bobby on his beat came along and booked her for her behaviour and foul language. She ended up by having to go to prison for a day.

In Wallasey Village, one Charles Brammah was found working an unfit pony. He was later fined twenty shillings for the offence.

Gathering youths have often caused people to walk in the road by them congregating on the pavements. The Policemen would ask them to move along. He would get tired of telling them to do so and in the end their names would end up in his notebook. Once, three youths were each fined a shilling for their behaviour. This habit continued in Liscard centre for many years but it seems to have been controlled by the Policeman on duty and I have not heard of youths appearing before the Court for a long time for this minor offence.

Children got up to mischief. Two 11 year-old youngsters managed to find some tin discs which were about the size of a penny coin. They had the idea of using them to get chocolate out of the machines on the railway stations that were the property of the British Automatic Company Limited. They were caught in the act at Seacombe Station and duly appeared before the Court. They received three strokes of the birch and probably never tried the trick again!

In the same year all vehicles had to have lights during the hours of darkness which came under the Road Transport Lighting Act of 1927.

As regards the policing of the County Borough of Wallasey, the situation was a little different from that of other County Boroughs, that one portion of the Borough consisted of a line of dockland whilst the other portion was a seaside resort. During the summer it had to be properly patrolled. Apart from New Brighton itself, there was also Wallasey Beach to take into consideration as the Harrison Drive area attracted a large number of people. Tents on the beach were popular and they would be seen right along the

Policemen lining up for the 1930 Government Inspection with their greatcoats and capes neatly folded in front of them

beach by the Embankment. There was also several miles of foreshore and promenade which had to be policed.

The jurisdiction of a Constable for the Wallasey force extended to the Borough boundaries (which actually ran through the middle of the Birkenhead Docks) to the shore at New Brighton and Wallasey. Birkenhead Police, under the provisions of the Mersey Docks and Harbour Board Acts, allowed them to be responsible for a portion of the Dock Estate within the Boundaries of Wallasey. Any corpse that was seen floating on the surface of the water came under the jurisdiction of either the Birkenhead force or the Wallasey Force, depending on which side of the dock it was pulled from.

A Police Officer of the Wallasey Borough Police had the power to act on the Wallasey side of the Dock Estate. The matter had to be reported to the Birkenhead Police, unless it called for immediate action to be taken.

Many items were stolen from the docks and the bobby at the gate, if he thought the docker was hiding something under his coat, would call him over and ask him what he was he was up.

Coal was taken from the Dock Estate; one was not allowed to pick up lumps of coal that had fallen from the shunting engine.

In the case of the River Mersey, which formed the boundary line of more than Courts of Jurisdiction, the offence could be tried.

An offence that was committed in the River Mersey which formed a boundary line between two or more Courts of Summary Jurisdiction, the offence could be tried by any one of such Courts. Cargo from ships was often washed ashore and men would rush down and get it away before the Law arrived.

Constables were encouraged to take a keen interest in crimes that were committed in other districts other than in Wallasey, otherwise a law breaker would think that they would have a better chance of getting away with the crime if he could slip out of the district where it had taken place as the other force would not be interested. To overcome this, there was cordial co-operation between the various forces, especially when a serious crime had been committed.

A Policeman could be lent to another Police Authority under an agreement between the two forces. They would, of course, become Officers of the district in which they had been sent to (under the Police Act, 1890).

The Police also had a department for the Local Taxation, Motor Taxation and Licensing and Hackney Carriage Department.

The Chief Constable was also Vehicle Taxation Officer for the Borough. He was also in charge of the petroleum and responsible for the issue of Hawkers' and Peddlers' Licences, the Theatre and Cinema Licences and in addition, the Children's Performing Licences.

The Mobile Officer acted as Coroner's Officer.

The CID had an Aliens' Register in order to keep a check on all the foreigners residing in the borough, together with information concerning dangerous drugs, cinema inspection, the supervision of scrap metal dealers, the operation of the Firearms Act and other duties.

There was one Officer to every 912 persons in the town, compared with the national average of 707.

In the days before the Second World War, there was far less traffic on the roads compared with today and large inspection parades could be held in Manor Road outside the Police Station. As traffic increased other sites were used. The Navy League Parade Ground in Withens Lane was used for the Annual Inspection by HM Inspector of Constabulary.

The men would line up in three columns and place their greatcoats and capes neatly folded up before them. This practice seems to have stopped when the Parades were held in the Navy League Grounds.

The Navy League had been established in 1894 and the Lancashire and National Sea Training Homes for poor boys was in Withens Lane which was the first sea training home on land being supported by public funds.

The CID lined up wearing bowler hats and plain clothes. In later years it was the trilby hats and raincoats.

All concerned hoped for cool weather as the parade could last for over two hours. The men would have to stand at attention for 30 minutes then march around the block with the Salute taken in Grosvenor Street.

On one occasion, the Superintendent, who headed the parade, had upset the men and everyone 'stepped short' around the block without him noticing. He rounded the corner into Grosvenor Street and realised that he was all on his own some 200 yards in front of the men. All that he could do was to 'mark time' until the rest caught up!

Those persons who reported having lost an article had the details recorded in the Lost and Found Book.

Summonses had to be served by the Warrant Officer. They could not be legally served on a Sunday and Officers were recommended that they should not be served between 10pm and 6am.

Seldom were the Police in this country armed; they relied on the wooden truncheon. Should it be deemed necessary to arm certain Officers of the Force, Smith and Wesson revolvers would be issued. The Police were exempt from having to have a Fire Arms Certificate when issued with a fire arm in the course of their duty. Animals were protected under the Protection of Animals Act, 1911. A Constable had the power to arrest a person causing cruelty to animals without a warrant if guilty under Section 1 of the Act. There was also Inspector M Lea and the Tax Officer was Detective Sergeant A Keafe. Alderman EG Parkinson was elected Chairman of the Watch Committee.

The telephone number of Manor Road Police Station was Wallasey 1340 (three lines) but this was later changed to Wallasey 6161, then to 638 6161.

Det Inspector TW Roberts was promoted to Superintendent in place of Mr. Sandland in 1924. Det Constable WG Short was also promoted to Sergeant.

Long Service was recognised in 1929. PC H Bland had 21 and a half years service; Det PC HM Brennan for 21. PCs Mann, Price and Webb for 17 and Det PC W Shelton, PC W Hallam and Sergeant WA Ligett for eight years' service.

In the same year Alderman J Pennington became Chairman of the Watch Committee and alterations were carried out at the Police Station at the cost of £225. Patrol cars were yet to come; Policemen patrolled on foot. If an extra Constable was needed in other parts of the town, he would cycle there.

In May, 1929 the Wallasey Police decided that it was necessary to get around quicker so they invested in a green Triumph motorcycle with open sidecar combination. It cost £93.2s.6d. The rider was a very tall Constable and wore breeches or black boots and gaiters

Albert Mackey (see below)

or leggings. His leather gloves were attached to the handlebars of the motorcycle. He took great pride in his dress. He would take Superintendent McDonough down to New Brighton in the sidecar to supervise the crowds at the resort.

Mr. Albert Mackey

Albert Mackey was out with a friend one day and happened to pass the Police Station in Manor Road which gave him the idea of becoming a Constable. During his interview he was asked if he could do shorthand and typing. Having demonstrated these skills he was enrolled without having to fill in an application form on 23 April 1928 as a Probationer, eventually becoming Constable No.63. He, and PC Bob Edwards, first found lodgings at Miss May Burston and her sister, Beatrice who lived at 30 Strathcona Road. The Misses Burton once lived in Liscard Vale House in Vale Park where their father, Mr WG Burston, was Park Curator. Albert and Bob were both keen swimmers and would participate in the Annual Police River Swim.

(PC. John Mann also lived in Strathcona Road at 32 and at a later date, Det Sgt Leslie Horricks lived at 49).

Albert Mackey then went to lodge with Mrs Thompson in Wilton Street in Liscard. There, he became friends with Mrs Thompson's daughter, Ruth Mobbs, and husband, Edda. All three would go cycling around Wirral countryside. Mr. Mackey married in 1940 and became a Sergeant. In 1947 he became Acting Inspector and went on the teaching staff at No.1 District Police Training School, Bruche, outside Warrington, where he taught Maths, Police Law and English.

Mr. Mackey's daughter, Pam Gruber, was employed in the advertising business. She also worked for the Cunard Company in Liverpool and became well-known as a jazz singer before joining TWA Air Lines as an air hostess. She is now a very successful business woman in cosmetics and makes regular visits to this country bringing her father when his health allows.

******

Training

All recruits wishing to don the cloth, went to No.1 District Police Training Centre for 13 weeks for initial training. The Police Training School at Bruche outside Warrington, being the largest in the country. Refresher Courses for two weeks were taken at the end of the first year of service and the second at the end of the Probationary Period. During this time one's Superiors could dispense with you at any time as being 'unlikely to become a good and efficient Officer'. If this was the case, there was no appeal.

Brigadier Dunn, Commander Willis and General Sim were at Peel House Training School. Brigadier PDW Dunn, CBE, DSO, MC, became Commandant of the Police College at Ryton-on-Dunsmore. The College had been set up in April 1948. Mr GO Griffith was the first lecturer in English. He was author of a small book, entitled 'Queen's English', which was published in 1953 by the College. Appointments were made officially by the Watch Committee as were the promotions and dismissals but the advice of the Chief Constable was always heeded. Promotion Examinations were taken at Mather Avenue and were the Liverpool City Examinations. These were in two parts - educational (taken after two years) and Police Duty. The latter could only be taken for promotion to Sergeant after completion of four years service and to Inspector only when a Sergeant had ten or more years' service.

On returning from Bruche, the Officer started shift on Night Duty and was under the supervision of a senior Constable for several weeks before being 'released upon an unsuspecting public'!

In January 1928 application was made to the Home Office for permission to increase the Wallasey force by one Superintendent, one Sergeant and 13 Constables. Sergeant Beer was promoted to Inspector.

The Men on the Beat

The strength of the Wallasey Borough Police Force on 23 April 1928 consisted of:-

Chief Constable:- Percy L Barry (Ex-Indian Army & Stoke-on-Trent)

Chief Inspector:- and 2nd in Command, John Ormerod.

Inspectors:-
Matthew Leigh, John Bebbington, Freddie Beere.

Det Inspector:- Kenneth J Cauldwell.

Fire Inspector:- William Nicholson.

Sergeants:-
Nos.
1   Bert Worrall.
2   Sam Brown.

3   Fred Wood.
4   WGG Short. Promoted to Det Insp CID.
5   Alex Keith, Motor Tax Officer.
6   Walter Payne, became Insp. General Enquiry Office
7   Bob Collings
8   Joel Atkinson.

9   Tommy Latham.
10 William Lidgett. Became Insp.
11 Thomas Wilkinson, Fire Brigade.
12 Michael McDonough, Superintendent and Deputy Chief Constable. [there was no No.13 as this was deemed to be unlucky]

14 Alf Bebbington (Moreton).

Acting Sergeant I Wedgewood (Formerly PC 100).

George Walker as a Mounted Policeman in the 1920s

Police Constables:-
1   J Wainwright (Act Sgt 2 stripes 1913 Cheshire Constabulary).
2   Eric Barke, CID.
3   George Craft.
4   Jack Williams, Mounted, Fire Brigade.
5   Larry Carroll
6   Martin Brenan, CID.
7   Harry Farran (Cycle Patrol)
8   Ted Whittaker.
9   Ted Fradley.
10 David Tweddle.
11 Arthur Reece, became Sgt.
12 Walter Jackson.
13 Jack Davies.
14 Jimmie Banks.
15 Monty Caugherty.
16 Jimmie Gallagher.
17 Bill Evason, Fire Brigade.
18 Herbert Bland.
19 Freddy Cooke.
20 Syd Lodge.
21 Bill Griffiths.
22 Len Marsden, Fire Brigade.
23 Dave Dawson.
24 Will Tomlinson.
25 Bill Packer.
26 Percy Swetman.
27 Walter Webb.
28 Jack Latham.
29 Alf Cotton, became Insp.
30 Bill Hallam.
31 Bill Price.
32 Bill Batty.
33 Edwin Griffin
34 Ted Pearce.
35 Jack Hesketh.
36 Jack Palin, became Sgt.
37 Jack Pickford.
38 Bill Barber.
39 Dick Thomson..
40 'Bud' Maddocks, Fire Brigade.
41 Dave Starkey.
42 Harry Benfield, Fire Brigade
43 Jack Holmes.
44 Bob Jones, Fire Brigade
45 Billy Field.
46 Charlie Sandland, became. Chief Insp.
47 Jack Mann.
48 Steve Prideaux.
49 Harold Le Grice. (PC DE Heenan became No.49).
50 Billy Machill, became Sgt.
51 Arthur Jones.

52 'Chummy' Ingram.
53 Herbert Ashall
54 Joseph Barke.
55 Stan Hill.
56 Bill Anderson, CID.
57 Harry Dolan, Fire Brigade. (Joe Newton became No.57).

58 Bill Wesley.

59 William Bassett.
60 Tommy Highton, Fire Brigade.
61 Jimmy 'Plum' Warner, Fire Brigade.
62 William Pender.
63 Albert Mackey, became Acting Insp. & Instructor.
64 Alex Yule, became Det Sgt
65 Joseph Ryan.
66 Dave Pendergast.
67 Bob Herron, Fire Brigade.
68 Walter Shelton, CID.
69 George Chilton.
70 Jonathan Thorley, Fire Brigade.
71 Mickie Golden.
72 Ted Petherbridge, became Sgt.
73 Thomas Haig.
74 Ernie Jarrett, became Sgt.
75 George Hodges
76 Herbert Winstanley, Fire Brigade.

77 Thomas Bale.
78 Thomas Beresford.
79 Alf Williams, became Insp
80 George Walker, Mounted.
81 Bill Rigg, became Sgt.
82 George Sharples.
83 Sidney Digman.
84 Ben Phillips
85 George Walker, Mounted.
86 Harold Cash, Fire Brigade.
87 Teddy Prescott.
88 Tommy Kenyon, CID.
89 Bob Jackson, became Sgt.
90 (Not allocated as it had been the Chief Constable's).
91 John 'Gunner', Marshall, Fire Brigade.
92 Jack Hughes.
93 Tommy Minor became Sgt
94 Norman Hill.
95 Jimmie Reid, became Sgt.
96 Vic Smith
97 Tommy Simm.
98 Frank Peck, became Insp. CID. (Bill Woolley was allocated this number soon after).
99 'Jock' Ingram.
100 Ben Bliss.
101 Walter Newall.
102 Bob Edwards, became Insp.
103 Jack Armstrong, became Sgt. No.11.
104 Harry Lang, became Det. Chief Insp.
105 Hughie Stevenson.
106 Anthony Thompson became Sgt.

The above was the numeral strength of the Force at 23 April, 1928. Following this date, the following were added:-

107 Jack Bowden, CID.
108 Frank McEvoy (resigned).
109 Ernie Reynolds, became Det Superintendent.
110 Louis McCormack, became Insp.
111 Bert Brown, became Sgt.
112 Walter Thacker.
113 Hughie Henderson.
114 Tom Young (resigned).
115 Dick Waft, became Sgt.
116 Albert Kennedy, became Superintendent.
117 Arthur Trowell, became Sgt.
118 Albert Mackey (new No.)
119 Ken Pearce.
120 Doug Wainwright (Grandson of AS. No.1), became Sgt.

Superintendent McDonough received twenty shillings rent allowance upon his appointment in 1931. He retired as Superintendent and was tragically killed in a road traffic accident whilst cycling.

Inspector Cauldwell lived at 12 Manor Lane and Inspector Walter Payne lived in Fieldway. Alexander Keith came from Scotland and was in the Wallasey Police from 1916 to 1943. He had seen the advert in the *Police Review*. He came as a Detective Constable and received £2.6s.0. a week with a detective allowance and worked in the Courts, taking down notes in shorthand.

Norman Hill's brother, Stanley, joined the Wallasey Force later.

Jim Banks must have joined the Force at the end of the First World War. No doubt, his father was Bob Banks, employed by Shaw Brothers. Their flower-decorated horse with horse-drawn van would be entered in local carnivals.

Jack Williams, who lived at 3 Manor Road, was the first Mounted Policeman (PC 4) in Wallasey. Soon afterwards he was joined by two others. Strangely enough, both were named George Walker, one lived in Carrington Road; the other in Daresbury Road, whose son also joined the Police.

George Walker joined the Force in 1919 during the Transport Strike and became a Mounted Policeman – the last one in Wallasey. The horse dropped dead whilst on patrol in 1938 and the mounted unit came to an end. In one of the Civil Parades, a horse had to be borrowed to lead the parade which George rode.

George Walker used one of his wife's old stockings when plaiting the horse's tail. One of the horses had the name of King Kong which was chosen for the Annual Police Inspection, another was called Prince. The Mounted Policemen could either wear the helmet or a flat peak cap, with the horses being used in such places as Wallasey Beach and sandhills as well as along the roads.

Jack Williams had been a butcher and was also a Fire Bobby. He was good with animals and had some veterinary knowledge, cutting the tails of dog pups, Sometimes biting the tail off with his teeth!

Often pet dogs would be brought to him. One lady asked what she should do with her overweight dog who had lost its appetite The animal was fat and obviously over-fed so he told her to leave it with him for a fortnight. Jack said to his friend, Fireman Walter Meacock, "I won't give it a meal for about a fortnight and by that time it will be hungry!" No doubt, Jack did give it a nibble or two and by the time the lady returned the dog had lost some weight and was ready for a hearty meal.

Jack also showed Walter how to harness a 'unicorn'. At first he thought that Jack was joking but in fact 'a unicorn' was a Horse Ambulance, hauled by three horses - two together and one at the front. PC Dave Liston was Jack's brother-in-law.

James Gallagher, wounded in the 1914-18 War, was admitted to the new Town Hall Military Hospital. When he was discharged, he joined the Wallasey Borough Police as PC 16. He was a fine figure of a man and looked smart in his new uniform. He became a Seacombe Bobby and would often be seen controlling the traffic

PC James Gallagher (later to become sergeant)

at Duke Street Bridge crossroads. While in the Force he would travel on the tramcars where he got to know one of the conductresses who wore a dark uniform with metal buttons and long skirt. Romance blossomed and they married. Jim came from Carlisle and had seen the advertisement in the Cumberland Gazette for the Wallasey Borough Police, whilst working in a solicitor's office. He became Police Sergeant 11 and was a member of the Wallasey Force for 27 years.

Frank Peck was promoted to Sergeant and received an extra half crown a week for having completed 15 years' service in 1928.

Constable William Evason, who lived at 52 Urmson Road, was a Fire-Bobby and was able to run to the Fire Station when he heard the bell.

Constable J Ryan

One of the most respected and popular Constables in New Brighton was PC Joseph ('Joe') Ryan who was born in 1894 and at the age of 18 joined the Royal Irish Constabulary in Dublin and after training was sent to County Waterford where he met his future wife Mary Kate. At the age of 21 he a volunteer to replace policemen who had joined the forces and was transferred to the English Police. He came over to this country in August 1914 and joined the Wallasey Borough Police. PC. Ryan was usually on foot patrol in New Brighton. He enjoyed living in Wallasey and asked his young lady to join him. They were married at the Catholic Church of St Peter and Paul's at the top of Hope Street and went to live initially in Virginia Road, then a house in Wellington Road which proved too small when they started a family so they moved to 16 Hope Street, one of the stone cottages which some folk now

Police Constable Joe Ryan

refer to as the 'Coast Guard Cottages' where they brought up three daughters and a son. It was very convenient for the family, as the Church, School and Police Station were all in the same street.

His brother came over from Ireland, working as an Attendant at the New Brighton Tower.

The Tower also had their own uniformed Police Force that patrolled the grounds and were on hand when needed.

PC Ryan asked for sanction of his previous service in the Royal Irish Constabulary and was allowed two years service.

On bank holidays he would be seen coming up the street holding the little hand of a lost child, followed by a number of lost children. His wife would get a couple of their daughters to give them refreshments. Sometimes there were almost 20 lost children in his care who would all hold hands as PC Ryan brought them up Hope Street to the Police Station.

PC Ryan had many friends and when he took his young daughter to the Trocadero Picture House in Victoria Road, she lost count of the number of people that would greet him by his Christian name as he walked along the road. Whilst on point duty one day at 'The Horse-Shoe' at the bottom of Victoria Road (so-called as the tramcar track was laid out in pattern of a horseshoe to enable the tramcars to turn around), a man came up to him and asked where he could find a place to stay. Joseph Ryan took a hard look at him and recognised him as the wanted man on the poster at the Police Station who had murdered a child.

"Look here. I'm coming off duty in a minute or two and we have a list of houses that take in lodgers up at the Station. Come up with me and take a look", said he.

The man agreed and while he was at the Police Station, using the toilet, the Constable informed the others and he was arrested. PC Ryan had to travel to Yorkshire to give evidence.

He left the Wallasey Borough Police in 1937, after 25 years service. He had been a good Officer and was well respected. On leaving the Force he became Master-at-Arms on one of the new B and I Dublin boats that sailed between Liverpool and Dublin and remained on them until they were taken out of service in the early months of Second World War.

As years went by, Joseph Ryan was remembered for the many acts of kindness he had offered during his time in the Wallasey Force. He died in 1959.

There was another Ryan in the force and in my previous book,

Sandstone and Mortar, I seem to have got confused with the two men. RE ('Paddy') Ryan was a Special Constable in the First World War. He was injured whilst apprehending a drunk and disorderly man on 5 February, 1915. I understand that he had been a member of the Black and Tans and was drafted into the Force. On leaving the Police, he became a commissionaire at the Trocadero Cinema in Victoria Road.

Another New Brighton bobby was Joe Newton, born on 14 January 1915. After serving in the forces, he joined the Wallasey Police and became PC. 57. A local grocer used to call him 'Heinz'. He later bought Ogden's newsagents in Victoria Road, which was owned by his wife's aunt. He stood as Ratepayer for the New Brighton Ward and was elected to the Wallasey Council in 1962.
******

> We observe too great a stress,
> On risks that on us press.
>
> **WS Gilbert**

In an extract from the Report of the Royal Commissioner on Police Activities and Procedures 1929 we have the following extract:
"The Police of this country have never been recognised either in law or by tradition as a force distinct from the general body of citizens. Despite the imposition of many extraneous duties on the Police by legislation or administrative action, the principle remains that a Police Officer, in view of the common law, is only a person paid to perform, as a matter of duty, acts which, if he were so minded, he might have done voluntary."

In 1929 each Constable was issued with a hard-backed instruction book for guidance. Each book carried a number and was recorded in the record of equipment that was issued to him. The book was not to be shown to persons other than in the force. Much of the information that it contained was supplied by Sir Leonard Dunning, one of HM Inspectors of Constabulary (Leonard Dunning was the Head Constable and Director of the Fire Brigade at Liverpool in 1912).

It contained a great deal of information including a brief history of the town and this fine book was printed and bound by Wallasey Printers costing £105 per batch.

In the old days the village Policeman would know all the locals and they would be on first name terms. He would patrol on foot and the friendly atmosphere would help in obtaining useful information. Their help often went beyond their call of duty.

New Brighton suffered from crime, with as many as a dozen pickpockets being active on a Bank Holiday. When the weather was nice, many folk left their windows open and it was easy to break in. House breakers could often be hard to convict as many of them would come over from Liverpool and Birkenhead and after committing the offence, would return. Members of the CID would go over to the Liverpool Landing Stage to watch out for them as they returned from New Brighton. Warnings were displayed at the ferries.

Lodgings for Policemen were easy to find in winter but in the summer it was more difficult as landladies could get better money from the visitors.

Sergeant John Hesketh lived at 3, Alice Avenue and was the Bridewell Sergeant in Hope Street. Another popular Bridewell Sergeant at New Brighton was Jack ('Sandy') Armstrong. He was a native of Doncaster and joined the Wallasey Borough Police on 19 March, 1927. He often wore a peak cap instead of the helmet. Jack, whilst a Constable, helped to save a boy from drowning in the river and was awarded the Liverpool Shipwreck and Humane Society's Silver Medal.

The Citation reads:-

"At a meeting of the committee of the Liverpool Shipwreck and Humane Society held at the Underwriters Room, Exchange Buildings on the 25th day of July 1934, it was Resolved Unanimously that the thanks of the Committee presented to PC 103 John Armstrong together with the Society's Silver Medal for bravely jumping into the River Mersey at Egremont and assisting to rescue a boy (14) in danger of drowning on 1 July 1934."

Jack
'Sandy' Armstrong

It is signed by the Chairman, TH Harper and Secretary, CK McCallum.

Jack's son, Colin, followed his father's footsteps and entered the Police Force and joined the Lancashire Constabulary and retired as Superintendent.

On retirement on 18 September 1955, Sergeant Armstrong received a Certificate of Service personally signed by the Chief Constable, Mr. John Ormerod.

Inspector RC Edwards also retired from the Wallasey Police Force on the same date. Both had joined on the same day.

Constable Maddocks went into the Fire Brigade on request.

Police Matrons

There were no Women Police Constables in the early days of the force, instead there were Police Matrons. These were usually the wives of the Constables who lived near the Police Station and one of their duties was to take in meals for the prisoners. However, Birkenhead Borough Police had women police officers as early 1915. They wore a navy blue skirt and a tunic consisting of four pockets. They were issued with leather belt and a smart modern soft topped peak cap donning the silver badge of the force. I understand that a lady was eventually appointed as Matron at Manor Road and PC George Walker (the one who lived in Carrington Road) became her husband. The Matron acted under the direction of the Senior Officer on duty. She took charge of female prisoners and was responsible for searching them and had to accompany them when they were removed to other institutions or brought before the Courts. Should a Police Officer need to enter a cell of a female prisoner the Matron had to accompany him.

Village Police

The original Police Station in Wallasey Village was at the top of Leasowe Road consisting of a small stone building dating back to the 1800s, which had a projecting gable. Next door was the Weights and Measures Office with the weighbridge in the fore. James Smythe was the keeper at one time and Thomas John Williams held this position in the 1920s. This building was later used as the library which opened on 7 January 1889.

There was a rest room in the building where the road-sweepers had their cuppa and at a later date, public toilets were erected.

One of the road-sweepers, known as 'Little Peter', who was getting on in years and was often late, would be seen running along to get his barrow out.

The Police Sub-Station was later replaced by a Police Hut on the other side of the road being a small wooden affair that was painted cream.

Sergeant John Palin was in charge. He lived at 111 Wallasey Village and would sometimes be mounted on a horse to enable him to patrol farther afield. He had a slight figure and was a quiet gentleman.

Sergeant Reynolds was an ex-Guardsman who would drill the boys in St George's School playground for the Wallasey Village Festival. There were two local bobbies, PC Bill Rigg and PC Arthur Reece, who patrolled the village on alternative days and nights. PC Reece was a well-known character and due to his heavy build the local lads rudely called him 'Pigeon Belly'. He had once worked as a miner.

He was often on duty at Harrison Drive, especially during the school summer holidays, where he was told to keep his eye on the school children that were in the water as he was a very good swimmer. He also took part in the Annual Police River Swim.

PC Reece would stand no messing and if he caught any boy after apples in the orchard of Buxton House, he would give the lad a good thrashing. Misbehaving boys in the village often felt a couple of swipes across their legs from his cape that he carried over his shoulder. He knew most of the children and often they would worry in case he told their parents.

He would give a lad a good clout with his belt if he was caught misbehaving. If the fellow was cheeky he would get another belt. "You lads are up to no good", he would say, "hop it!".

The lads kept clear of him but those who got a belt from him seem to have accepted the punishment without complaint as it was a result of their behaviour and in later life they realised that it had stood them in good stead.

PC Reece would patrol the village, calling in for a cup of tea and a smoke at Bill Clooney, the cobbler, whose small shop was the front room of the cottage at 29 Wallasey Village. He was known as 'The Little Fella' on account of being small and he had lost a leg in the First World War. Arthur Reece was promoted to Sergeant and transferred to Moreton on 17 April 1942. He lived in Fieldway and was eventually replaced by Sergeant Bebbington in 1947. On retirement, in 1954, after 30 years service, Mr Reece took up security work and was often seen in that capacity at Chester races. He went to live in Rossett on the Chester/Wrexham Road.

PC Bill Rigg was a tall bobby and could often be seen at the bottom of Perrin Road, making sure that the children crossed the road safely. He had once been a seafarer aboard sailing ships.

There was another Policeman that was often on duty in Wallasey Village. The local lads rudely christened him 'PC Rubberneck'.

Francis J McEvoy became a Reserve Constable in September 1929 and at the same time alterations were carried out at Seacombe Police Station.

With cat-like tread,
Upon our prey we steal,
In silence dread
Our cautious way we feel,
No sound at all,
We never speak a word,
A fly's foot-fall
Would be distinctly heard.

WS Gilbert

The Wallasey Village Police Station is behind the Policeman on duty at the top of Leasowe Road, Wallasey Village

Larceny (common stealing) and housebreaking were the main crimes in the Borough. A lot of the residents in large houses had expensive jewellery. Many houses had leaded-lights in the windows and these were easily broken with the minimum of effort and noise, especially when fitted to front doors. Sash-windows could be opened with the aid of long flexible palette-knife which, when worked between the frames, threw back the catch. Small windows could be easily smashed and the hand slipped through to release the catch. The noise of the broken glass was deadened by placing some sort of material over the glass before striking it. By climbing up rainwater pipes access could be obtained through the first-floor window which had been open for fresh air. Doors could be forced open by using a jemmy or crowbar.

Other small crimes were what was known as 'sneak-ins' - folk leaving the front or back doors open for the opportune thief.

A common offence was breaking into gas meters.

When Wallasey was a County Borough in its own right, apart from Moreton, the town was easy to control in the event of serious crime as there was only one road (Leasowe Road) leading out and the Dock Bridges were easily sealed off. The ferries and railways were under close liaison and therefore it was not easy for a gang to make an easy getaway.

The Liverpool City Police circulated lists of stolen property on Merseyside which were printed daily and sent to the other forces. Pawnbrokers' notices were then taken around to all the pawnbrokers, second-hand shops and jewellers by a member of the force.

The Constables had to fill in a sheet that itemised arrests, summonses, street lamps that needed attention and properties that were not properly secured etc. These would be read by the Inspector and he would write comments on the reverse.

Inspectors were not allowed to address the Constables by their Christian names nor make themselves too familiar. They were to inspect the parades and give orders to Sergeants and Constables. It goes without saying that a Constable was not allowed to address a superior by his Christain name.

The Constables found that if they stood unseen in a shop doorway at night they were able to hear what people were saying. All manner of things would be said and sometimes they would hear mention of a crook or stolen goods.

If a Constable made an arrest whilst on Night Duty he had to appear at the Court at 9.45am and give evidence of arrest. Time off would be allowed for this to be taken at discretion of his superiors.

Annual River Swim

The Wallasey Police Recreation Club augmented the Annual River Swim when members of the Wallasey Police Swimming Club were invited to participate.

The first River Swim was held on Wednesday 24 August 1921 when Alderman NH Blackburn donated a silver cup which was to be presented to the winner of the event. The swim covered a distance of four and a half miles from Woodside Ferry to New Brighton Pier. The first Officer to win was Detective Constable Frank Peck who covered the distance in under 39 minutes, but clocked in at 40. Five competitors took part but Constable Larry Carroll had a severe attack of cramp and was helped out of the water at Seacombe Ferry.

The swimmers wore a one-piece costume that had a badge designed from the shield and dolphin entwining a trident from the town's Coat of Arms and the letters WPSC (Wallasey Police Swimming Club).

The swimming costumes were rather loose fitting in those days. Some had longer shorts, albeit they were woven as one piece. One or two swimmers opted to wear a rubber swimming hat. Each swimmer was followed by a dinghy for emergency purposes.

In 1922, the current was so fierce that no one reached the New Brighton Landing Stage from Woodside. Swimmers were carried out into midstream. Sgt Savage led as far as Egremont. Constables Peck and Mann came forward in midstream but could not get inshore and were carried out to beyond the Rip Rap Buoy. However, Constables Warner and Jackson finished opposite the stage. The latter gave up at 6.10pm. Referee WJ Trist suggested that the decision should be given to those who had made the best attempt to reach the landing stage. PC Warner was presented with The Blackburn Cup and Gold Medal by Mr M Phillips, second was Constable Jackson, third Constable Peck, fourth Sergeant Savage and fifth Constable Mann.

Det Constable Peck won back The Blackburn Cup in 1923 in a time of 39 minutes, second was Constable Clay and Sgt Savage came in third.

The competitors that year were:-

Sergeant G Savage, Sergeant J Wedge, Sergeant T Wilkinson (Fire Brigade), Constable JH Mann, Constable CT Sandland, Constable F Marsden (Fire Brigade), Constable LH Bliss, Constable F Peck, Constable H Clay, Constable NB Phillips, Constable FE Wood and Constable RH Jackson.

Detective Constable Peck won in 1924 with Constable Jackson second and Constable Jackson third. Constable Reece was last to complete the swim. Inspector Bebbington was in the motor-launch.

1925 was Constable Jackson's year. He swam the distance in 40 minutes.

Constable CT Sandland was one minute behind and Constable Starkey came in on 42 minutes. Det Constable Peck was fourth in 43 minutes. Fifth was Constable Clay and sixth was Sgt. Savage.

Constable Dave Starkey set up a record time of 22 minutes 19 seconds in 1926 over this course.

The 1929 entries for the River Swim were Messrs, Woolley, Mackey, Reece, Maddocks, Warner, Hill, Starkey, McCormack, CT Sandland, Lang, Peck, Mann. The winner was Sergeant Charles Sandland who won in 41 minutes, Dave Starkey, who had won the previous year, was second and JL McCormack came in third. Only two seconds divided Starkey and McCormack who was 90 seconds behind the winner.

Others to finish were A Reece (43 Mins), N Hill (44), J Mann (45), F Peck (48), RJ Edwards (49), W Woolley (50) and J Warner (54). Constable AE Mackey was taken out of the water opposite the Mariners' Home.

Competitors for the Wallasey Police Annual River Swim from Woodside Stage to New Brighton Stage 1928. Lt. to Rt:- Billy Trist (Navy League); Harry Lang; Albert Mackey; David Starkey; Chief Constable Mr Barry; Bob Edwards; Arthur Reece; Norman Hill; Charlie Sandland and George Savage

The Blackburn Challenge Cup had been won outright by Constable Starkey for the previous three years and a new one was presented by Mr FH Blackburn, the original donor. The prizes were presented at the Yacht Club's Head Quarters in Hope Street New Brighton.

Constable Starkey was the Hon Secretary.

Councillor J Pinington remarked at the meeting, "....that whoever said that a Policeman's Lot was not a happy one did not speak `The Truth, The Whole Truth and Nothing But The Truth'."

He had not seen an unhappy Constable at the event. The occasion had led a gentleman to compose a light-hearted poem that appeared in the Wallasey News on 27 July 1929.

The Police Swim

Last Wednesday was a great day for our gallant men in blue,
Instead of catching burglars they tried hard to catch the flu;
For thirteen hardy constables the River Mersey swam,
From Birkenhead to Wallasey, and caused a traffic jam.

They nearly struck the Seacombe Stage and rammed the lifeboat too.
While the burglars on the ferryboats into the cabins flew,
Each time a swimmer raised his hand the steamer promptly stopped,
They couldn't disobey the law,
For fear of being "Copped".

The swim was most enjoyable,
The weather bright and clear,
The Sergeant Sandland first man home, first to reach the Pier,
A great ovation greeted him, as near the stage he came,
And now the Blackburn Challenge Cup will bear the swimmer's name.

When Wallasey has grown a lot, with heaps more people here,
And twenty ferryboats queue up to take them from the Pier.
Our constables won't worry at the traffic there will be,
They're just jump in the Mersey and direct it from the sea.

FEH

******

Wallasey Police – Royal Life Saving winners 1950
Lt. to Rt. Back Row: Another, Barns, Warrington, Waft.
Front Row: Chief Constable John Ormerod, Betty Daulman,
Linda Elliott, Inspector Woolley

Rescues/Swimming

Constable David Prendergast, who lived at 9 Rappart Road in Seacombe, was on duty at New Brighton one summer's afternoon and went to investigate a commotion going on by the pier slipway. People had gathered when they heard that Betty Moore, a 16 year-old Birkenhead girl, had been bathing close to the slipway when she was carried off her feet and taken out into the river. Six men, including a 70 year-old, had entered the water in hoping to reach her but had failed. Constable Prendergast, who was noted for his rescues, saw what had happened, dashed through the crowd and jumped fully-clothed into the water. He succeeded in getting hold of the girl and brought her back to the slipway where he applied artificial respiration. The ambulance was summoned and the girl was taken to the hospital.

At the Prize Giving evening, Constable Prendergast's rescue was mentioned. He had twice been able to save a life through life saving methods. He had also had a narrow escape in his effort in another rescue a few weeks before the meeting.

He received the Bronze medal of the Liverpool Shipwreck and Humane Society.

When, in 1932, Inspector CT Sandland, Chief Clerk of Wallasey Police, won the four and a half mile race from Woodside for the third time in succession, he won the Blackburn Challenge Cup outright and retained the trophy. The first Blackburn Cup had been won outright by Constable Starkey four years previously and a third cup was promised by Mr Blackburn. His time was ten minutes slower than his previous swim when a record was established. Inspector Frank Peck also took part. It was the first time that Constable Warrington, who was the Yorkshire Breast Stroke Champion, had competed. Inspector Sandland's time was 41 minutes, second was Constable Reece with a time of 42 minutes and Constable McCormack was third in 42 and a half minutes, the same result as the previous year. Constable Warrington was fourth with a time of 43 minutes.

Inspector Sandland clocked up 43 and a half minutes, followed by Constable Starkey at 44, Constable Lane in 49, Constable Edwards in 52 and Constable Stevenson completed the course in 59 minutes with twelve swimmers finishing. The judges were Mr. Pennington, the Chairman of the Watch Committee, John Ormerod and Mr W Blackburn. The race had been started by Superintendent McDonough.

The trophy continued to be known as The Blackburn Cup and the swim continued until just before the outbreak of the Second World War.

There is also the Dearing Cup that was presented in 1934.

In later years, the winner receives The Highet Cup.

There are a number of other trophies that the Policemen competed for.

The Swim was not staged again until 1952. The distance of the course was altered to approximately three miles. Sergeant Ernie Warrington was the winner who went on to win for the following nine years. Within the Annual River Swim there was also the Handicap. Constable Maurice Toyn won this competition in the 1960s. He was presented with an alarm clock and the following morning he was late for parade! In the same race Constable Rowland Field, who had a motor boat in attendance, swam off course and ended up on the other side of the River by Gladstone Dock. A rope was thrown to him and he was towed to shallow waters by Perch Rock Lighthouse where he was able to wade ashore.

The force always had a number of good swimmers and five Officers decided to enter, namely Messrs Holmes, Keeley, Kehoe, Waft and Woolley. They had arranged the swim but the Chief Constable cancelled it. The following year, the committee decided to hire the

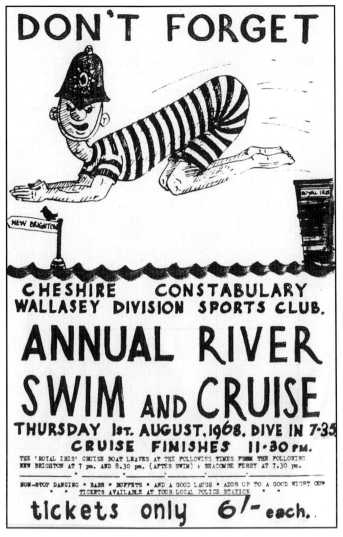

DON'T FORGET

NEW BRIGHTON

CHESHIRE CONSTABULARY
WALLASEY DIVISION SPORTS CLUB.

ANNUAL RIVER
SWIM AND CRUISE
THURSDAY 1ST. AUGUST, 1968. DIVE IN 7·35
CRUISE FINISHES 11·30 PM.

THE 'ROYAL IRIS' CRUISE BOAT LEAVES AT THE FOLLOWING TIMES FROM THE FOLLOWING
NEW BRIGHTON AT 7 pm. AND 8.30 pm. (AFTER SWIM) : SEACOMBE FERRY AT 7.30 pm.

NON-STOP DANCING • BARS • BUFFETS • AND A GOOD LAUGH • ADDS UP TO A GOOD NIGHT OUT
TICKETS AVAILABLE AT YOUR LOCAL POLICE STATION

tickets only 6/- each.

*Poster for the Wallasey Police Annual River Swim
and Cruise 1 August 1968*

Wallasey Ferryboat, *Royal Iris*, which had to be booked well in advance and this time the event could not be cancelled.

In addition to Mr Warrington, the outstanding swimmers have been Alan Williams, who won on eight consecutive occasions from 1972 to 1980 and Shaun Kehoe with 13 wins.

Alan Williams has over 250 medals and trophies at home, winning his first medal at the age of nine. His father was a Welshman so Alan was able to represent Wales in 1969/70/71 and in the Commonwealth Games at Edinburgh. He swam many times for Police teams and held the European Police record in the 400 metres free-style for a number of years. Apart from winning the Police River Swim, he has also won the Dee Mile and the Thames Mile races as well as holding all sorts of swimming records at county level. He also played water-polo for the Northern Counties and Cheshire.

Shaun Kehoe is the current record holder setting up 22 minutes nine seconds over the modern course.

The swim had a long association with the *Royal Iris* over the years.

The first Policewoman to enter the swim was in 1979 when 19 year old Lesley Farlam, who lived in Moreton, completed the course. Since then a number of Policewomen have participated in the event including Pam Ash croft, Tracy Waring and Tara Davey have all finished in the first three.

Roy Humphries and Phil Smith (the 1962 winner) clocked up over 50 swims between them. Alan Steen, who won in 1970 and 1971 swam on a number of occasions. His father, Bob, and Frank Chapman have served as Time-Keepers/Judges for many years.

A televised Police Swimming Match was held at the Empire Pool, Cardiff with the Police team and water polo opposing South Wales team in the 1960s.

Peter Pinnington won The Highet Cup for the River Swim at the first attempt in July 1963 and went on to win it for the next two years.

In 1965 the Wallasey Police swimmers between them won 13 plaques at National Police Swimming Championships at the Empire Pool, Cardiff. Alan Steen was third in the Back Stroke, Peter Pinnington won the 110 yards Free Style in 60.2 seconds, being 1.4 seconds outside the record and Alan Williams was third in the Cadet Race. George Ferrier and John Whitfield were successful in the Team Race and Polo Team. Team Captain was Len Littlewood.

John Whitfield set up a new record of 25min. 53sec. in the 1966 River Swim, Alan Steen was second and Peter Pinnington third. Wallasey Police were easy winners of the Cheshire Constabulary Inter-Divisions Swimming Competition which was held at Crewe in 1967. Wallasey scored 145.5 points with Birkenhead second with 39 points.

The winning team was:-
Sergeants MA Barnes and WP Holmes, Constables E Fletcher, R Parry, P Smith, A Steen, J Whitfield and A Williams.

Due to the Toxteth Riots, the River Swim had to be cancelled in 1981.

Forty-one year old Wallasey Constable, Steve Blakemore, won the 1997 Annual Police River Swim by beating Acting Sergeant Tara Davey. His time was 24 mins and 26 secs. Constable Tim Baldock who had won the previous year did not compete due to holidays. Tim was stationed at Hoylake and was third in the previous year (Second in '96 was PC Kevin McGuinty).

Det Con Sean Kehoe won the River Swim for the 14th time in 1995. He decided not to compete again after his father, another veteran police swimmer, died in 1994. The Kehoes had dominated the swim for decades with his father second in the race 14 times.

Sean said: "I never had to compete against him but after he died I felt I couldn't swim again. But as soon as I realised just one more win would mean I had 14 wins to match my dad's runner-up titles I thought I would race one more time."

Sergeant George Savage was one of the originators of the Annual River Swim and although he retired in December 1927 he was allowed to take part in the 1928 Swim. On his retirement, he was given a gold watch which was presented to him by the Chief Constable, Mr. Barry. His wife also received a presentation. George had been in the Police Force for twenty seven and a half years, serving in the Cheshire Constabulary and the Wallasey Borough Force. Chief Inspector, John Ormerod, described him as one of the most popular men in the Force. He joined the Police in 1900 and was five years at Seacombe before he was moved to Hoole. From there he moved to Chester, Frodsham, Runcorn and Walton Castle. He was promoted to Acting Sergeant in 1912 and spent a year at Sale before returning to Wallasey where he was stationed at New Brighton as full Sergeant. Although he never won the Annual Swim, he loved to take part in the event. In his younger days, he would swim from Eastham to New Brighton. In 1916, Sergeant Savage received the Diploma of the Royal National Life Saving Society and Merit Badge for Life Saving. He was also the Instructor for the Police swimmers for three years and was a keen rifleman and a member of the Police Rifle Club. He won the Lady Brooke's Silver Challenge Cup in 1911, 1912 and 1913. His hobby was keeping pigeons.

Sergeant E Warrington and Constable R Waft won the Colonel Hall-Walker Shield for the Wallsey Police in 1947 & 1948 for Life Saving when Chief Inspector CT Sandland was their Instructor. They also won in 1949 with Inspector Woolley as the Instructor. WPC Lillian Daulman won the Policewomen's 100 yards Free-

Wallasey Police Cricket Team 1953: Constables: MA Barnes,
BR Carpenter, GK Carter, R Collister, KR Halliday, PG O'Dwyer,
EE Sutton and DM Williams. , Sergeants: D F Dransfield, S Fisher,
S R Foster. Scorer – Mrs Carter

Style Swimming Championships of Great Britain and Northern Ireland at Blackpool on Wednesday 4 September 1951. She achieved this feat only six weeks after being involved in a road accident on 17 July whilst motor-cycling down to Devon on annual leave where she suffered from a fractured skull. She had only resumed work in the week of the Championships and her time was only two fifths of a second outside the record. She was also a member of the Northern District winning team.

Competing in the same gala was another Wallasey WPC, Joyce Esseen, who was placed fourth. The men's Relay Team gained third in the Medley Relay Race.

The 1950s winning team was Messrs Barnes, Kehoe, Waft, Warrington and two Policewomen, LEA Daulman and JT Elliott. In 1952, the Life Saving Team won the Col. Hall-Walker Shield again along with the Colonel Woodcock Police Cup and the JM Learmont Trophy. They also won the Trophy in 1955, being winners four years in succession.

The Colonel Woodcock Cup was an annual competition which was open to all the Police Forces in the British Isles. Points were awarded for bronze medallions. The size of each individual force was taken into consideration and the percentage per capita was calculated to determine the winners.

******

The Sporting Force

The Police have always been encouraged to participate in sports as it is one way of keeping fit. Football has been played for many years.

The Wallasey Police Football Team of 1927 was:-

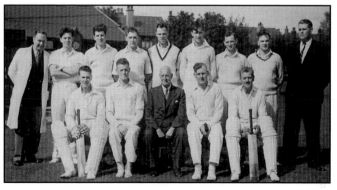

Wallasey Police Cricket Team 1957 consisted of:-
Sergeant S Fisher (Captain), Constables: PH Edwards, KR Halliday,
PN Harvey, TR Humphreys, E Marshall, PG O'Dwyer, C Rae,
SH Smith, D Watson and DM Williams. Scorer – Constable RP Field

ND Starkey, GH Chilton, G Sarples (Goalkeeper), WE Field, J Hughes, CT Sandland, JW Barke, JJ Read, I Maddocks, W Shelton and E W Barke. A football match would be arranged with the Police and the Fire Brigade. Ex-New Brighton footballer, Ernie Longden (who later became the team's trainer) refereed the game which was played at Spiller's Sports Field in Station Road. Mr Albert Owen Litchfield, who refereed matches for the Police, was alsoa keen sportsman and umpired local cricket matches.

They also played cricket at Heathbank Sports Field in Station Road.

Mr Alfred J Stears (known as 'AJ') became the Police Cricket Umpire. In his younger days he refereed local football matches. If spectators were not pleased with some of the decisions he had made during a match he would find the tyres of his cycle let down. Mr Stears was a long-serving member of Toc H and had served in the Army in the First World War. He could relate many stories about the Front and how the Rev Tubby Clayton ministered to the troops in Poperinge.

Golf Team winners of the Hart Trophy 1962
Lt to Rt Back :PC. D Knight, PC. P Lakins PC. DA Wainwright
PS. ME Toyn, Suppt. WJ Bryan, Chief C. W Marshall,
Det Ch Insp. HT Lang, Insp. LE Harrison

'AJ' used to play a small zither-like harp which he took with him while in the Army. On one occasion when he was wounded on the battle field, two stretcher-bearers found him, placed him on a stretcher and covered him with a blanket. They picked up the harp and placed it on top of him.

One Tommy called out, "Where's he off to?", referring to the harp which he might use in Heavenly Places!

The Wallasey Ladies Section of Toc H was actually born during a conversation between 'AJ' and his wife over the breakfast table for which she became a Founder Member.

Sergeant DF Dransfield was Umpire and Secretary. Mr. Ormerod, the Chief Constable, was President of the club.

The Police also had a golf team. They won the Hart Trophy in 1962. The winning team was:-

Superintendent WJ Bryan, Inspector LE Harrison, Constable CD Knight, Det Chief Inspector HT Lang, Constable P Larkins, Chief Constable Walter Marshall, Sergeant ME Toyn and Constable DA Wainwright.

The Police have had a bowls team for many years, playing an annual match against the Magazine Bowling Club for 'The Batons' (truncheons) mounted on a board The Police would play at the Leasowe Hotel in Reeds Lane. The Chief Constable, Mr. John Ormerod, loved to play in the team and was a good bowler. It was one of the occasions where he was able to relax. A photograph was taken on 12 August 1949 of the players with the Mayor of

Wallasey, Robert Yates Knagg, Chief Constable and Inspectors Marshall and Sandland.

The annual match was an enjoyable occasion.

Other Bowls Cups include: The Duncalf Challenge Cup, The JW Collins Challenge Cup, The WA Read Cup and The J Roberttson-Dunn Police Charity Cup. There is also a Cup for the Rifle Club. All these cups are kept in the Trophy Case at Manor Road.

As regards snooker, the Police play the Old Wallaseyans for 'The Cap and Cuffs'. An old school cap from what was the Wallasey Grammar School and a pair of handcuffs make up the winners' prize.

******

Motoring

Before the Second World War there were a dozen bobbies on duty at New Brighton on a Bank Holiday to deal with the crowds of visitors. A 20 mph speed limit for heavy cars with pneumatic tyres was imposed but if they were pulling a trailer they were restricted to 12 mph.

In May 1928, a second Police motor car was needed. This was purchased from Mr E Ward's garage in Leasowe Road at a cost of £54.10s.0. The Police had to get rid of the old Worsley car that they had used for a number of years. Mr Ward allowed £6 off the new car as it was 'worn out'.

There was a speed limit of 8mph on the Marine Promenade in the 1930s when motorcars became popular. A Singer Bantam could be purchased for less than £140, a Roadster of the same make cost £169 and their Super Ten could be had for £185.

On 1 January 1930 Constable Craft arrested Alfred Burrows for burglary and was awarded two guineas on 13 February for his alertness and attention to duty on making the arrest.

In the same year, three Constables were recognised for their long service.

PC 37 J Pickford, 20 years' service and PC 38 W Barber and PC53 H Ashall each having reached 17 years' service.

The construction of a garage at Manor Road Police Station in 1930 cost £525. The Council agreed to purchase a Dennis general utility van with a low-line chassis at the cost of £595.

Miss Hilda M Jones, the Police typist at Manor Road Police Station had an increase in pay of £10 per annum in April 1932 and a young man from Chester, William Wingfield Partington, became a Probationer Constable.

In the July of the same year, Constable William Packer retired from the force on health grounds.

Another Constable to have to retire on pension in 1932 was PC Thomas Simm through very defective vision.

Expenses

In the account books it is recorded that Knagg's the jeweller was paid 3/- for winding clocks at the Police and Fire Stations. Mr E Laurie used to be paid two pounds annually for this service and later the job was taken over by Walter Newport. 15/2d was paid out for metal polish and a further 7/9d for dog biscuits!

Rank

The order of rank:-

Chief Constable, Chief Superintendent, Chief Inspector, Sergeant, Police Constable.

The Police Rank Markings, displayed on the epaulettes and on the peak of the cap:-

Chief Constable:	Silver Imperial Crown with crossed tipstaves encircled.
Asst. Chief Constable:	Crossed tipstaves.
Chief Superintendent:	Silver Imperial Crown and one star.

Superintendent who is also Deputy

Chief Constable:	Silver Imperial Crown and monogram DCC.
Superintendent:	Silver Imperial Crown.
Chief Inspector:	Three Stars.

Inspector who is also is also Deputy

Chief Constable:	Two stars and monogram DCC
Inspector:	Two Stars.
Acting Inspector:	One Star.
Sergeant:	Three white chevrons (stripes) on each upper sleeve.
Acting Sergeant:	Two white chevrons on the upper sleeve.

The Assistant Chief Constable used to have Silver Imperial Crown and two stars.

******

Drink Problem

Drunkenness has always been a problem, especially in New Brighton and to some degree, Seacombe.

In the case of New Brighton, where there were many public houses and other licensed places it was more of a problem, especially from ten o'clock onwards when there were often many drunks. The troublesome, local drunk was taken up to Hope Street and put in a cell to sleep it off. Where the fellow had come over from Liverpool, the Police would take him down to the ferry and put him on the boat. I often wondered how the deck-hand coped, but the drunk was no longer a problem for the New Brighton Police. Clubs in Wallasey were raided from time to time for drinking outside licensed hours and names of those doing so would be taken.

In 1956 Old Mother Redcap's Social Club was raided and names and addresses taken. The club was later struck off the Register for 12 months.

When the enterprising burglar's not-a-burgling.
When the cut-throat isn't occupied in crime.
WS Gilbert

'Pitch and Toss', also called 'two ups', was started in the 1850s in Australia. It was played near the docks by dockers and other workers. Bets were taken on the outcome of two coins being tossed as to whether they would turn up as two heads or two tails. A lookout would keeping watch for the bobby as the coins were tossed into the circle and the crowd would disperse quickly should he appear.

The back street 'Bookie' existed in various parts of the town but by and large, the Police turned a blind eye. From time to time a bookmaker would be raided and possibly fined for taking bets on the day. The Law, in those days, only allowed bets to be placed on horses at a race meeting. The bookmaker would have a special 'Runner', who would collect the bets. There were a number of reliable bookmakers in Birkenhead and Wallasey noted for paying out large sums of money on trebles or accumulators.

Anti-post bets were allowed and Scottish bookmakers would pay out all winning bets providing the envelope had been franked before the time of the race. They also provided prepaid envelopes.

Moreton

When the Borough took in the Townships of Moreton and Saughall Massie in 1928 and 1933 respectively, the Police had over 90 miles of streets to patrol. The force also had high-powered patrol cars to cover the Borough. Previously, these townships were under the Cheshire Constabulary and policed from Upton. Sergeant Bebbington and six new Constables were enrolled for the Moreton area.

In those early days at Moreton, after heavy rains, the Arrowbrook and Birkett would overflow causing flooding right across the low-lying fields and isolate the bungalows and other wooden buildings. The Police would have to take a flat-bottom boat to rescue the people trapped by the water.

Mr George L Reakes

George Leonard Reakes was a popular and well-known citizen of Wallasey. He was born in Bath in 1889 being the son of a carpenter and was one of five boys. He was educated at Bath City Secondary School where he was good at Art and English. He entered a Pupil Teachers'

examination which he passed and was found a post at Weymouth Boys School. He later worked for five years at a second-hand bookshop in Bath. George then worked for the International Correspondence Schools. At the outbreak of the First World War he failed his medical for military service and came to live in Wallasey and, for a short spell, in St Helens and Preston working for the Correspondence School. He felt he should help the war effort so joined the staff at the Recruiting Office and eventually passed fit for the Artists' Rifles Officers' Training Corps. He was later discharged on medical grounds.

As a young man, George entered into politics by joining the Labour Party and took a great interest in local issues, writing to the local newspapers about them.

One of the things that he did not agree with was the way that prisoners on remand were taken from the Wallasey Court and over to Liverpool on the ferryboat. Passengers could see the handcuffed prisoner. George demanded that they should be taken by closed motor car. He wrote to Jack Hayes, the MP and asked for his assistance. The Member tabled a question to the Home Secretary who gave instructions to the Chief Constable on the matter.

At the time of the Police Strike, George helped to organise a meeting at the New Brighton Tower Theatre in 1924 when two MPs, Arthur Henderson and Margaret Bonfield, were to address a large crowd. John Roberts, JP had agreed to take the chair. There had been a Police Strike in Liverpool in the previous year and many of the Constables had been dismissed for going on strike. They appealed to Mr Henderson, who was Home Secretary at the time, but he would not take action against decisions that had been made by the Liverpool Watch Committee.

The meeting took place on 20 June 1925. A large number of the dismissed Policemen were present and for fear of trouble extra Constables were brought in. When Mr. Henderson stood up to address the gathering there was booing and the stamping of feet that lasted for several minutes. There were too many disorderly men, that it was not possible to remove them from the meeting. It was impossible for Mr Henderson to be heard and he was howled down. He left the stage and he, along with Mr. Roberts, Miss Bonfield and George Reakes were escorted away by the Police. They left by taxi and crossed over to Liverpool by ferry from Seacombe. Mr. Henderson was sorry that he was unable to deliver his speech but George Reakes saw that it was published in the *Liverpool Daily Post* along with a report of the meeting.

George Reakes became Chief Magistrate of Wallasey on 9 November 1936 and was the second senior JP on the panel of 34 Justices.

Four cases of murder appeared before him.

In 1937 a man appeared before him accused of murdering a child. When Mr. Reakes asked if he wanted bail, the defendant shouted across to him "No - please hang me."

One Saturday evening George received a telephone call from the Magistrates's Clerk of Wallasey who told him that a War Damage committal case was due on the Monday and that all the witnesses and Council were already in the town waiting for the trial to begin. They included an MP barrister from London and as no magistrate was available, the Clerk asked George to take the case.

"How long is it likely to last?" asked George.

"About five days", answered the Clerk.

George agreed. In fact the case lasted 15 days and he was completely bored as it was uninteresting.

George Reakes served for 12 years on the Juvenile Court panel at Wallasey and went on to be Chairman for five years.

In the course of his career, he served Wallasey as Town Councillor, Mayor, Member of Parliament and Journalist.

He entered Parliament as an Independent in 1942, when JTC Moore-Brabazon was elevated to the House of Lords.

He beat another local man, John Pennington (Conservative) and Major LH Cripps (Independent) with a 6,012 majority.

In the 1945 General Election, George Reakes, who polled 14,638 votes, was defeated by the Conservative candidate Captain Ernest Marples.

George was for many years on the editorial staff of the Wallasey News writing a stimulating weekly column entitled 'Looking Around'. He became a director of the company.

In 1953 he had a book published entitled *The Juvenile Offender*. He also wrote other works and published his autobiography in 1956.

*****

Mr John Ormerod

Mr. Barry served as Chief Constable until his retirement in November 1930 and died in the winter of 1933. A short list was drawn up for the position of Chief Constable. It consisted of RG Greensmith who was the Chief Constable of Glossop, Superintendent Hall from Sheffield, Detective Inspector Ashton of Wolverhampton, Chief Inspector Peel of Liverpool, Inspector Crosbie, also from Liverpool and Superintendent John Ormerod

Chief Constable John Ormerod OBE, CBE

of the Wallasey Borough Police.

The salary was £600 per annum, rising by four bi-annual increments of £50 to £800 per annum, together with a rent allowance of £15 per annum and actual travelling costs.

The Watch Committee were unanimous in selecting 40 year-old John Ormerod, who had been Acting Chief Constable and was married with two children.

Mr Ormerod was born in Manchester in 1890 and had come from a family with a long association with the Police, covering 200 years continuous service. His father was stationed at Prescot and became a racecourse detective. He was the third generation to become Superintendent. John Ormerod came out of the Army and joined the Wallasey Police Force in 1919 as a Patrol Constable, having previously worked in the Justice Clerk's Office at St Helens after being the secretary of St Helens YMCA. Before then he had been employed as a clerk in a colliery counting-house and had also been in the Purser's Office of a passenger shipping line.

At the outbreak of the First World War he was a member of the Waterloo St John's Ambulance Brigade and was mobilised with that unit before joining the Army where he served in the 19th Battalion King's Liverpool Regiment, first as an Infantryman then became attached to Earl Haig's staff of the BEF and attained the rank of Staff Sergeant (1st Class) and had seven decorations including the French Medialle d'Honneur avec Glaives en Argent, the Military BEM and the Meritorious Service Medal. He served overseas in 1915 and was mentioned in despatches. In 1917 he was transferred to the Commander-in-Chief Head Quarters. Fourteen months after joining the Wallasey Police Force he was appointed detective and Aliens Officer in 1920.

At that time he was living at 18 Bishop Road and in his spare time studied methods for the prevention and detection of crime and the system of Police Records. He introduced photographing criminals and was in charge of the Crime Register. He also prepared the evidence for indictable cases.

Whilst a detective he single-handed arrested two well-known housebreakers and was complemented by the Wallasey Justices. In 1924 he was given the rank of Sergeant, having passed the Liverpool Police Examination with high marks. The following year Mr Ormerod passed his Inspector's Examination following a period of being an Acting Inspector and soon after he became a full Inspector and Chief Clerk in charge of the Chief Constable's Office. Mr Ormerod was complemented by Sir Leonard Dunning upon his abilities of organisation and he became Chief Inspector in 1926.

He organised the Special Constabulary for the General Strike of 1926 and acted as Liaison Officer during that period. In October 1929 he became Superintendent. Mr Ormerod was appointed Acting Chief Constable in 1930 and in January, 1931, at the age of 41, he became the youngest Chief Constable in the country. He had served in every department in the force.

Before he was appointed he had said "If I become Chief Constable, and that's my ambition, I'll make this a first class force which Wallasey will be proud of", This statement proved to be true as the years progressed. He was as strict with himself as he was with his men but was also fair, outspoken and fearless. In February

Chief Inspector John Ormerod's signature which was said to resemble a gunboat

Chief Constable John Ormerod watches from the back right as the children are being fitted with new clothing and boots provided following the Chief Inspector's appeal

1931 he was created a Serving Brother of the Order of St John of Jerusalem for work in developing and maintaining a high standard of First Aid work in the force. During the Depression, the Police did all they could for the unemployed and their families. So as to enhance the good will among those who were out of work, a football match was arranged in 1933 between the Police and the unemployed workers at Sandheys Park in Rake Lane – the home of New Brighton Football Club. The famous `Dixie' Dean acted as referee. Almost 4,000 spectators turned up on a cold afternoon to see the match, which was well-fought, played in a sporting manner and won by the Police by the odd goal in seven. There was a collection after the game. The players retreated to the Police Social Club where they had tea and entertainment.

A billiards handicap was arranged and played off in eight halls in Wallasey and Moreton. The 16 finalists won eight geese and eight good joints of beef.

The Chief Constable helped more than one youth to go straight and saw that unemployed men had clothing.

In the days before the Welfare State, there were many families on the bread line when things were not easy for the unemployed. Money would not always stretch to buying a pair of shoes and if a second-hand pair was not obtainable, they could go to the Police Station and get a new pair free. Mr. Ormerod took a special interested in the welfare of the local children and set up the Chief Constable's Appeal for the Poor Children's Clothing Fund which attracted many supporters who provided warm clothing for the needy children. Some 687 youngsters were chosen from schools in the town and the distribution took place in the Police Recreation Club. More than 400 complete suits of clothes were given out and nearly 600 pairs of new boots. The good class clothing cost £250. The public responded so well that before each Christmas more than 1,200 children had been provided with a new set of clothing and boots. The Fund was carried on for some considerable time and many needy children benefited. Sad to record, there were some mothers who sold the child's boots in order to raise cash. They were unable to take them to the pawn brokers as all the items were stamped with the letters WBP and could get into trouble if they were found out.

The Police Benevolent Society continued with the practice and they provided a full set of clothing (underwear, shirt, jersey, trousers or skirts, socks and gloves) to all the needy children of the Borough. The Officers' wives would go to the Concert Hall and help to dress the children.

Mr Ormerod attended the occasion of the presentation of a billiards table to the Unemployed Social Centre in Magazine Lane in October 1934 and played the first shot on the table. It had been donated by Mr GH Young of Liscard Road.

It is good to record that there was little crime among the unemployed in the town.

As Chief Constable, Mr. Ormerod had an additional dress uniform with the tunic fastening at the neck and decorated cuffs. His hat was not unlike that worn by an admiral of the Navy. He would wear this hat when HM Inspector paid a visit. Other times he would wear a spiked decorated Police helmet. He also carried a sword which was fastened to his leather belt. I understand this was the same sword that Mr. Barry had used.

Mr Ormerod used to give lectures at various clubs and groups. In later years the men would bring an enclosed platform (possibly one that was used for Point Duty) from which he would address the audience.

There is a story that one of the Constables was in lodgings and he started to court the landlady's daughter. As time went on, he decided to pop the question. She accepted and he then sort the permission of the Chief Constable. The latter agreed and wrote across his Form 28

"Permission to change bedrooms!"

Chief Constable, John Ormerod's signature was known as the 'Battleship Signature' as some like to think that it resembled a gunboat (*see previous page*).

When writing, he usually used green ink and the 'E' in the name Ormerod was always a capital letter. His handwriting was big and bold and some said that it reflected his character.

He was awarded the OBE in 1941 and was raised to the rank of Officer Brother of the Venerable Order of St John of Jerusalem and became President of the local corps. He later donated a cup which is competed for annually.

He was awarded the King's Police Medal in 1948 and the CBE in 1952.

******

Law Breaking

HM Inspector of Police Forces, Colonel GHR Hallwood, CIE, OBE inspected the Wallasey Force in 1931.

There were 99 cases of house breaking in 1930/3.

218 persons were prosecuted, 56 over the previous year. There were 61 cases of housebreaking. 249 cautions were sent out.

9,949 Road Fund Licences were issued in Wallasey in 1930 and 7,058 were issued to applicants.

Dr Tom Martlew was Police Surgeon, who was Chairman of New Brighton FC and supported the club for many years. His brother, Robert, was also a medical practitioner in Wallasey.

Fire Police Constable JH Williams completed 17 years' service in the Police in November 1931.

In 1923 there were 8 fatal accidents on the roads in the borough and the figure for 1931 was 11, when there were also 307 people seriously injured and 836 slightly injured. However in 1932 the figure was only one.

There were 6,666 motor licences issued in 1932 with 7,149 the following year. There were 519 motorcars stolen in the town in 1932.

Too many cyclists were depending on the reflector on the back of their machines when cycling in the dark, which gave them a sense of false security.

The Chief Constable, Mr. Ormerod, said that he could foresee that in the future the busy thoroughfares would have railings along the edge of the kerb with sliding gates in front of the shops for the unloading of goods and subways or bridges to allow pedestrians to cross busy streets.

Annual Government Inspection 1932 carried out by Lt. Colonel WD Allen OBE

In the early 1920s there were no Patrol Cars though the force had four motorcycles. Other forms of transport was the simple cycle or the use of the tramcar or bus.

The motorcycle patrols watched out for motorists who, having turned into Leasowe Road from Reeds Lane, would speed down to Wallasey Village.

A second-hand motorcycle with combination was purchased for the force in 1932 for £32.10s.0d. (less £38 less £5.10s.0d for two derelict machines) and provision for a new motorcycle was made for £95.

Inspector WA Lidgett retired from the force in June 1932 after 25 years' service on a pension of £210.16s.0d. per annum.

PC Herbert Bland also retired on a pension of £153.11s.3d having completed 25 years' service with the Force.

Lt. Colonel WD Allan, OBE, HM Inspector of Police Forces, carried out the 1932 and 1936 Annual Inspections.

Another offender was the lad with the catapult who, for the shear devil of it, would let fly at the glass in the street lamps. As many as 50 would be smashed in one night. The Chief Constable wrote to Mr. Samuel, the Director of Education, concerning the matter and was told that teachers had taken action and had confiscated 200 catapults.

Crimes, such as housebreaking and shopbreaking totalled 196 in 1932 but the figure dropped to 137 the following year.

There were 915 lost or stray dogs in Wallasey in 1932. The number had fallen to 848 in the following year.

Some 682 needy children had received clothing and boots.

There was trouble with gangs of youths in the winter of 1933 when 50% of the house and shopbreaking was committed by youths under the age of 20. There were at least six gangs going around the town with the Police rounding up a good number and when they appeared before the Courts, 15 were sent to Borstal Institutions.

The gangs seem to have been influenced by the American Gangsters, such as Al Capone and others. Getting the idea from the films or cheap books on the market. They used such phrases as 'Lay off, Cop', 'shoots up in the burg' and 'bumped off'. They also liked to use the expression 'Oh yeah' and they tried to impress others as being 'Tough Guys'. The Chief Constable had much to say about them in his Annual Report. It was also reported in the national press.

Among reported crimes committed in the town during 1933 were 68 house break-ins, 853 indictable offences and 174 bicycles stolen. There were 7,149 Driving Licenses issued and 10,050 Road Fund Licenses.

There were 848 stray dogs destroyed. They were kept for a period of time and if they were not claimed by the owners, were destroyed.

This was carried out at Manor Road Police Station, using gas with the policy changing to electrocution at a later date. However, a stray dog could be purchased for five shillings.

Some 82 road accidents occurred and Police Constables rendered First Aid on the spot.

There were six Probationers in the force that year.

In November 1934, during the unusually long Mayoral Procession, there were a large number of people watching which resulted in traffic jams. As the procession came away from St Hilary's Church and arrived to Liscard, a bus had been held up for a quarter of an hour by the crowds. By the time it reached Church Street and Brighton Street, the traffic was at a complete standstill. Chief Constable John Ormerod, who was dressed in full regalia and sword, led the procession assisted in the direction of traffic.

The Chief Constable was concerned that 13 people had been killed and 285 people injured on the roads of Wallasey in 1934. Speeding had to be checked. During that year 7,529 Driving Licenses were issued as well as 10,130 Road Fund Licenses.

Two Constables were involved in sea rescues from the river for which they were awarded the Liverpool Shipwreck and Humane Society's Silver Medal and Certificate for gallantry. The rescues took place at Egremont when two fourteen-year-old boys were carried out by the strong tide on different dates in July 1934.

In their reports, one wrote '..while I was in the water, I regret I lost my Warrant Card'.

The other modest Constable reported 'I beg to report that my staff was lost in the River Mersey.'

Mrs. Jean Hime of Birkenhead, who assisted one of the Officers in the rescue, was awarded the Society's Silver Medal.

Another recruit, who had only been on street duty for two or three days, was awarded the Society's Bronze Medal for stopping a runaway horse. The animal dashed off at great speed pulling a spring cart. The young bobby ran and leapt onto the cart but to his dismay, found that the horse was without bridle and reins so he had to crawl along the shaft and hang on to the animal's mane and nose. He managed to turn it into a side road and bring it to a standstill.

He simply reported 'I received a slight abrasion to my left knee, caused by the horse's hoof, which appears to be of little consequence.'

Another Constable had distinguished himself by arresting two shopbreakers single-handed.

The members of the force had, in 1934, given First-Aid to 299 persons.

The strength of the force then was Chief Constable; One Superintendent and five Inspectors; 11 Sergeants and 98 Constables plus the Fire Service. There were nine recruitments during the year.

In 1935, there were 270 road accidents. Of the six persons fatally injured, three were killed in Seabank Road and in the same year a man was brought before the Court who confessed that he had committed 61 crimes and a youth was responsible for 25 cases. There were 105 cases of housebreaking; 174 bicycles stolen; 118 juveniles were brought before the Court; 122 cases of shopbreaking cases compared with 167 in 1934.

The Council sanctioned the Police to purchase a Police horse providing it would cost no more than £75 and weekly allowances were reviewed.

Mr Ormerod, the Chief Constable, addressed a meeting of the Liverpool and Merseyside Safety First Council at Southport in January 1935. He pleaded for white clothing for errand boys as a means of preventing accidents.

The first Pedestrian Crossing in Wallasey was laid in 1935 and the first traffic lights to be installed in the town were those at the Rake Lane/Penkett and Earlston Roads, being manufactured in the USA. In the 1960s these were removed and replaced with 'Give Way' signs. The crossroads are now very dangerous, especially with a wide sweep on one corner. [Several accidents now happen at this spot and traffic lights should be reinstalled.]

There were 130 members of Wallasey Borough Police in 1935 of which fourteen of this number were employed solely on Fire Brigade and Ambulance duties. The average height of a Constable in that year was 6ft. two and a half inches. The men patrolled 100 miles of streets and there were 25,000 houses and 100,00 people to take care of. That figure did not include the visitors to New Brighton in the summer.

There was a decline in house and shopbreaking in 1935 with the figure falling to 122 cases. There were 227 people were prosecuted. Lost and stray dogs amounted to 864 and some 670 lost children were returned to their thankful parents.

The Chief Constable, John Ormerod, stated 'The general conduct of members of the force is all that can be desired.'

Lt. Colonel F Brook carried out the Government Inspection of 1935 as well as that of 1938.

In the case of juvenile crime in 1936, the Chief Constable called for more birching. He said "I am old fashioned enough to believe that these sinful traits would yield to the sound application of a few well-selected birch twigs." He went on to add, "A firmer hand is needed with youngsters, but it goes deeper than that. I believe the remedy is in the younger Magistrates."

Several of the youths left the Court sneering at the kindly advice given by the Magistrates and using the most abusive adjectives that one could hear.

The Police were told that there were five 'P's' - **P**reservation of the **P**eace, **P**rotection of Life and **P**roperty and **P**revention and Detection of Crime.

There was a 100% increase in the number of motorcars, albeit there were fewer people killed and injured on the roads in the Borough in 1937.

Five people had lost their lives through road accidents and there were 268 injuries. The roads where most accidents happened were Liscard Road, Hoylake Road, Poulton Road, Leasowe Road and Seabank Road. However, the Police were concerned over the intoxicated driver.

There were now 278 more drivers on the roads in the town.

Crime figures showed as many as 941 indictable offences and 727 crimes being detected; 363 letters of caution being sent out; 1523 lost articles were found with 726 being reclaimed.

There was an increase in the number of crimes in the town. A

Chief Constable Ormerod with the Mayor, Alderman S Panter Brick and Government Inspector, Lt. Colonel F Brook in 1935

figure of 941 offences was recorded, against 849 in 1936. There was also an increase in the number of cycles stolen and youths breaking automatic machines to steal the coins. There was also an increase in unnatural offences and the Chief Constable, Mr. Ormerod, took measures in cleaning up the Borough "of this perversity" as he stated in his Annual Report. The vice had been reduced by 75%.

The Licensing Bench refused to remove the licence from the *Griffin Hotel* in Borough Road in Seacombe to the proposed site in Hoylake Road.

There were 662 children reported lost and were reunited with their parents.

Lost and stray dogs numbered 853.

The Police numbers remained the same at 116 and 14 in the Fire Brigade.

Two Sergeants and ten men retired from the force.

The fleet of four Police Cars in 1937 consisted of: the fine black SS Jaguar with chromium plated radiator and headlamp surrounds and was fitted with a loud speaker attached to the bumper; the Ford V 8 patrol car, registration number HF 6526 was a very powerful motorcar that only did eight miles to the gallon. The slightest touch on the accelerator made it shoot forward and the steering wheel needed more turns to get around a corner that an ordinary motorcar; another patrol car; and the older Hillman saloon with the Registration number HF 7999 that was nicknamed 'The Queen Mary' by the men. I understand that the Chief Constable used a Vauxhall saloon car, AHF 1 at one time. An addition to the fleet was the car, registration No. AHF 999.

In the February of 1938, Mr Ormerod was invited to be the speaker at the Liscard Wednesday Evening Society. His subject was 'The Police Service, Then and Now'.

Mr. Robertson Crichton, the well-known barrister, was the Chairman and during the course of his address, Mr Ormerod passed him a bottle and carefully taking it from him said "Now I have your fingerprints." The Chief Constable then powdered the glass and placed a piece of adhesive plaster over the spot where the Chairman's fingerprints had rested. He then showed the audience the evidence.

A call was sent out over wireless and a Motor Patrol picked it up at Moreton and reported himself at the lecture hall.

Mr. Ormerod went on to speak about other modern policing methods.

On 26 February 1938, following the hearing of several serious cases committed from the Wallasey Police Court, Mr Ormerod was asked to appear before Mr Justice Atkinson at the Chester Assizes in order to pass favourable comment. He said "I congratulate you on the clean up, I only wish others would follow your example."

Brave Girl

Wallasey was proud of one of its youngest heroines. Shy 14 year-old maid Doris Clarke of Hawthorne Road was bathing near Egremont Ferry and had left the water when she heard the cries of an 11 year-old girl who was being swept away with the tide and was heading for the ferry pier. Doris did not hesitate, she dived into the water and swam after her, grabbing hold of the rubber tube the girl was wearing around her waist and dragged her to the wall. There she held on and was helped by Joseph Weir of Liverpool. He took the child and Doris returned unaided.

For her brave rescue, Doris was introduced to the Mayor of Wallasey, Councillor George L Reakes, who presented her with the Royal Humane Society's Bronze Medal and

Doris Clarke receiving her certificate and silver wrist watch in November 1938 from Mayor George L Reakes for saving an 11 year old girl from drowning. John Ormerod looks on

Certificate and a silver wristlet watch. The watch was inscribed by members of the Wallasey Borough Police Force who were greatly impressed by her courage and action. The presentation was made at a Coronation Supper given by the Mayor to the Wallasey Police in November 1938. Mr. Weir had also received an award from the Society at an earlier date.

Another rescue that seems to have passed unnoticed was when a number of small children were cut off by the incoming tide by Fort Perch Rock Battery as they played on the sands. Action had to be taken quickly.

Mr Clark, the well-known owner of the horses for hire on the beach, quickly jumped on to one of his animals and rode out into the water, rescued the children and brought them back to the beach.

******

Motorcars

In 1938 there were 10,979 Road Fund Licences issued and 9,887 people took out driving licences. Eight people were killed on the roads in that year but there were 30 fewer injuries. More pavement rails were called for as a result.

Most road accidents happened in Leasowe Road, Liscard Road, Hoylake Road (where there were two deaths) and Wallasey Road. The Chief Constable was glad to report in 1938 that there was a decrease in the dangerous class of offence concerning intoxicated drivers. Only two motorists were convicted and fined for the offence.

There were 41 cases of drunkenness (all men) which was an increase of 15 over the previous year which was mainly due to visitors.

PC George Hodges, whose father had been a Police Officer, joined the Cheshire Constabulary in 1938. He served in the RMP and was transferred to Wallasey in 1947 and held the Bronze Medal of the RLS.

When a Constable was on night duty, he had to check the doors of each shop on his beat to see that they were locked for the night. Some Policemen called this 'shaking hands with the doorknobs'. If a door was found to be insecure after a Constable had gone off duty he got into trouble. It was not unusual for a Constable to be aroused from sleep to report to Head Quarters for questioning concerning incidents on his beat the previous night.

Other premises, including the fronts, sides and backs were also checked.

Householders could notify the Police when they were going on holiday or away on business, leaving a vacant house. All these houses had to be visited once in each shift. For instance, in 1932 832 of these dwellings had to be checked out, as well as other properties.

Some Constables who were on 'earlies' or 'afternoons' would have to perform traffic crossing duties at schools.

In the cold winter, the rain water that had collected on the promenade near the bottom of Holland Road would often freeze over making it the ideal place for local children to use as a skating rink. Residents living in Marine Terrace found the noise from the children enjoying themselves annoying so they contacted Manor Road Police Station. It would not be surprising to see the Chief Constable arrive at the scene, break up the fun-seekers and restore the calm again.

Sergeant 'Ted' Petherbridge was in charge of the Traffic Department (which was a separate unit) and was also the Coroner's Officer who dealt with the sudden deaths for which doctors couldn't issue a death certificate.

The Police had a mortuary in Mortuary Road at the side of Rake Lane Cemetery which was the province of the Coroner's Officer. Mr Petherbridge had been Coroner's Officer for 18 years and had joined the Wallasey Force in 1926 when there were only 36 members compared with 160 in 1951. Ted served under two Chief Constables and three Coroners, preparing a thousand inquests and taking in the region of ten thousand statements. He was a married man living in Thorncliffe Road with one daughter.

On his retirement in March 1951 it became part of the CID section and Det Constable George Edwards became the Coroner's Officer.

Sergeant Brown took charge of the Motor Patrol and PC Stanley Fisher was promoted to Sergeant. He had joined the Force in 1939.

Col. F Brook FSO, MC carrying out the 1938 Government Inspection with Alderman AW Vickary, Alderman S Coins and Chief Constable John Ormerod

The Police were worried over the number of young people that were roller-skating on the roads as it was very dangerous.

Some 99 members of the Police Force qualified in First Aid with St John Ambulance Association Awards and between them had treated some 140 cases of lacerated feet caused by broken glass on the beaches. The Constables carried an iodine pen as part of their equipment which proved to be very useful.

There were 153 people who wrote in with complaints and 914 had made verbal complaints, some being about noisy animals. All were looked into and if possible the matter put right.

When HM Inspector of Constabulary, Lt Colonel Sir Frank Brook, DSO, MC, came to the Navy League ground in 1939, he inspected four Inspectors, 12 Sergeants and 82 men who gave an admiral display of drill, under the direction of Constable Carr and the Band of the Navy League. Mounted Police were also present. The Chief Constable was accompanied by Superintendent McDonough. The Colonel was greatly impressed with the Wallasey Force and speaking at the luncheon at the Ferry Hotel, he said, "I never find perfection in a Police force. I have yet to find the force that is absolutely right in every department. Such a thing was quite impossible, but I assure you your force is a good one. Discipline is being well maintained."

He also said that they were a good body of men, well-trained, and he hoped that they would be encouraged.

Alderman John Pennington was Chairman of the Watch Committee and Mr JP Wilson was Magistrates' Clerk.

In the 1930s, there was a Police Hut near the Railwaymen's Home (Leasowe Castle) in Leasowe Road with sub-stations in Church Road, Seacombe, Hope Street, New Brighton. Egremont was served by a Sub-Station in the old *Bee Hive* at Egremont Ferry. It was not the best of places in rough weather as the high tides would batter it and being so cold for the bobbies, an electric radiator was purchased in 1930 to warm the place up. At a later date a Police Box was built next to the Ferry buildings.

On one occasion, a Bobby was loaned a bicycle to go down to the Bee Hive Police Box. Little did he know that the machine had very poor brakes. He rode down Tobin Street and as he gathered speed he applied the brakes but they had no effect so all he could do was to swing around the corner at the bottom of the street and shoot along the promenade until he could stop and turn around. When he met up with the others, he had a few choice words to say!

Wall of Death

Leonard Sidney Sutton, a 24 year-old motor coach driver from Coventry, was killed when a female motor cyclist lost control and 'shot' out of the 'Wall of Death' in the Tower Grounds. Mrs. Zoe Campbell, aged 21, of Greenbank Avenue in Wallasey was unable to give evidence at the inquest as she was in hospital with a fractured leg. Police spoke to her in hospital the following day but she said that her mind was a complete blank.

Sergeant EV Petherbridge, the Police Motor Patrol Sergeant, said that he found that the outer cable housing of the throttle control had been secured by a clip which was held by a small single bolt. The bolt was loose and had allowed the cable to fall away with the result that when the throttle was opened by twisting the grip handle bar control it would not close again, even though the control was turned back to the zero position. The sudden acceleration of the machine and the subsequent leap up the wall could be understood because of the inability of the rider to close the throttle.

John Campbell, the rider's husband said that he had been riding for more than ten years and he had examined both the machine and the wall the day before the accident and found that the motor cycle was in good order as was the wall itself. In previous accidents, the rider had been thrown back into the pit by the safety cable running around the top of the wall.

The Chief Constable said that such seaside entertainment should be subject to inspection by a Government department to ensure public safety. The Jury returned a verdict of misadventure.

******

Report

In the Chief Constable's Annual Report for 1940, it showed that there were 273 cases of cut feet on the shore due to broken glass. Many small children were treated by Constables.

In 1939, there were four people killed on the roads and 194 injured. There was an application to build a new hotel on the site of the Palace in New Brighton which was turned down by the Wallasey Licensing Bench in 1940. It was to have seating for a thousand people and 500 diners. The application was made on behalf of Mr George Wilkie, who had leased the site off the Corporation in August 1938 and was hoping to spent £40,00 on the project.

'Police Boxes'

'Police Boxes' were small buildings scattered around the borough. There was one on the promenade adjacent to Victoria Gardens; two in Poulton, one being in Poulton Road near the Oxton Road and Gorsey Lane traffic lights and the other in Gorsedale Road near the school. There was also one in Rockland/Hoseside Roads by Elleray Park; one at Egremont Ferry; another in Ashville Road; one in Church Road and one by the Derby Pool.

The wooden hut in Leasowe Road was replaced by a Police Box on the other (South) side of the road; there was a Police Box at Twickenham Drive and another at Pasture Common.

The 'Police Boxes' were sturdily-built and had the appearance of an air-raid shelter.

When PC Dave Liston was on duty in Wallasey Village he would sit down to eat his sandwiches in the 'Police Box', but he was often disturbed by someone seeking advice, reporting thefts or

Police Box at New Brighton

accidents. It was all a part of being a bobby.

The 'Police Box' by Victoria Gardens, New Brighton was bright and sunny where the bobby was glad to take a rest and put his weary feet up for a few minutes and enjoy a cup of tea.

Lord Derby opened the new extension to Manor Road Police Station on Saturday 9 September 1940 and inaugurated the new Police Telephone Communication System in the Borough that linked eight Police Boxes and 30 blue-painted Police Pillar-Phones to Police Headquarters.

His Lordship was accompanied by the Mayor of Wallasey, Councillor PG Davies, Alderman John Pennington, the Chairman of the Watch Committee, Chief Constable John Ormerod and others. A short prayer was offered by the Rural Dean, the Rev WS Coad.

The ground floor of the new building was used for Motor Taxation and the first floor had offices for the CID and Summons Department. Registration of aliens was also taken into account. The photographic department and darkroom was also on this floor. Lord Derby was taken to a 'Police Box' in Wallasey Village to inaugurate the system. The uniform Officers did not carry a radio then, as apparatus was so bulky. All they had was a whistle, However, in the 1940s patrol cars were fitted with radios. These consisted of a large box fitted in the boot of the car. The Wallasey call sign was CW and the Birkenhead Police, who used the same frequency, had the call sign BN. The Constable on the beat had a key which opened the small door marked 'Police' on the Police Pillar-Phone and from there he was able to telephone Police Headquarters in Manor Road. To contact the bobby on the beat in an emergency, the operator at the Station was able to control a switch that caused the lamp on top of the Pillar-Phone to flash intermittently and there was also a buzzing sound. At the back of these Police Pillar-Phones was a spring-loaded door with the word 'Public' on. A caller could contact the police switchboard and consequentially a direct link to the Fire, Ambulance or Police. The Constable had to report from these pillars at regular intervals and if he did not telephone at the arranged time, a patrol car would be contacted and sent to check see if he was alright.

PC John Shakeshaft using a Police Pillar telephone

It has been known for a bobby to have a quick word with his fiancee who was working on the switchboard at HQ!

These Police Pillar-Phones were discontinued when Constables were equipped with a portable telephone and the public could dial 999 from a public telephone box.

In 1942, a temporary Sub-Station was opened in Chadwick Street to cope with the increased population of Moreton.

Councillor JH Wensley served as Chairman of the Watch Committee from 1942 to 1944 and was succeeded by Alderman HJ Hall in 1945 who served for about 12 months. Alderman Wensley was Mayor of Wallasey in 1950/51 and died in 1960.

Second World War

In March 1937 the Wallasey Town Council took the wise decision and formed the ARP (Air-Raid Precautions) Committee with Councillor JH Wensley, JP as Chairman. They were set up for the protection and well-being of the civil population in the event of war. The official statement read:-

"The general idea of an Air-Raid Warden is that he should be a responsible member of the public chosen to be a leader and adviser to his neighbours in a small area, street or group of streets in which he is known and respected. He could also lead a check for missing persons". There were as many as 600 trained Wardens in Wallasey by the autumn of 1938 which brought the dark clouds of the approaching war.

The members of the ARP dressed in what was called a 'Siren Suit' (a navy blue sort of boiler suit with pockets).

The Concert Hall in Manor Road became the ARP Headquarters and in 1938 a large number of ARP workers, Police Officers and others were working until the small hours assembling some 96,000 civilian gas-masks for the people of Wallasey. They were distributed to the general public from some 22 centres around the Borough within a very short time. Special gas units were available for babies, known as Cradle Gas Masks. They had light metal frame with a large window and canvas hood. Air was drawn in through the built-in filter by means of bellows. There were even gas-masks for horses which were huge, with two windows and a filter at the end nozzle.

A decision was taken by the Government in 1939 that all large towns would have an ARP Controller and that an Officer should be appointed by the local Authority. In most towns, the first appointments were mainly given to the Chief Constable of that area, as was in the case of Wallasey where Mr Ormerod was given the position which was responsible for the Air-Raid Wardens who worked with the Police.

In the case of Birkenhead, the Town Clerk was the Controller as was Liverpool and Bootle. Bebington's Controller was the Chief Constable of Cheshire.

The Chief Constable attended a special course at Gloucester in connection with Air-Raid Precautions and Inspector Alf Williams had been to a course at Civilian Anti-Gas School at Falfield.

War was declared on 3 September 1939 with the *Liverpool Echo*, printing a special Sunday edition for a penny.

School children were 'evacuated' to rural districts. On Friday 1 September 1939 a large number left Seacombe Station for destinations such as Heswall, Shotton and North Wales. They kept their gas-masks in a cardboard box with a string attached to go over the shoulder for carrying. They each had a label pinned to their coats. Pupils from the Oldershaw Schools went to Hawarden and Nantwich, Boys from Wallasey Grammar School went to Harwarden, whilst some of the girls went to stay in Oswestry. Girls from the Wallasey High School were evacuated to Abergavenny in South Wales and those who stayed in Wallasey were taken for lessons at the Grand Hotel in New Brighton and

some large house which had an air-raid shelter that could accommodate ten people. A house in Paignton Road was used as was a bungalow near Wallasey Village Library named *Oruba*.

Rest Centres were set up at various points in the town which were staffed by the ladies of the WVS. Some wore a green uniform and others had overalls. They were to do gallant work in looking after those made homeless by the bombing raids and serving countless teas, from mobile canteens, to the rescue workers.

Mr David Forsyth was Chief Air-Raid Warden a the time. He had a Deputy in Mr FD Larcombe. Owing to ill health, Mr. Forsyth was compelled to resign and Mr Ormerod appointed Mr Larcombe to fill the post. Mr Larcombe put long hours into the organisation and set up an office in the vicinity in order to be close to his Warden service. All this proved too much for him and he had to resign on health grounds. Mr J Reginald Smith became the Chief Warden who had almost 1,000 men under him. His Deputy was Mr George Proudlove. The Civil Defence was divided into groups and were responsible for an allotted area.

A large parade was arranged in Central Park with Mr Hartley Shawcross (later Sir), taking the Salute.

Trenches for shelter were dug in Central Park, Belvidere Recreation Ground, Ellery Park, Gorsey Lane and other sites in the town.

Col Arthur Behrend, who was the head of a Liverpool shipping company, was in charge of the AA Regiment in Wirral and it took receipt of a Vickers machine gun. Later AA guns and searchlights were placed at certain points in the town. On the end of New Brighton Pier, there was a machine gun and searchlight. A painting was done of this by Albert Richards from Wallasey, an official war artist. He was tragically killed on his way to paint the Allied Forces' attack on the River Maas in 1945.

The Chief Constable reported that four people had been killed on the roads. Over 10, 000 Road Licences were issued and 47 people were prosecuted for breaking the Emergency Lighting Regulations (Black-Out).

The Black-Out came into force on 1 September 1939 when vehicles had to have a bulb not greater than 3 watts and the lamp glass had to have at least three thickness of tissue paper.

One of many War-time posters - this one encouraging the people of Wallasey to join the Home Guard Artillery

---43---

1940s

The first bomb to be dropped on our Isles was that on a raid in the Orkneys on 17 October 1939 but it was not until the fall of France in 1940 that the German air-raids started in earnest. In Wallasey, 31 Warden Posts were set up throughout the Borough and Air-Raid Sirens were installed on the top of various buildings in the town. The warning of an approaching enemy plane was given by the siren being switched on and off, thus giving a whining rising and falling sound. It put fear into one's soul. When the danger had passed, an 'All Clear' signal was given which was a long continuous sound. Everyone was so thankful to hear it. The first time they were sounded, other than a short test, was on 25 June 1940 but it was only a false alarm. They were to be heard for something like 500 times during the war.

The warning were as follows:-

'P' - Purple Warning - initial warning; lights out.

'R' - Red Alert - Air-Raid imminent.

'W'- White - Raiders passed.

Wardens patrolled their area, looking to see that the Blackout restrictions were being adhered to. Even a small amount of light showing would bring a knock at the door. If a front door opened allowing the light to be flashed across the pavement, one would hear the familiar call of "Put that light out!"

It was said that "even a pin-point of light can be seen a thousand feet up", but this was an exaggeration.

Motorcars had shields fitted to the headlights in order to restrict the beam and mudguards had a white-painted trim. Street lamps were mainly turned off, lamp posts, trees and telegraph poles had white bands painted around the bottom and some kerbstones were picked out in white.

During the Blackout, a small leather cover was fitted over the lamp on top of the Police Pillars so only a slit of light could be seen at its base.

At Mr Ormerod's Head Quarters, there was a personnel of about 90, ranging from clerks to telephonists. There were arrangements whereby he could sleep on the premises.

By the end of the year there were some 857 fully-trained Wardens in the town, with another 136 still under tuition.

People tuned in their radios to listen to Lord Haw Haw's (William Joyce) propaganda broadcasts from Germany with the familiar introduction "Jairmany Calling, Jairmany Calling". He would spread rumours about the damage caused to this country, mentioning Wallasey several times.

The Home Guard, originally known as the LDV (Local Defence Volunteers), was formed in May 1940 after a broadcast over the wireless by Anthony Eden, the Secretary for War. In the first week there were 2,500 men in Wallasey who had answered the call. Mr. William Duncan Taylor, JP was in command assisted by Mr. Sidney Goodman with Head Quarters at the Concert Hall in Manor Road.

The first bombs to fall in Wirral were on 29 July 1940 in fields near Neston, Irby and Thurstaston which made small craters and many curious people went out to see them.

During the early part of the war some of the Policemen wore tin hats with the word 'Police' painted on the front.

Many local policemen had joined the forces but those who remained in Wallasey played their part on the Home Front during the war by helping in the rescuing of people after the raids; clearing away the debris and many other tasks in addition to policing the town.

WH Davies, the Wallasey Golf Club professional and Ryder Cup player, became a Police War Reserve Constable.

There were 22 local Police Officers who were recalled to the Colours, 12 were Grenadier Guardsmen. They were:-

HS Brown, JD Brown, H Burrows, WN Carr, R Ellis, LE Harrison, JA Harrison, L Reavil, EA Sharples, R Waft, L Whittingham and EJ Young.

Constables JG Bradley, CE Brown, AM Farquharson, RC Myles and GH Steele joined the Scots Guards. Constable JD Newton rejoined the Welsh Guards. Constables C Rycroft and TG Wearing joined the Royal Artillery and Constable H Hargreaves went into the King's (Liverpool) Regiment, Constable WG Craft had rejoined the Navy. PC Stanley Fisher of the Motor Patrol joined the Royal Air Force in 1941 becoming a Pathfinder Squadron Leader and won the DFC twice for bombing raids over Germany. He had also received the King's Commendation for rescue work during the Blitz in 1940.

He was promoted to Chief Superintendent and his brother, Leslie, also joined the Wallasey Borough Police. The family had connections with the Police dating back to the early period when they wore top hats.

PC 105 was Hughie Stevenson. He joined the Royal Air Force and became a Pathfinder Pilot and a Flight Lieutenant, being awarded the DFC.

******

Royal Visit

King George the Sixth and Queen Elizabeth made a surprise visit to see the bombed areas of Wallasey on Wednesday 6 November 1940. Their Majesties were met by a number on dignitaries on entering the Borough which included the Mayor of Wallasey, Councillor PG Davies; the ARP Controller, Mr Ormerod; Alderman John Pennington; Councillor Mrs Dorothy Barton (WVS); the Chief Warden, Mr J Reginald Smith; Wardens Rescue Party members and First-Aid personnel.

The King was dressed in the uniform of a Field Marshall and the Queen wore a two-piece suit of hyacinth blue.

The Royal Couple saw Sergeant Woolley's house in Bedford Road where most of the roof had been blown away with the blast. The debris had fallen into the house, with the blast going through the building, tearing the plaster from the walls and smashing the window panes. Fortunately, the Officer and his wife and young son and daughter escaped injury due to the fact that they had taken refuge under the stairs and in the inside corner of the downstairs room in which special bunks had been erected. The King and Queen talked to the Sergeant and Mrs Woolley and having learned of their experience, the King said "I have heard a lot about the safety of under the stairs, let me see where you were."

The king was taken into the hallway and went under the stairs and he congratulated the Woolleys on their escape. The Queen spoke to five year-old Stanley Woolley. "Can you read?", she asked.

"Yes", replied the little fellow.

The Queen asked Mrs. Woolley if it were true.

Their Majesties also spoke to the Chief Constable's two young

King & Queen leaving Littledale Road on their visit to Wallasey 6 November 1940

daughters, Nancy and Audrey and the Queen asked them if they went to school.

The Royal Couple also spoke to 84 year-old Mrs Jessie Lloyd and chatted to several families who had lost their homes in the bombing. The Queen waved to two old ladies who were sitting on their doorstep some distance away.

When the crowd surrounded the King, he was heard to say in a humorous way, "Don't step on my corns!"

A little girl was standing on her own in Seacombe and the Queen asked her where she lived.

"Back of the Gandy", came the reply.

******

OBE

Chief Constable and ARP Controller John Ormerod was made a an Officer of the Order of the British Empire in the New Year's Honours List of 1941. He was still very keen on First Aid and was made an Officer Brother of the Order of St John, eventually becoming President of the Wallasey St John's Ambulance Association.

Mr Ormerod was already a member of the Military Division of the Order.

Constable Starkey and Special Constable Jones

Great courage was shown by Constable David Starkey, a Policeman for 17 years who lived in Riversdale Road, in the March raids of 1941. A house received a direct hit and was completed demolished with three people trapped in the ruins. Assisted by Special Constable Frank Fleetwood Jones, an analytical chemist who lived in Frankby Avenue, they set to work to rescue those trapped as High Explosive bombs were falling. Constable Starkey, followed by the Special Constable worked carefully for two hours passing bricks and burning timbers to other helpers. At last they reached the three people under the debris and brought out two women and a man to safety as the bombs still fell. Both men received the George Medal for gallantry.

A Police canteen was set up in the Concert Hall with Inspector CT Sandland responsible for its organising and running.

Arthur Trowell joined the Wallasey Borough Police in 1941 as a Patrol Constable and remained in the force after the war. He was twice commended and held three RMS awards.

Mr. Winston Churchill

Mr. Winston Churchill, the wartime premier visited Wallasey on Friday 25 April 1941 when he came to Seacombe wearing his nautical cap and carrying a gas-mask over his shoulder. He arrived

Winston Churchill visiting Wallasey 25 April 1941

in an open car with a private detective, escorted by the Chief Constable, Mr Ormerod who was also the ARP Controller. They stopped by the Swan Hotel in Dock Road where there was a Constable present to see that there was no crowd trouble. It was a 'hush-hush' visit but news that "Churchill's here" soon spread and a number of people gathered to see the Leader.

Mr. Churchill was then driven to Poulton and inspected the Civil Defence and saw the bomb damage in Erskine Road. With a cigar in his mouth, carrying a stick and waving to the cheering crowd, he held up his hand and gave his famous 'V' sign salute and called out, "God Bless you All" and as he climbed into the car to leave, he asked, "Are we downhearted?"

"No" shouted the crowd.

VIPs

Among the other VIPs to visit the town were Admiral Sir Edward Evans in 1941 and Mr AM Trustrom, QC of the War Damage Commission. In the December of the same year Mr. Herbert Morrison, Minister of Home Security came.

On 17 August 1941 the control of the Fire Brigade passed from the Police to the National Fire Service.

In Moreton, there was an Inspector, three Sergeants and more than six Special Constables.

There was an increase in the number of crimes reported by the Chief Constable in 1941. The figure had risen from 1,273 to 1,449 when 242 males and 33 females were prosecuted. There was a rise in the number of juvenile offenders but a fall in the adults. This was due to the adults being involved in war duties either away or on the Home Front leaving the youths with less supervision and more opportunities to turn to crime. There were over 250 minor cases where letters of caution were sent.

Housebreaking had increased from 50 to 79 cases; shopbreaking 44 to 89; receiving stolen goods had also increased from 19 to 80. No doubt the war had contributed to this increase as there was a blackout in force and a ready 'black market'.

The Police Force had 143 men, including 14 members of the Fire Brigade with 25 vacancies; one Policeman had resigned and one Probationer was disposed with. There were 22 Reservists as well as 31 Police Reserves.

Speaking of the Special Constables, Mr. Ormerod said "This admiral body of men have proved themselves of immense value, especially during grave emergencies."

Eleven people were killed on the roads in the year, two being children who ran in the front of a moving vehicle and a 13 year-old boy was killed by a van whilst roller skating on the road. Wallasey Road was the most dangerous road in the town.

Inspector Payne attended a course on Operation Control by the Police at Air-Raid Incidents.

St John's Ambulance set up their Head Quarters in the old rectory of St Hilary's Church in the summer of 1942. Mr Ormerod, who was their President, performed the opening.

There were 145 members of the Women's Home Defence Unit which was set up and organised by Mrs Edith Roberts who worked alongside Lt Col Duncan Taylor of the Home Guard.

In the Second World War, 44 members of the Force served on many fronts. Eleven were killed on active service and of the other members, two were awarded the DFC and another received the DSM.

A bronze tablet was placed in the Manor Road Headquarters in memory of those members of the Borough Police who lost their lives in the two world wars, 1914/1918 and 1939/1945.

Headed by the badge of the Wallasey Police, the bronze tablet has the following wording:-

The tablet was unveiled by the Rt Hon the Earl of Derby and dedicated by the Rev Canon WS Coad of Chester Cathedral on 30 April 1951.

Hughie Henderson had tried to join the RAF soon after the outbreak of the war but was turned down as being too young. However, he applied again and this time was accepted and became a Pilot Sergeant. He took a Commission as a Pilot Officer and was killed while on a raid over foreign soil.

Inspector Alfred Williams and Sergeant Rigg were awarded the BEM for their courageous deeds while performing civil duties, one was a Training Officer of the LARP Instructors.

During the war, the King awarded one George Medal, one British Empire Medal and three commendations to three members of the Force. In 1943, an Inspector received a British Empire Medal for distinguished service.

Brave Constable

34 year-old Police Constable Eric Leslie Valantine of 10 Bletchley Avenue made a heroic attempt to rescue a young Wallasey lady named Joan Boote on Friday 20 August 1943. He was on Cycle Patrol at Harrison Drive when he was called to the scene. Seeing the girl in difficulties, he removed his cap, tunic, leather leggings and boots and plunged into the rough water, swimming out to the girl. However, his breeches had filled with water and caused him to sink beneath the waves and he was drowned. Miss Boote was also drowned.

The sea was very rough at the time which led the Chief Constable to say of him at the Inquest "…..that he must have had the heart of a lion." The Constable left a widow and two young children aged five and a half and four years. He was a devoted husband and father.

The *Wallasey News*, with the permission of Mr. Ormerod, set up an 'In Memoriam Fund', which Mrs Valantine used for the children. She also received a small pension from the Carnegie Hero Trust Fund.

******

Wallasey Warden Service

Courageous work was carried out by members of the Wallasey Warden Service. The Air Raid Wardens, and other Civil Defence

A booklet was produced in 1944 to record the work of the gallant people in the Warden Service. This is reproduced in the book 'Wallasey at War' published by the Wallasey Historical Society.

Workers continued their operations despite the fact that enemy planes overhead were dropping bombs. They risked their lives in carrying out their duties and 12 Wallasey Wardens lost their lives as a result of the bombing.

An oak screen was dedicated in St Nicholas's Church with all the names of the wardens who gave their lives in the sector during the war.

Other Brave Men

Some of the other brave Wallasey men of the Second World War were:–.

Ian Fraser, who was awarded the Victoria Cross for destroying the Japanese cruiser, *Takao,* in Singapore whilst in the Navy. He also holds the FSC, DSM and the Legion of Honour.

George William Beeching had been an active member of the ARP, serving at the First Aid Centre in Princess Road. He joined the Navy and served in *HMS Ibis* and showed great heroism when the ship was sunk off the coast of North Africa after the Algiers landing. He was 23 years old and the first and only Wallaseyan to receive the Albert Medal in Gold (Posthumous). George had been a member of St John's Ambulance as a young man and attended Oakdale Mission.

Joseph Lynch was awarded the BEM and Albert Medal whilst serving in the Royal Navy.

Harold Rogers also received the George Medal. He was a 41 year-old Dock Gateman who lived in Hertford Drive. He rescued three women, one being over 80, and a child from a burning house in Radnor Drive.

John N Stevens, who lived in Seaview Road, came to the rescue when a house in Manor Road received a direct hit. The 34 year-old worked for two hours without regard for his own life, while Nazi planes were overhead dropping bombs. He rescued a woman and child from the badly-damaged house. For his brave action he was later awarded the George Cross. During the war, he received four other life-saving medals. John, who was a talented footballer and had played a few games at centre-forward for New Brighton FC (also known as The Rakers) in prewar days, came from a family of 13 children and two of his brothers, William and George Leopold, played for the same club. Leo, who had been a tramcar conductor in Wallasey, joined them professionally and was the club's leading goalscorer for two seasons.

William Albert Clare, a dairyman aged 51, was an Officer in the Home Guard who lived in Fieldway. A house was hit with a High Explosive bomb, trapping several people inside. The house caught fire, but this did not deter Mr Clare who rushed in and rescued the occupants, despite the fact the house could have collapsed at any time.

Both **Lieutenant Dennis James O'Hagan** and **2nd Lieutenant ARP Watson** received the George Medal. Dennis for bomb disposal work and the 2nd Lieutenant for his effort in the rescue of an RAF pilot.

Arthur Graham Harrison served as an officer in the RNVR and received the DSC. He was to become an excellent Town Clerk for Wallasey Town Council, succeeding Mr. Emrys Evans, who had held the position from 1931. Arthur, who also held the OBE, is an old boy of Birkenhead School and became a solicitor in 1936. He served on the Civil Defence Committees as well as the Law Committee of the Association of Municipal Corporations. Mr Harrison, a past Captain of Wallasey Golf Club, was a married man with two sons and his wife, Joan, was a Wallasey JP.

Wallasey-born **General Sir Miles Dempsey** lived in Sandringham Road and as a child attended Ellery Park Preparatory Boys' School.

******

Choir and Orchestra

The Wallasey Civil Defence Choir and Orchestra gave concerts during the war. Their conductor was Mr Stainton de B Taylor, the well-known musician and organist. Originally, there was only the choir which was formed in 1941. They gave their first concert in the First Aid Post in Princess Road by singing a selection from the Gilbert and Sullivan Operas. It was the first town in the country to form such a choir. The orchestra began in a very humble way in January 1942 with a collection of second-hand instruments. It consisted of six violinists, two cellists, two viola players and a pianist. Within a short time they grew in numbers and became an excellent choir and orchestra, giving concerts all over Merseyside. They rehearsed in the blackout between air-raids and performed Handel's 'Messiah' and Haydn's 'Creation' to audiences. They gave a concert at the Floral Pavilion following the drumhead service in Central Park in July 1942 when the Service and Defence Units took part in the Service which was conducted by the Rev Canon WS Coad, the Rural Dean and Vicar of St James' Church. The Mayor, Alderman PG Davies read the lesson, the hymn singing was led by the band of the Cheshire Regiment and the sermon was given by Bishop Crick.

The Chief Constable marshalled the parade and the Salute at the March-Past, which took almost 30 minutes, was taken by The Earl of Derby.

The Choir, in the evening, sang selections from Wagner's 'Lohengrin', Elgar's cantata, 'Spirit of England' and other works. In 1945 the Wallasey Civil Defence Choir and Orchestra gave a Victory Concert at the Tower Theatre which was decorated with the flags of the Nations. A large crowd witnessed a fine concert. The Choir and Orchestra continued to give concerts for some time after the war with performances including 'Hiawatha', Haydn's 'Creation' and other works. The Orchestra was bold enough to perform symphonies such as Beethoven's Fifth and many charities benefited from their efforts.

Winning Team

The Wallasey Civil Defence Services Team won the Regional Commissioner's Trophy, North Western Region on 14 May 1944. They were trained by Inspector Alfred Williams. The team consisted of W Halliday (Ambulance), WT Matthews (Decontam..), R Bennet (Rescue), G Askham (Warden), S Banks (Control), Miss SS Boyce (First Aid Post), FJ Saunders - Team Captain (Warden), AS Brown (Fire Guard) and HH Beale (Reserve). Constable David Starkey represented Wallasey in the Victory Parade in London in 1945.

Special Constabulary

The Wallasey Special Constabulary served in the First World War (payment not more than five shillings a day) and in 1919, when the Special Constabulary Medal was instituted by Royal Warrant for appreciation for war time services, six members of the Wallasey Force received this award.

During the First World War they were issued with a walking stick so that they could turn off the gas street lamps when an hostile aircraft approached. Some enemy planes managed to drop bombs on 25 and 26 September 1916 but they did not explode.

The force played its part during the Sinn Fein trouble in 1920/21 and their work during the 1926 General Strike was also appreciated.

Sir Thomas David Owen

Sir Thomas David Owen was the Commandant of the Special Constabulary in Wallasey. He lived with his sisters in Fowell House, Fowell Road, New Brighton and was a very popular citizen and noted sportsman. As a batchelor, he was able to devote much time to local sport. He played cricket with New Brighton at Rake Lane, later becoming President of New Brighton Cricket and Bowling Club from 1913 to 1921. Mr Owen was well-known locally as a keen crown bowler and was an active member of the local Association, becoming their President. He donated a silver trophy for the Wallasey Open Festival and other fine prizes. He was also a good golfer.

In addition to being a sportsman, he was interested in politics and stood as an Independent for Wallasey after the First World War polling 3,407 votes. He stood against JM Hoy (Liberal), Dr Bouverie McDonald (Conservative) and Walter Citrine (Socialist). The doctor was returned with a majority of 10,249 votes, becoming the town's first Member of Parliament.

Mr Owen worshipped at St James' Church where he was a sidesman. He was Head of David Owen and Sons, the metallurgical chemists. He was a very generous gentleman, helping local charities and in 1920, he gave the handsome sum of £10,000 to Banger University, to found a chair for developing electricity from rainfall.

Mr Owen was knighted in the New Year's Honour List in 1921 for services to chemistry. Sadly, Sir Thomas died on 22 September of the same year.

******

Reorganised

In the following years, there was little for the Specials to do, so the numbers were reduced and it was not until the fear of war that the Special Constabulary was reorganised in Wallasey in 1938 as it was in the rest of the country. The first Police Reserve in the country was set up just before the outbreak of the Second World War, which was made up of ex-Policemen who had volunteered. They were full-time and by the end of 1938 there was as many as 10,000, compared with 4,000 in the First World War but as time went on, numbers began to fall. (Nationwide there were some

FVW Crook BEM, Commandant, Wallasey Special Constabulary

130,000 Officers.) In Wallasey they were under the command of Commandant CH Newport and Captain G Nickson as his Deputy. Head Quarters were established in a room in the Grosvenor Assembly Rooms. The Specials received a thorough training in Police and defence (ARP) duties. Guide duties were performed and they assisted the regular force in many ways during the war. From 1938 until the end of the war, almost a thousand men had joined the Wallasey Special Constabulary. A good number of these Constables had to resign when they were called up to serve in the armed forces with the figure staying at about 400.

A new Police Reserve was set up nationally which was for wartime duty only and a Women's Auxiliary Police Corps came into being in August 1939, being made up of women between the ages of 18 and 55.

Mr Luke Pope was one of the first men to join at the outbreak of war.

Special Constable William Wallace, aged 63, was killed when an enemy bomb fell on his home at 23 Elgin Drive on 20 December 1940 and 34 year old Special Constable William Athol Snelson lost his life when a bomb fell on his home at 19 Asbury Road on 12 March 1941.

It was not uncommon for Special Constables to find a man who, having lost his whole family in a bombing raid, had hung himself over the crater where the house had stood. As they usually worked in pairs, one Special would have to hold the legs while the other cut the rope.

An Inspector received the King's Commendation for gallantry. Commandant CH Newport had served the Specials with enthusiasm and faithfulness and this was recognised when, in 1943, he was awarded the MBE. Mr. Newport died in 1952 and Mr FL Wilson became the new Commandant.

Ernest Kendal, a Special Constable, was blown down the cellar steps in the Concert Hall when the Land Mine dropped on Lancaster Avenue during an air-raid.

Mr Kendal, a well-known Liverpool Solicitor, had an unusual badge which was not the bright metal type, but had the words 'Wallasey Special Constabulary' on a navy blue, enamelled background and in the centre was the shield from the town's Coat of Arms in pale blue and yellow. At the foot of the badge was a fold with a English rose embossed. It carried no Crown and may have been issued to Specials that had not then been issued with a uniform.

After the war the Specials were under Commandant FVW Crook.

His Deputy was Mr H Beggs and there was also Inspector Tyrer. In 1958 there were 126 members in all ranks who were well-trained and well-equipped and could be called upon when the occasion arose. Their work was varied and they were always on call for duty at various functions in the town. They helped to control traffic and carry out patrols where necessary.

The Warden Section continued under the care of the Chief Warden, Mr WC Gillmore, JP. Of the 124 members, 50% held a fully-trained members Certificate.

Moreton had its own Civil Defence Headquarters which was opened on 9 October 1958 when Mr F Mathieson was the District Warden.

Since the reforming of Specials in 1938, there have been hundreds of Long Service Medals and Bars awarded to its members. In 1960 they were presented to: Commandant FVW Crook, Deputy Commandant H Beggs, Inspectors S Hughes and WE Littler. Sergeants Jones, Kehoe, McHarrie and Woosman.

Constables Blair, Colebourne, Ferguson, Higgins, Jefferies, Lever, Peers, Robinson, Scorell, Tetlow, Thackray and Wain. Also to Constables Banks, Bidston, Micheals, Penny and Watt.

In 1960, the number of Specials had fallen to 115 and more men were needed.

1962 promotions saw Mr JM Kehoe (his son, Jeff, was a Wallasey Constable) and Mr SJ Stead made Inspectors and Norman Ferguson, D Jones, H Langland, D Renton and FL Wilson made Sergeants.

The numbers rose steadily and it stood at 292 at the time of the Wallasey Police Golden Jubilee in 1963.

The Special Constabulary Long Service Medal is presented after nine years' service and at that time there were 121 members who qualified for a bar to this medal, which represented 19 years' service and 40 qualified for a second bar, presenting 29 years' service, out of 66 members.

Special Constable H Laugham may have joined the regular Police at a later date.

Frank Woosman, who joined the Special Constabulary at the outbreak of war, performing night duty for them and was later promoted to Sergeant. He worked in the Cashier's department for Bibbys in Liverpool and helped with the Home Guard there. Vera, his wife, would knit him white gloves. He was on duty when the Queen came to Wallasey and would be on weekend patrol at Harrison Drive during the summer months. Frank was a member of the Special Constabulary until his death in 1968.

During the war, Moreton had seven Specials, two Sergeants and an Inspector. John Lee was one of the Specials. One evening he was driving along Wallasey Road in his Ford Eight saloon when an air-raid started and a bomb, which fell lower down the road, blew his car through a shop window and ended up at the back of the shop. He had a lucky escape when shrapnel shot through the spare wheel at the back, through the back seat and lodged in the dashboard.

Commandant FVW Crook was awarded the British Empire Medal in 1966 which was presented to him on behalf of the Queen by Lord Leverhulme, Lord Lieutenant of the County. In the same year there was a special parade when the Mayor of Wallasey, Alderman Tom Garnett, presented Long Service Bars to six Specials. Three Bars to Commandant Crook, BEM, Deputy Commandant H Beggs and Special Constable EN Lever and Second Bars to Special Constable AE Jeffries, FA Scovell and CJ Simkins. Mr. Crook had been a Special Constable since 1938. He was made a Sergeant in 1939 and was a leader during the air-raids. He was made an Inspector in 1952 and became Commandant in that July. He was interested in cricket and rugby football and became President of New Brighton Rugby Union Club.

Leslie Boumphrey, Cliff Goodwyn and Jack Tibbet were among the large number of Special Constables that served in Wallasey in the dark days of the War.

******

Post War

Mr JH Wensley, now an Alderman, was elected Chairman of the Watch Committee in 1946. This was his second period in that office and served until 1958. He actually resigned from the position in May 1959.

With the shortage of housing in the borough after the war, 79 Penkett Road was taken over after the Second World War and converted into four Police flats for Constables and their families. A new Police house was erected on the corner of Stoney Hey Road.

Moreton

Before Moreton became part of the County Borough of Wallasey in 1928, it was under Cheshire Constabulary.

When Wallasey took over five Constables were added and Sgt Bebbington took charge.

Some of the Constables then were: William Bassett, 'Dickie' Bird, 'Monty' Caugherty, George Chilton, Syd Lodge, Harold le Grice, Teddy Prescot and Cyril Rae.

PC Lodge used to be on patrol at New Brighton in 1928, before being transferred to Moreton; 'Monty' made sure that there was no trouble from youths making a noisy exit from the Moreton Picture House. A swipe over the head with the cape was enough to bring them to order. Troublesome youths hanging around Moreton Cross were easily dealt with. A clip around the ear soon sent them on their way.

Sergeant Bebbington retired in 1947 and his place was taken by Sergeant A Reece, who had come to Moreton in 1942.

The first WPC to take up duty in Moreton was Marie Cushing, who had previously been at Liverpool in 1955.

At one time, Moreton had a Cycle Patrol covering Leasowe with Sergeant Joseph Gibson and two Constables.

Change of Uniforms

In 1948, the Home Office announced that Police Constables would be getting a summer uniform of open-necked tunics in the place of the 'dog-collar'. They were to be issued with RAF blue collared shirts with black clip-on ties for safety reasons.

The new uniforms, which were seen for the first time on August Bank Holiday 1949, had one button less, two additional pockets and the Constable's number moved from the collar to the epaulette. When Officers were allowed to work in their short sleeved shirts detachable epaulettes were introduced. The bobbies did not like the narrower trousers that came into fashion as they were not able to get them over their boots. The advantage of the old tunic was when the weather was very hot, Constables were able to just wear a vest as it fastened right up to the neck.

The uniforms were later changed from navy blue to black with Inspectors wearing a white shirt and black tie, as they do today.

The two-way radios came in 1948 with the main transmitter in Birkenhead.

The Watch Committee paid for medical expenses, dental treatment and the Police Surgeon could be consulted if necessary.

When the National Health Service started in 1948, the Police had to contribute like everyone else but they preferred the old system. Four people were killed on the roads in 1948.

The Concert Hall in Manor Road housed the Road Safety Department and Training Rooms.

HM Inspector of Police forces, WC Johnson, inspects PC R Myles' cycle with PC Stocker on the right

Cycle Patrol

On each shift at Manor Road there was a Cycle Patrolman. Their beats covered a large area and in addition they could be used as messengers. In later years they were equipped with a mobile telephone with the frame acting as an aerial. A speaking horn was attached to the handlebars and the batteries were kept in a case that hung beneath the crossbar. In the 1950s Constables bought their own cycle and were allowed 3/9d a week.

The Borough was roughly divided into two sections by taking Manor Road and Wallasey Road as a centre line. The New Brighton side was the North Division and the Seacombe side was the South Division with a Sergeant covering each division. Each of the Sub-Stations were manned by two men from 8am to midnight. Sergeant Reece, who had been a local Bobby in Wallasey Village, was in charge at Moreton.

Donning the Cloth

All Constables had to be on duty a quarter of an hour before the shift time when the personnel gathered in the small Parade Room at the Police Headquarters in Manor Road where they would be inspected by the Inspector or Sergeant. 'Daily Orders' were then read to the men by the Shift Inspector. Local crimes and other information would be given. These were typewritten as they had purchased a typewriter, then known as a Remmington Brief Typing Machine. Originally slates and slate pencils were used.

They would line up in the Parade Room and the Sergeant would call out the Constables' numbers, the men would reply. The Sergeant then said: "Produce your Appointments".

The Constables assembled would hold their staffs (truncheons) in front of them in a horizontal position with their whistles and chains draped over them. They also produced their note books, warrant cards and handcuffs. One pattern of handcuffs were called 'Snaps' which hung on the lip of the left trouser pocket and were only used when there was fear of the prisoner escaping or when conveying a prisoner by rail.

The Warrant Card was given to each member of the force on joining. It is a signed statement by the Chief Constable. Warrant Cards had to be produced when requested. Statements had to be taken down in the witness' own language and signed.

The whistle was kept in the left-hand breast-pocket of the tunic. The chain being fastened on to the top buttonhole of tunic. The wooden truncheon measured fifteen and a half inches in length with a leather strap at the end to go over the wrist. It was carried in a special long pocket down the right side of his trouser leg.

They were supplied by George Dickson and Company at the cost of £4. 3/4d. The Mounted Police had a longer truncheon measuring twenty-four inches but some forces only had a twenty inch truncheon for the Mounted Branch.

A general inspection was carried out of their clothing and boots to see that they were in accordance with Regulations.

Constables on leaving the Police Station would take with them a Beat Book which outlined the boundary of that particular beat and laid out the order of the 'Conference Points'. These were every half hour in the day shifts and every three quarters of an hour at night time. The Constable had to arrive at these points two minutes before time and left two minutes after time. A Constable who failed to arrive at one of the points without a valid excuse resulted in action taken against him for failing to work the beat.

For example, a Constable would be at the Mariners' Home at 2.30pm and by 3pm at Magazine Lane/Promenade and at 3.30 at the Police Pillar-Phone at the bottom of Steel Avenue.

These 'visits' were recorded in the Constable's notebook and they were also entered into the Ledger by the supervising Officer back at Headquarters. The Beat Book also carried items of special note, ie, workmen on shop premises; a spate of stolen milk from doorsteps in a certain area. At the back of the book was a list of all the Temporary Unoccupied Houses (TUH).

Some beats started from a Sub-Station (Police Box). The Constable would take his lunch with him and have it there and parade off duty by telephoning HQ, otherwise the parade to go off duty was at Manor Road Police Station where one's pocket book was examined and initialled after reporting any incidents.

If there were steep hills on the beat, the Constable would find it rather strenuous to get to the Conference Point on time. The Conference Point was where the Constable met with his Sergeant. Sometimes both the Sergeant and the Inspector would be waiting. They would be always on foot. After a few minutes, the Inspector would be off as he had the whole Borough to cover. The Sergeant stayed on the beat for about a half an hour and then moved to the next beat and met up with another Constable. The Sergeant would be able to pass on useful tips or advice and sometimes he would check the Constable's knowledge of the beat by asking him to name all the different streets. If one of the Constables was going to sit for a promotion examination, the Sergeant would go over the questions that the Constable would be asked in the examination. The Sergeant was allowed to be on friendly terms with the men under him but he had to maintain discipline in such a way as to support his rank. He had to insure that he had the trust of his men. A Sergeant would take about eight Constables and march off in two lines on their allocations from Manor Road Police Station. The men would peel off two by two at certain points. One Sergeant would take men on the Liscard North District, the other on Liscard South District.

They would meet a Sergeant every half hour. Sergeants and Inspectors would tap their metal-ended sticks on the pavement and the noise could be heard a good distance away by the Constable whom they were looking for.

Signals with the stick or whistle were:-

1 short note or tap - Are you there?

2 short notes or taps - indicating an affirmative to number one.

3 short distinct notes or taps - I want you.

4 short distinctive notes or taps given in quick time - I want you at once.

Constables were told never to answer continuous blowing of a Police whistle as this could be a child or other playing with a whistle that had the same tone as a Police whistle.

Beats

Beats were, over the years, altered from time to time. They were also varied according to the shift. The following list refer to the period in the 1950s.

North Beats.

No.1.	Seabank Road. Point to meet Holland Road/Seabank Road Police Pillar-Phone at 2.30pm Magazine Lane/Cemetery Gates at 3.0.

This was later altered to Seabank Road to Molyneux Drive.

No.2.	North of Manor Road, from the Queen's Arms public-house, covering the Rake Lane Area to Magazine Lane/Field Road.

No.3.	Earlston Road Area (patrolled at certain times only).

No.4.	Rockland Road Police Box, Vyner Road to Albion Street. Parade on and off from Wallasey Village Police Box in Leasowe Road.

No.5/5a.	Warren Drive Area to top of Victoria Road.

No.6.	New Brighton. Hose Side Road to Victoria Road.

No.7.	New Brighton. Rowson Street, Albion Street. Usually 10pm to 6am

No.8/9.	Wallasey Village.

South Beats.

No.1.	Egremont Ferry Police Box to Liscard. Normally a Night Beat, 10pm to 6am Hourly point at the Police Pillar-Phone at Serpentine Road.

No.2.	Liscard Road (from Police Pillar-Phone by Martins Lane) to Rappart Road.

No.3/3a	Liscard, St Mary's Street, Burns Avenue, Westwood Grove.

No.4.	Seacombe Police Station, Poulton Road to Ashville Road Police Box and on to King's Arms. (Afternoons and Nights).

No.5.	Poulton Police Box from HQ (Gorsey Lane) to St Hilary's Brow.

No.6.	Seacombe. Seacombe Ferry, St Paul's Road, Borough Road, Ashville Police Box to Dock Road.

No.7.	South Liscard. Liscard Road (from Wallasey Road) to Central Park.

No.8.	Liscard Centre (Wallasey Road) to Bus Depot in Seaview Road.

(Beat No.8 may have once been called No.7a.)

There was also a Cycle Patrol in the South Division as well as one in the North Division.

Two beats covered Liscard being important as it was the centre of the town.

One of the two Seacombe beats also covered from the Ferry to the Guinea Gap. After the Seacombe Police Station was knocked down, the Constable paraded from the Police Box in Church Road.

In Leasowe, there was a Cycle Patrol and in Moreton there were two Foot Patrols and one Cycle Patrol. Men paraded from Chadwick Street Police Station. Police Boxes in Leasowe and Moreton were built in 1928 costing £240.

The Constables for New Brighton paraded from Hope Street Police Station and later from the Police Box in Victoria Gardens.

Wallasey Village had one beat that paraded on and off from the Wallasey Village Police Box in Leasowe Road.

The Constable walked a pace that would take him 30 minutes to reach the Conference Point from Tobin Street to Town Hall Police Pillar-Phone where he would meet the Sergeant on the even half hour and from the Town Hall to the Gaumont Palace cinema on the odd half hour.

There were two beats for New Brighton and part of Wallasey Village was covered by the North Beat. The Night Shifts usually covered North Beats 6 and 7.

In the South Division, the 10pm to 6am shift met hourly at the Police Pillar-Phone in Serpentine Road and half hourly at the Police

The former Police Box in Poulton Road

Pillar-Phone by the Town Hall. South Beats 7 and 8 were covered on the Night Shift.

The Constables were designated on a rota system. Half Beats operated on the Night Shifts.

There was one Sergeant in the North Division and one in the South. A Sergeant was in the General Office. One Inspector to each shift.

Four shifts were covered viz:

1- 10pm to 6am.

2- 2pm to 10pm.

3- 6am to 2pm.

4- 2pm to 10pm and 6pm to 2am.

Monday/Tuesday - Rest Day. Wednesday to Sunday - 2pm to 10pm. Monday/Tuesday - 6am to 2pm. Wednesday/Thursday - Rest Days. Friday/Saturday/Sunday - 6am to 2pm. Monday/Tuesday - 6am to 2pm. Friday/Saturday/Sunday - Rest Days.

The men worked a seven-week cycle with one day off. 48 hours a week.

The patrol staff worked three main eight hour shifts viz:-

6am to 2pm, 2pm to 10pm and 10pm to 6am. These times were supplemented by a day shift of 10am to 6pm and an evening patrol of 6pm to 2am. Eight hour day in shifts from 6pm to 2am, 2am to 10am and 10am to 6pm.

Another shift was 3pm to 11pm, 11pm to 7am and 7am to 3pm.

The pattern of shifts was Nights/ Evenings/ Afternoons/ Earlies / Days.

The Senior Shift Officer was the Inspector.

Other Police Forces worked a twelve-hour day with a four-hour break or eight hours in two spells of four.

There was no overtime; instead a Constable got time off.

Rota

	Mon.	Tues.	Wed.	Thurs.	Fri.	Sat.	Sun.
1-	N	N	N	N	N	N	N
2-	R D	R D	A	A	A	A	A
3-	E	E	R D	R D	E	E	E
4-	A	A	E	E	R D	R D	R D

Key N - Night, R D - Rest Day, A - Afternoon, E - Evenings.

The Constables had a long weekends from time to time. The shift that finished at 10 O'clock in the evening meant the bobby had to get home, have a meal and relax and had to get up early to be on at six in the morning. Cycle Patrol had similar shifts. 11pm to 7am, 3pm. to 11pm. and 7am to 3pm. The men often would walk with their cycles as the area which they patrolled was too quickly covered if cycled.

Police Cars were on call. The men had an evening shift of 7pm to 3am and 11pm to 7am. These covered the Beat Patrols who finish and start shifts.

The night shift was easier in those days as there were no late night clubs or other establishments as there are today and there were far less people about. However, there was one person who was always to be seen, 'Willie the Waterman' who came out of Mill Lane Water Tower carrying a hurricane lamp and a long hollow metal rod with a funnel at one end. His job was to go around after all the traffic had dispersed and all was quiet, then he could listen for underground water leaks. He did this by placing his rod to the ground and putting his ear to the funnel. Following many years of working for the Water Department one ear was quite misshapen. Many a bobby had a shock when they saw Willie appearing out of the fog! Another of his duties was to check and report burst or overflowing pipes.

The Constable on duty was responsible for switching the traffic lights off at midnight that were not automatic, as they did not operate through the night. Many streets were lit by gas and when the foreman at Mill Lane depot opened the gates, lamplighters on either foot or cycle, armed with a long bamboo pole and metal hook on the end, set about their business. The bobbies called it 'The Charge of the Light Brigade'!

Those on cycles could knock the lever that switched out the light without stopping and by 12.30am most of the borough was in complete darkness, except for lamps on dangerous corners.

There used to be a big troublesome man, often drunk, that frequented *Pool Inn*, Poulton. Once he approached a bobby who was about to enter the pub following a disturbance and offered to assist the Policeman, as the man inside would cause trouble.

Another time a Police Officer was called to New Brighton to deal with a call from the Tower Grounds where an animal had escaped from the zoo. The animal was eventually recaptured in Victoria Road.

After the Second War World MANWEB took over the electricity from the Wallasey Corporation. There were three voltages in use in the borough at that time, 112 volts DC, 200 AC and the modern 240 AC voltage. This meant that new cables had to be laid which caused extensive road works. 'Cockey Watchmen' were employed to keep their eye on the sites at night. Their brazier would be lit all year round and there would be an iron kettle on top for making tea. Many Watchman suffered with chest complaints due to the coke fumes and hence one got the nickname of 'Whispering Jack'. The bobby on night duty would often check on the watchmen; a cup of tea and a chat would be very welcome before continuing on his way. The local bobby with a railway station on his beat could get a pot of tea and have his supper in the Waiting Room.

The Criminal Investigation Department had an Inspector, two Sergeants and ten Constables. They had a 'Rogues' Gallery' of all known criminals in Wallasey and surrounding areas and had its own fingerprint expert and a photographer. All the CID department received special forensic training and were also able to make plaster casts of foot prints.

The Wallasey Coroner was Mr. Stuart Cook.

The Traffic Department had one Sergeant and ten Constables. One of the force's Patrol Cars was a black Triumph Dolomite which was fitted with a loud speaker attached to the front bumper.

The Administrative Branch dealt with all the correspondence, the personnel files of the force, criminal records, pay, pensions, charging and maintenance of prisoners, lost and found property as well as many other jobs.

In 1947, the strength of the Wallasey Force in all ranks was 142. John Ormerod was Chief Constable; Deputy Chief Constable, Superintendent M McDonough; Chief Inspector C Sandland, the administration Officer and Ernest Reynolds, Detective Inspector. There were three Patrol Inspectors (one for each shift) – Messrs Edwards, McCormack and Woolley. Walter Marshall, who became Chief Constable on the retirement of Mr Ormerod, was training Inspector.

When a prisoner was brought in he would be kept in a cell at a

Sub-Station. A van would go down from Head Quarters and take him up to Manor Road for questioning. Drunks could be taken to St Catherine's in Birkenhead.

A new Austin 'Black Maria' was purchased in 1947/48 which was used for several years. They later used a utility van for the conveyance of prisoners.

The Mobile Section had two radio Patrol Cars to cope with the increase in motor vehicles with Policemen finding it an advantage to be able to drive. Ernie Longden from Seymour Place East in New Brighton would take them on a drive before taking their test using Portland Street for hill-starts.

The first Police Ball was held c.1926 at the Tower Ballroom. This was a special annual event in the calendar and was always attended by the Mayor of Wallasey and other dignitaries of the Borough. The attraction at the 1947 Ball was the famous American film actress Mae West. She posed for a photograph with the Chief Constable Mr Ormerod; Alderman JH Wensley, the Chairman of the Watch Committee and others.

Mr Ormerod was appointed Secretary of No.1 District of Chief Constables (Lancashire, Cheshire, Cumberland and Westmoreland) in 1947, when he was also Secretary of No.1 District Home Office Training School at Bruche and in June the same year, was appointed President of the Chief Constables' Association of England and Wales at the 51st Annual Conference that was held at New Brighton. This was the highest honour that the Police Service could bestow on a member.

From 1945 to 1948, Mr Ormerod was a member of the Police Council and in addition was a member of the Special Home Office Committees on: Police uniforms; Rent Allowances and the Special Committee that dealt with the pay of Chief Constables.

He was awarded the King's Police Medal for distinguished service in 1948. Lt Col G Egerton Warburton, the Vice Lieutenant of Cheshire, said, "An Award made for exceptional courage and skill and conspicuous devotion to duty."

By 1948 the force totalled 127 members but twelve years later it had grown to 183 which included six Policewomen.

Both John 'Rex' Norris and Len Stocker, who were on the Cycle Patrol, later joined the CID. Rex was once investigating the theft of some rolls of material in Egremont. In a cellar he discovered a jam jar from which some of the contents had been spread on a window pane to avoid any noise when breaking the glass to gain access to the property. He found a finger print on the jar which led to the conviction of the thief who had used a handcart to transport the cloth along the promenade! Rex lived in Seabank Avenue (as did Len Stocker and Sergeant Waft) and later moved to Cambridge Road. His son became a printer, working at sea aboard the big liners.

In the same road was a Liverpool Police Sergeant, Fredrick Davies who died in 1949 and the Assistant Chief Constable of Liverpool, Mr. E Nicholls, OBE, attended his funeral at Rake Lane Cemetery. Constable David Norman Starkey, GM, served in the Cycle Patrol for a time. He had been commended by the Magistrates and also by the Salford Watch Committee for rescuing five Salford children trapped on a sandbank while on a day trip to New Brighton. He was a member of the Wallasey Swimming Club for over 25 years and was Chairman in 1945 and also a member of the Wallasey Police Swimming Club. He served as Hon Secretary of the Liverpool and District Swimming Association and officiated at many Swimming Galas, including the ASA Northern Counties and Cheshire Championships. He lived in Mosslands Drive and retired from the Wallasey Force in 1949 after 25 years' service, becoming manager of the Riverside Restaurant in New Brighton Bathing Pool.

Inspector Alf Williams also retired in 1949. He had joined the Wallasey Borough Police in 1919 and served with the 4th Cheshire Regiment in the First World War, taking him to Gallipoli, Egypt, Palestine and France. During the Second World he was responsible for recruiting and training and also helped to organise the air-raid precautions for the town, being awarded the MBE for his services. On leaving the force he found employment as Assistant Civil Defence Officer for Wallasey, retiring from the position in 1963. He and his wife, Nora, celebrated their Golden Wedding in 1973. They had three daughters and six grandchildren, one becoming a Flight Lieutenant in the RAF.

Eight people were killed on the roads in Wallasey in 1949, a 100% increase on the previous year.

Inspector WH Woolley

Constable William Henry Woolley received the Liverpool Shipwreck and Humane Society's Silver Medal and Certificate for saving a 13 year-old Wallasey boy from drowning in the River Mersey.

About 3.30pm on 8 August 1933 during a strong ebb tide, Joseph Gregory of 176 Withens Lane was bathing between the Perch Rock Battery and the New Brighton Pier and got into difficulty at a point where a man had been drowned three weeks previously attempting to save his nephew. PC Woolley, who was on shore duty, heard the boy's cry and seeing him disappear went into action. He threw off his tunic and helmet and swam out 30 yards to the unconscious boy. Finding it impossible to swim against the strong current, he supported the boy until they were rescued by George Stonall in the motor launch *Silver Foam*. They were taken to Victoria Central Hospital by ambulance where the boy was retained until he recovered. However, Constable Woolley, with fresh clothes, was back on duty in about a hour.

Mr Woolley, a popular member of the Wallasey Force, was a native of Liverpool and having joined in June 1930 came to live in Walmsley Street, Egremont. He was very keen swimmer and while he was in the Army in India he did voluntary beach patrol work near Karachi. In 1917 he gained the parchment from the Liverpool Shipwreck and Humane Society and it was the following year that he won the Silver Medal. He went on to hold every honour of the Society. For many years, he was an Instructor and Examiner for them as well as secretary and treasurer. He trained the Wallasey Police Life-Saving Team which won the Hall-Walker Shield several times in competition with other Merseyside Forces and on one occasion they reached the National Finals. The RLSS awarded him the Silver Recognition Badge in 1952 and in 1959 was presented with the Service Cross. He also held the prestigious honour of the Society's Diploma.

He was well-known and very popular in the town, becoming a

Inspector Woolley

Sergeant in 1939 and Inspector in 1943.

Inspector Woolley was invited by the Queen to a Sherry Party at Buckingham Palace. As Chairman of the Liverpool and District Branch of the RLSS he attended the first Commonwealth Conference which was opened by the Queen Mother at St James' Palace.

******

Point Duty

The centre of Liscard Village had little traffic in the early days and it was not until the turn of the century that it became a shopping centre when a pagoda-like shelter, with hard wooden seats, was erected on a small island in the centre of the road for people awaiting tramcars. It was also used as a meeting place.

It was Alderman Eastwood who first called it 'The Monkey House' as he thought the people looked like monkeys in a zoo. It was removed in 1926 but the gentlemen's toilets under the shelter remained until the 1930s.

One of the first citizens in Wallasey to own a motorcar was Dr Bouverie Francis Primose McDonald, JP, who lived in *Ivor Lodge* 172 Seabank Road. He was the town's first Member of Parliament, being elected after the First World War.

Liscard became more active when Woolworth's and other shops opened then more shoppers were attracted to the centre of the town.

In the 1930s when the Constable was on point duty in Liscard Village, he would place his cape on the high window sill of Martin's Bank (opened as the Bank of Liverpool in 1908 and much later to become Barclays). In those days the pigeons did not perch above! Liscard was much quieter then with fewer motor vehicles around. Constables on point duty would use Gauntlets (slip-on white cuffs) so their traffic signals would be seen easier. Later, point duty Constables wore a white raincoat during wet weather.

A Constable was on point duty in Liscard Village one day and along Liscard Road came Ernie Longden, a young Co-op Milkman on an errand-boy's bicycle which was loaded with 96 bottles of milk on the front and sixteen at the rear. The cobblestones caused one of the flat-lying bottles to jump up and Ernie, injured his hand on the side of the crate when grabbing at it. The bobby came to his aid and held the cycle as the boy wrapped his cap around his cut fingers. All that concerned Ernie was that the hole in the centre of the cardboard milk top was intact so he could prove that the bottle had not been opened and would be able to claim a 'broken bottle', thus saving two and a half pence. He later had his fingers dressed.

Traffic was quieter in those days and errand boys would carry groceries in the large baskets in front of their cycles.

Constables would also be on point duty at the top of Leasowe Road, Wallasey Village; the bottom of Victoria Road (now Borough Road) Seacombe; Duke Street Bridge and the bottom of Victoria Road, New Brighton, which was one of the hardest to control especially on a hot sunny August Bank Holiday with thousands of visitors coming off the ferry and thronging the promenade, congested traffic trying to get through and a single-decker bus making a turnaround. All this happening while the Chief Constable and Chief Inspector stood watching!

At a later date, on the site of the 'pagoda' shelter in Liscard Village, a new large traffic island was created which did away with the Constable on point duty. This island remained until the new road layout in 1979. [The present system, to my mind, it not wholly satisfactory and I can foresee alterations taking place in the future with, perhaps the return of two-way traffic in Wallasey Road.]

Point duty was fairly easy in Wallasey compared with Liverpool where there were four or five crowded lanes of traffic converging on some crossroads – all at the same time.

When the traffic lights were turned off at the Wallasey Road and Belvidere/Torrington Roads junction, the Constable on point duty had to do a sort of dance as he directed the traffic to make sure vehicles' tyres did not go over his feet, as the Torrington and Belvidere Roads were not in true alignment.

Readers who have spent a holiday in the Isle of Man in the past may have seen the poor bobby on point duty in Douglas at the cross roads at the foot of Prospect Hill who would often get pushed forward by the side of a double-decker bus cutting the corner as it went up the hill. He had to watch out that there was not one coming down in the opposite direction!

The By-Law which forbids bicycles and other vehicles on the promenade between Seacombe Ferry and the bottom of Egerton Street was often taken literally by the Police. A young lad was told to remove his cycle from the promenade when he was neither riding nor wheeling it, but had leant it against the low wall of the Tower Grounds.

A lady was once warned for reversing onto the promenade from one of the roads that led down to the front in order to go up the road again. Since then special reversing bays have been added at the bottom of the roads. This By-Law has not been altered.

******

Two Fine Bobbies

PC. Arthur ('Joney') Davies Jones, of Dinmore Road, also retired in 1951, after 30 years' service with the Police. For the last 30 years he had been chief mechanic and was chauffeur to the Chief Constable.

Mr Ormerod must have been impressed with him as I have been told that he had a photograph of him on his desk.

Arthur joined the Wallasey Borough Police in 1921, having served with the Royal Flying Corps in Egypt as a driver and maintenance mechanic in the First World War. When the Police became mechanised he was switched from foot patrol to Police vehicles. The Chief Constable, Mr. John Ormerod, said of him, "He could maintain a car better than any other man in the country and his retirement is a great loss to us. He is one of the finest drivers on the road."

Another well-known bobby to retire was Alex 'Jock' Ingham of Brisbane Avenue, who after 30 years' service with the Force, left to take up a position as farm manager in Cullen, Banffshire in Scotland. This popular bobby was more than a Policeman as the New Brighton residents looked upon him as a guide, philosopher and friend.

Inspector McDonough said of him " 'Jock' Ingham was a fine Policeman. He had a genial and friendly personality and endeared himself to the people of New Brighton. I have never known a Constable who was so popular with the public."

To the left of the Policeman on duty in Liscard is the 'Monkey House' pagoda-like shelter

The crime figures in 1951 totalled 1,185 of which 1,041 were detected which showed an increase in crime.

Constables were allowed three quarters of an hour for refreshments which had to be taken at set times either at Manor Road Headquarters or in a Police Box that was on or near the beat.

After refreshments the Constable on the night shift would go back on beat. The Sergeant would hand out a list of those Policemen who wanted to be 'Knocked-Up' on the beat. These men would be going on 'earlies'. He was to call around and see if they were up by about 5am and if he saw no lights on, he gave a tap on the front door but if the houses he had to call on were well apart, it was often 4am and many men woken up were far from happy. This practice went on for several years although it was disliked by the men. If one of the Constables that was on the early shift did not report until late he would say that he wasn't called and the Constable responsible would get into trouble.

At 5am one of the first vehicles on the road was the bus from the depot that went around picking up the crew for the early buses and then came the fresh bread deliveries from the bakeries. The newspaper vans brought papers to the newsagents and the milkman headed for the diary to start his round. Postmen were hurrying to the General Post Office and the greengrocers were off to market. When the bobby saw this happening, he knew his shift would be soon over and he could get back home.

The Policemen were paid out at Headquarters on Thursday afternoons with a parade. Sergeant Chaddock had the job of handing out the packets. Those men who were on duty (or at home) could fill in a chitty and get another bobby to draw his pay. After the Sergeant had completed his task, he would go in a Police car to the other Sub-Stations at New Brighton, Seacombe, Wallasey Village and Moreton.

There was always the Constable who forgot to fill in his chitty and he would have to go down to the Town Hall to collect his pay. The Constables were paid £6 a week and if he failed to collect, his wife would have something to say about it!

Sergeant Chaddock ran the office at the Queens Street part of Police Headquarters.

Actor Anthony Oliver who played the part of a policeman in the 1950 film The Magnet *(see above)*

When someone was rescued from the river they were taken to the Victoria Central Hospital in Liscard Road and anyone else who had assisted and was wet through was allowed to dry off in the hospital boiler room.

"The Magnet"

I was told the following story: When Ealing Studio were making the film "The Magnet" in Wallasey in 1950, actor Anthony Oliver played the part of a Policeman (*see picture below*). He was dressed in the proper Wallasey Police uniform and whilst waiting in New Brighton for his part, took off his helmet and lit a cigarette.

Along came an Inspector in the real force who was not aware of an actor playing the part of a Police Constable in the film and although not recognising him as one of the his men, ordered the Policeman to extinguish the cigarette immediately and put on his helmet. It a was a few minutes before he realised his mistake but they had a good laugh.

******

On the Beat

Originally the CID had only one motorcar so all the staff were issued with an annual bus pass. Det Constable Jack Bowden would often arrest a person, bring them back to Headquarters on the bus. He would have to pay for the prisoner and keep the ticket to claim a refund!

A Det. Constable was in charge of issuing the summonses for all offences and executed all warrants. He also apprehended all the absentees and deserters from the forces. Those who dealt with him, held him in high regard as being a very fair and considerate man.

Sunny Bank Holidays often brought thousands of people to New Brighton on the ferry and large crowds would queue from as far back as Dalmorton Road, along the promenade, past the Tivoli Theatre and down the pier to the floating stage, for the return to Liverpool. Police would use temporary metal posts and chains to separate the ferry queues from others on the promenade. These posts and chains were rather rusty and the Constables' uniforms often got soiled.

Crowd control was always very important as there were thousands of day trippers who came by ferry, motor-coaches, private cars and rail. Evening attractions at the Tower and other places of entertainment were very popular especially on a Saturday or Bank Holiday, including the many public houses. In order to keep control, Constables walked in pairs and were in sight of the next pair so if there was any trouble, it could be dealt with very quickly by a number of Officers.

Lost Children was often a problem at New Brighton but there were special arrangements to deal with the many children who were separated from their parents.

Women Police Constables

Women Police Constables looked smart in their uniforms of black skirt, opened-necked tunic with belt, white shirt and black tie. The all-black cap carried the shield of the town's Coat of Arms in a circle with crown at the top.

The first Policewoman was WPC Joyce Carlett who joined the force in 1949. Next came Molly Bellman, who lived in Brompton Avenue and Joyce Esseen from Bromley Road, Joyce Garnet Evans, with two others by the name of Daulman and Jones, making six in number.

Three ladies were equipped with WPC uniforms but were not really members of the force. They were Noella Worrall, Gertie Herron and Gertie McKay. These had the job of going around the different schools in the Borough giving talks on Road Safety. They were later employed as telephonists at Manor Road Headquarters. Gertie

First Policewoman in theWallasey Force was Joyce Carlett who is seen here being welcomed by Ald. JH Wensley in 1949. John Ormerod is on the left and Mr C Sandland on the right

Herron married a Policeman.

WPC Betty Daulman lived in Magazine Brow and was in the Wallasey Police Force for five years. She was a member of the Police Life Saving Team and helped them to win a number of awards. She won the 100 Yards Free-Style Championship in 1952. The 26 year-old left the force in 1955 she emigrated to Africa to marry her fiance, James Crabtree.

WPC No.1 Barbara Jones (now Mrs Pilkington, living in Leonia, New Jersey, USA) had the honour of being chosen to serve at the Coronation of Her Majesty in 1953. She was a member of the Wallasey Force for three years. In 1955 Marie Cushing was the first Policewoman to be on the beat at Moreton, she had previously been with the Liverpool City Police.

The WPCs were issued with a shorter baton measuring some ten and a half inches in length which was carried in a special pocket inside the skirt.

WPC Norah Walbel also gave talks on Road Safety.

WCP Brenda Parkes, who had been with the Liverpool City Police for two years before joining the Wallasey Borough Police, married PC Maurice Toyn who became a Sergeant and was later promoted to Inspector. Mr and Mrs Toyn attend Manor Church Centre where they are Elders.

One of the first 20 women to join the Liverpool Police Force after the Second World War was 29 year-old Doreen Ann Prissick of Seabank Road, Wallasey. She joined in 1948 and was promoted to Sergeant in 1955, later entering the CID.

Two Policewomen, left Brenda Toyn (Nee Parkes) [in Liverpool City Police uniform] and right Betty Daulman, who were two of the first batch of six Policewomen to be recruited in Wallasey

The Paterson Twins

Two of the most popular members of the Wallasey Force were the Paterson twins, Alex who lived in Rake Lane and his brother Tom from Kenwyn Road. They were born 6 November 1922 to George and Grace Paterson of Hunts Cross in Liverpool. The Patersons had another son, George and two daughters, Mary and Brenda. The twins married two sisters, Tom married Joan Beckett and his brother Alex, Lucy. Tom had one daughter, Elaine, whilst Alex had two, Jean and Marjory. Tom joined the Wallasey Borough Police in 1950 and his brother soon after. Tom and Alex were so alike that they were often mistaken for each other. That was the case once with Alex's daughter, Marjory. Her mother would make a nice hot dinner for her husband and get Marjory to take it down to the Police Station. On one occasion, the young girl went in and seeing who she thought was her father said, "Here's your dinner." Grateful Tom took it and thanked her. Sat down and enjoyed it – poor Alex had to have sandwiches!

One of the twins was on duty at New Brighton having trouble interviewing a member of the public when the man spotted a No.1 bus going to Seacombe Ferry. He ran after it and jumped aboard, leaving the Constable standing. The Constable telephoned Seacombe Police Station and explained what had happened and his brother being on duty there apprehended the culprit as he alighted the bus. The man was amazed "My, that was quick. How did you get down here?" Not realising that he was confronting the other brother!

On another occasion, the mother of a child rescued from the sea by one of the twins, had seen whom she thought was the same Policeman minutes later smartly dressed on duty higher up Victoria Road!

They knew and were liked and respected by all the shopkeepers and local people. Tom, who was on the New Brighton beat retired from the force in 1975.

Alec's daughter, now Mrs. Coffee, is a WCP and is stationed at Manor Road Police Station, thus keeping up the family tradition. Even daughter Elaine Davies worked for a short time as a temporary in the office at the Station.

******

Tom (left) and Alex Paterson, the popular twins who were members of the Wallasey Force (see this page)

The Policeman's Gait

It has been often said that one could tell a Policeman by the manner in which he walked. There was a Constable in Wirral in the 1930s who took long strides. One day he was on his beat when he saw one of villagers trying to stake out a tennis court. He offered to pace it out for him as he claimed his strides were as accurate as a surveyor's tape. Indeed, a certain lady that lived in Durban

Road was convinced that Mr. Murray, who lived in Carrington Road, was a Police Officer by his gait! In actual fact, Mr. Murray held a clerical position with British Road Services in Liverpool. Never-the-less, he looked every inch an Inspector in the CID with the right appearance and height.

He once told me that a neighbour from the next road called at his house asking him to go round and settle a domestic dispute as her husband had thrown the radio out of the bedroom window. He was not able to convince her that he was not a member of the Force.

More of the 1950s

Mr Ormerod received the CBE in the Queen's First Birthday Honours in 1952.

In the same year a Wallasey young man was released from the RAF in order to become an Inspector of Police in Northern Rhodesia. He will be remembered by some readers as a soccer player with St Joseph's CYMS Football Club.

The police were puzzled when in November 1952, a labourer digging in Magazine Lane near Seabank Road, in order to lay cables, discovered human bones. They carried out research and consulted old maps but were unable to establish how or when they had been buried.

In the 1950s Police used Rovers for patrolling the town, later changing to Humber Hawks and Snipes. They were all black except the Chief Constable's Triumph which was blue.

Some of the Registration numbers of the Humbers and other Patrol Cars (eight in all) were, DHF 769, EHF 93, FHF 516 and FHF 517.

Phillip Edwards, the son of Inspector RJ Edwards was fatally knocked down on Friday, 6 January 1950 by an electric van near the junction of Foxhey Road and Mosslands Drive.

Emrys Edwards joined the Wallasey Borough Police in 1950. On the first day that he was to report for duty at Manor Road Police Station he took great care in his appearance. He brushed down his tunic and made sure that his trousers were pressed and had a fine crease. He adjusted the chin-strap of his helmet, checked everything was right in the mirror and set off to the Station on foot, not having a bicycle like a lot of the other men had, and was passing a house where there was a man working on the roof. "Excuse me Officer", cried the fellow as he raised his hand and started to descend the ladder.

Poor Emrys was worried. "My first day on. What on earth could have happened?" he questioned himself. All sorts of things flashed through his mind.

The roofer confronted the Constable.

"Could you please tell me the right time?"

A very thankful raw recruit obliged.

Government Inspection of a car boot, 1953

PC Raymond Lewis

Constable George Craft, who lived in Carrington Road, retired from the Wallasey Force in March 1951 aged 52. He had joined the Merchant Navy as a boy and went into the Royal Navy in the First World War and for a time served under Captain Evans of Broke. George joined the Wallasey Borough Police in 1920 and was recalled by the Navy at the outbreak of the Second World War. He rejoined the Wallasey Force in 1945. George had one son, Clifford, who was in the Air Cadets and later worked for Local Authority.

Dr EA Hoppins became Police Surgeon and was Surgeon for the Fire Brigade in 1951, taking over from Dr Tom Martlew.

Constable Rowland Fields

Wallasey had a likeable young Policeman in Rowland ('Rollo') Fields in the late 1950s. He was a tall stout fellow who weighed about 20 stone, thus his nickname of 'Tiny', and was scorer for the Police cricket team.

On one occasion, he was on duty in Liscard with Constable Ray Lewis on the two Liscard beats of 7A and 7B.

Up came Sergeant Waft.

"Where's PC Lewis?" he asked.

"Here, next to me", replied Tiny.

The Sergeant had not seen him as he was completely hidden by the frame of 'Tiny'. He found walking the beat taxing on his feet and emigrated to New Zealand where he joined the Prison Service as a warder.

Seacombe

The Seacombe Police Station in Church Road was demolished in the 1950s as it was no longer required. It was replaced with a Police Box opposite the office and works of Wallasey Printers in Church Road.

The old Mariners from the Mariners' Homes would place as little as three pence each-way on a horse at bookmaker's in Egremont. It was an interest for them rather than a gamble. I am sure the Police were not bothered in stopping them. In the afternoon, some of them would go to the Royal cinema, where, I think they would be admitted free. No doubt a few had a sleep!

War Damage Case
Clever Detection

Two brothers, one aged 38, the other aged 31, who were in partnership as estate agents in Wallasey, along with a 69 year-old building contractor faced a case involving 54 summonses arising out of claim for war damage repairs between August 1948 and August 1950.

The case began in August 1951 when the Chief Constable, Mr John Ormerod, received a communication from the Director of Public Prosecutions asking him to make preliminary inquiries into certain payments that had been made by the War Damage Commission which had aroused suspicion.

The Chief Constable appointed Detective Inspector Harry Lang and Detective Constable Len Harrison to look into the matter. They soon found that suspicions aroused in London were well founded. A network of frauds emerged. They decided to bring in Policewoman Molly Bellman, an expert typist and shorthand writer, to assist them. Their work involved taking them to Manchester and London where they studied thousands of documents. Weeks were spent at the War Damage Commission in London sifting through letters, building specifications and tenders.

Typewriters in those days did not have the figure '1' on the keys. One was taught to use the small letter 'l'.

It was discovered that the older brother always used a capital 'I' when typing out tenders and specifications. This idiosyncrasy was to prove that he was the chief culprit in the prosecution that he had typed out several important documents although they did not contain his own signature.

The team worked day and night conducting 500 interviews. Witnesses had to be traced and interrogated including: building contractors, workmen, lorry drivers and tenants of property where the work had been carried out. Statements had to be written down, collated and a complicated method of cross-references which involved linking up statements with documents.

The Police Photographer had the job to photograph the most important documents; the rest having been done by an outside firm.

The team had to work until 2 and 3am in order to get all the documents ready for the next day's hearing.

Over 400 statements on closely typed sheets of foolscap and 3,000 documents were presented in Court under the special care of Policewoman Bellman who had to quickly produce them when needed by the Counsel.

Finally, when the case was heard at Chester Assizes, the team had handled 64,000 documents, including photostats which had to be transported to Chester in a prison van as it was the only suitable vehicle to carry the load.

The case was first heard at the Wallasey Magistrates' Court before Mr GL Reakes and ended after 15 days with all three defendants being committed for trial at Chester Assizes.

The case ended on Tuesday 25 April 1952, 15 months after the first inquiry.

The older brother received three years imprisonment plus £2,000 of the prosecution put at £7,000. His brother was given one day's imprisonment, which meant immediate release. He had to pay £1,000 towards the cost of prosecution. The contractor was given six months imprisonment.

The jury found all three guilty of conspiracy after four hours retirement on the Monday night.

Committal proceeding took 29 days following a 14 day trial, the longest criminal trial in the history of Chester Assizes, and had engaged the minds of nine counsel. It was the longest and most expensive trial in the history of Wallasey.

The Judge, Mr Commissioner Ernest H Goodman Roberts, commended the conduct of Inspector HT Lang, Sergeant LF Harrison and WPC Molly Bellman.

******

A Fair Cop for the Captain!

I am the Captain of the Iris;
And a right good captain too!
You're very, very good,
And it must be understood,
I command a right good crew.

Adapt. WS Gilbert

The new Wallasey cruise boat, *Royal Iris*, featured in the National Press in 1951 over the problem of selling liquor outside the licensing laws that were permitted on land at the time.

The ferryboat was registered in Liverpool so the Liverpool Police decided to challenge the Wallasey Corporation over the matter. Chief Inspector Seymour Jones was given the task of collecting evidence. He took with him Sergeant Skelton, Constable Anderton and a WPC named Regan.

They boarded the vessel one pleasant May afternoon dressed in plain clothes and mixed among the people on the cruise.

Inspector Jones kept his eye on the time, for in accordance with the 1921 Act, no alcoholic drinks must be served after 3pm.

Behind the bar was Jim Innes, who was happily serving alcoholic beverages to those at the bar and the Chief Steward Percy Bell was also in attendance.

The *Royal Iris* sailed off on her cruise and by 4pm, the bar was still serving alcoholic drinks. Five minutes later, the Inspector decided to take action. He went up to the bridge with his Sergeant and gave a rap on the captain's door. He had not checked out his facts, as he thought that the captain automatically would be the licensee. The captain was annoyed with the situation and using his rights as a captain 'arrested' the Inspector and locked him in his cabin until the end of the cruise. In actual fact, the chief steward was the licensee.

The case was far from being simple for if drinking was stopped on the River Mersey, it would also have to apply to all the other ferries in our waters.

In was not until March 1952, that the case was heard. Mr Glyn Blackledge, QC represented the Wallasey Corporation. Mr. Arthur McFarland, the Liverpool Stipendiary Magistrate, said that the drinks aboard the *Royal Iris* had to be covered by the 1921 Licensing Act and the vessel ceased to serve alcoholic drinks after 3pm. Mr Blackledge objected at the summons alleged multiplicity of the offences without specifying the time and place of each sale.

The case was adjourned indefinitely.

Later in the year, Lord Goddard, the Lord Chief Justice stated in the Queen's Bench Division, that the sale of intoxicating liquors to the passengers on the pleasure boats on the River Thames outside the permitted hours was legal and in his opinion the 1921 Act did not apply "If it's all right for the Thames, it's all right for the Mersey", said the Officers of the Wallasey Corporation and told their ferryboat captains to serve intoxicating drinks to passengers while the vessels were afloat regardless of the licensing hours ashore. And so they did without further ado.

******

The Royal Iris, centre of a licensing dispute in 1951

New Declaration

When Her Majesty, Queen Elizabeth II succeeded to the throne in 1952, the larger Queen's Crown was used on the helmet plate, replacing the smaller King's crown. The Wallasey Police Declaration was also altered and the words that a new recruit had to say was as follows:-

I do solemnly and sincerely declare that I will and truly serve our Sovereign the Queen in the office of Constable for the County Borough of Wallasey during such time as I shall hold the said office of Constable, according to the best of my skill and knowledge.

A modern definition of a Police Constable is:-
'A citizen, locally appointed but having the authority under the Crown for the preservation of life, the protection of property, the maintenance of order, the prevention and detection of crime, and the prosecution of offenders against the Peace.'

******

Mr L Whitfield

Mr Leslie Whitfield was a flying instructor in the RAF serving for four years. On leaving the service he was five years in commerce and then joined the Wallasey Borough Police in 1952. He served in the Wallasey and District Centre at Bruche until 1967 reaching the rank of Inspector. With the amalgamation with Cheshire, Mr Whitfield saw service in the Chester Division and Hoylake to Chief Inspector. When the force became part of Merseyside Police he served in Bootle, Knowsley, Mather Avenue Training School, Liverpool City, St Helens to the rank of Chief Superintendent. He retired on completion of 30 years' service as Divisional Commander, St Helens.

Constable Dave Liston

Everybody knew 'Big Dave' Liston. He was six foot four and a half inches in height, a good bobby, was popular with the shopkeepers and the folk that lived on his beat in the south end of the town.

Before becoming a Policeman, he worked for a carpet company in Willamson Square in Liverpool. Dave was a talented a boxer and at the age of 16 he entered a tournament in Nottingham and won over six rounds. Unknown to him there was a Chief Constable watching the bout and afterwards asked him to join the Police, but he was too young. He wanted to become a professional boxer but when he went to fight at Blackpool the other boxer failed to turn up, so he gave up the idea. He later decided to join the Liverpool Police but discovered that the Liverpool City Police did not enlist

PC David Liston being presented with the BEM by the Lord Lieutenant of Cheshire, the Rt. Hon. Viscount Leverhulme

men from the city, so, not wanting to be far away, applied to the Wallasey Borough Police, was accepted and joined in September 1933.

An 18 year-old Birkenhead man was brought before the Court for being drunk and disorderly in Borough Road. He had been bumping into shop windows. Constable Liston went over to speak to him but he adopted an aggressive attitude.

"I've never lost a fight yet", boasted the drunk.

The Constable advised him to go home but the young man 'kneed' the Officer in the body.

Det Chief Inspector WE Reynolds said in Court, "If you had taken the fight a little further with Constable Liston, I am afraid it would have been one fight the defendant would have lost". The young man did not know that the Constable was once a well-known heavyweight boxer.

The 17 stone David John Liston was presented with the BEM by the Lord Lieutenant of Cheshire, the Rt. Hon. Viscount Leverhulme at the Town Hall on 27 April 1953 for his brave conduct in defending a fellow Officer, PC Marshall, from a razor attack while apprehending a prisoner.

PC David Liston's Medal

Citation Of Award
DAVID JOHN LISTON, Constable,
County Borough of Wallasey Police

While on night duty in the dock area of Wallasey, Constable Liston and another Constable, saw a man who was a deserter from the Army and who was suspected of housebreaking offences. They arrested him and took him towards the Sub-Station. When about 30 yards away from the office, Constable Liston, who was holding the prisoner, was dealt a severe blow on the side of his face from behind. He turned and saw his assailant was the brother of the prisoner. Liston, still retaining his grip of his captive, fought him off; but another man then attacked the other Constable with an open razor. He knocked him down and slashed his head and face, which were covered in blood. The prisoner's brother also ran at the prostrate Constable and commenced to kick him on the head, face and shoulders. Constable Liston, still gripping his prisoner, went to his colleague's assistance.

Resisting the attacks of the man with the open razor, he fought both men one-handed with such skill and courage that they broke off the encounter and ran away. Liston lifted up his severely injured comrade and continued on his way to the Sub-Station, the prisoner in one hand and holding the Constable with the other.

Arriving at the Sub-Station, he secured the prisoner and at once joined in the search for the two men who were later arrested.

By his determination, coolness and courage in tackling two desperate men, one armed with a razor, Constable Liston set an outstanding example of devotion to duty.

The two men who carried out the attack, aged 19 and 18, received four years and three years imprisonment at the Manchester Assizes. The injured Constable was Cecil Marshall who received several wounds. He was admitted for treatment at the Northern Police Convalescent Home in Harrogate.

39 year-old Constable Liston received £20 from the Watch Committee for his gallantry.

He said, "I only carried out my duty like any other Policeman." Dave married Miss Lilly Williams, sister of Jack (the Mounted Policeman) and lived in Daventree Road. He eventually went to live in Canada.

His son, also Dave, joined the Wallasey Fire Brigade.

'Big Dave' Liston died in White Rock Canada in August 1999 aged 86. He is remembered with affection.

*****

Police Dogs

Forces throughout the country began to have dogs and by 1954 28 of the 126 Police Forces were using 266 dogs. The majority of them were Alsatians but it was not uncommon to see Boxers, Dobermann Pinschers and Labradors out with a handler.

Mr Ormerod was chosen to command a detachment at the Queen's Police Review in Hyde Park in 1954. In the same year he was awarded the Royal Life Saving Society's Cross in recognition for his services to the Society and was Vice-Present of the Liverpool branch.

In the same year Inspector Alec Yule retired after 25 years service. He went into the Atomic Energy Department as an Investigating Officer. He was an active worker at St Chad's Church in Leasowe and became a Warden in 1961. He died in 1974 whilst visiting his daughter in Madrid.

Charles Sandland was recommended for Asst Administrator.

There were 66 people injured on the roads in the Borough in 1954. The population in 1955 stood at 102,400. All had a right for protection against crime and the Police saw that Law and Order was maintained throughout the Borough.

A larger Police Station had been needed at Moreton for some time so a modern Sub-Divisional Headquarters was built on the site of the old temporary Police Station in 1955 and in 1959 a new Police Sub-Station was completed in Twickenham Drive. Chadwick Street Station was built to replace the smaller building. It was designed and under the supervision of the Borough Architect, Mr WP Clayton. The district was policed by ten men with the two Sergeants living in Moreton.

The Sub-Station at Victoria Gardens, New Brighton was also enlarged. The Wallasey Force had as many as 225 members including Policewomen.

First Aid

The Police Ambulance Challenge Cup First Aid team was successful and went forward. The team was Sergeants Stan Rothwell and Joe Barke, Constables E Parker, B Faulkner, G Sharpe, J Nance

The Wallasey Police Team won The Molloy Cup in No.1 District Police First Aid Competition at Bruche where teams from Cumberland, Westmoreland, Lancashire and Cheshire competed in 1955. The competition started in 1932 and this was the first time that the Wallasey Police team had won. The team was :- Constable DJC Clarke, Team Captain; Constables T Williams, JE Nance, J Fearon, J W Barke and B Roberts. Chief Inspector Walter Marshall was their Instructor.

Six people were killed on the roads in Wallasey in 1955 compared with three the previous year and 91 were seriously injured in 1954; 91 in 1955. The figure of 250 for slightly injured was the same for both years.

When I, good friends, was called to the bar,
I'd an appetite fresh and hearty,
But I was, as many young barristers are,
An impecunious party.

WS Gilbert

PC Donald JC Clarke studied Law in his spare time and he passed his finals of Trinity Examinations in 1955. He had joined the Wallasey Police Force in 1947 and was attached to the Training Department and Six years later he was commended at Birkenhead for his part in the rescue of three men.

Mr Clarke was also a Civil Defence Examiner and held nine RLS awards was promoted to Inspector and became the Prosecuting Officer.

The 1956 Annual Inspection was carried out by Mr WC Johnson, HM Inspector of Constabulary. In that year, there were 1307 crimes committed in Wallasey.

The Annual Police Ball was held at The Tower Ballroom on Friday 23 November 1956 when Victor Sylvestor and his Ballroom Orchestra provided the music. The orchestra was the top ballroom dance orchestra in the country and made many broadcasts with the BBC. Tickets cost ten shillings and six pence.

Royal Visit

Her Majesty the Queen and the Duke of Edinburgh paid a visit to Wallasey on Thursday 11 July 1957. The train arrived at Grove Road Station at 2.27pm where they were greeted by Station Master, Mr E Martin, the Mayor and Mayoress of Wallasey, Alderman and Mrs. Harry Bedlington, Town Clerk, Mr. AG Harrison, and the Chief Constable, Mr. John Ormerod. They were presented to her Majesty by Lord Leverhulme, the Lord Lieutenant of Cheshire. In charge of the proceedings at the station was Inspector James Reddy of the British Transport Police.

Mr and Mrs Reddy lived at 30 Edinburgh Road in Liscard. This friendly man was a perfect gentleman and was loved by all who knew him. He was also a keen amateur photographer and was a member of the Wallasey Amateur Photographic Society. In 1955, he won the Intermediate Cup in the club's Annual Exhibition.

Standing at attention, he saluted Her Majesty as she left the station the Royal party was then driven to the Town Hall. The cavalcade

The Queen's car leaving Wallasey Village Station during a visit to the Borough 11 July 1957

The Queen being saluted at Grove Road Station by Inspector James Reddy of the British Transport Police on 11 July 1957

was led by the Humber Police car No. EHF 515.

Along the route 16,000 children waved to the couple as they drove by. Among the many people that were presented to Her Majesty, was the Chief Constable's wife, Mrs Ormerod, who wore a cornflower silk suit. Alderman JP Ashton was congratulated by Prince Phillip on his unusual distinction in being the holder of Military Cross and Bar. After waving to the waiting crowds from the balcony, the Royal Couple left.

The Chief Constable expressed his deep appreciation and thanks through the *Wallasey News* to all the members of the public who, during the Royal Visit, had co-operated wholeheartedly with the Police.

******

166 Men

In 1958 the Wallasey Borough Police consisted of the Chief Constable, two Superintendents, one Chief Inspector, six Inspectors, 21 Sergeants, 146 Constables and six Policewomen, making a total of 183.

At the end of the year, there were 166 men.

Three men retired on pension in 1958. Det Constable JA Bowden retired on completions of 29 and a half years' service, Constable N Newall with 30 and a half years and Sergeant H Wright with 26 years. The Sergeant had joined the Wallasey Borough Police as a Probationer on 8 October 1932.

Jack Bowden served as Warrant Officer.

In the same year three ex-Police Officers passed away, namely, J Hesketh, J Latham and EV Smith.

Alderman JH Wensley, OBE, JP, was Chairman of the Watch Committee. Det Chief Inspector Harry Lang, Det Constable David Evans and Det Constable William Russell were commended by the Watch Committee for the painstaking manner in which they had carried out their enquiries.

The Chief Constable also commended Constable Ray Molyneux for his efficient manner in dealing with a traffic accident on 26 February 1958. He was also commended for assisting in the detection of stolen motor cycles.

Others to be commended in 1958 were Sergeant Kennedy and Constables E Marshall, O'Dwyer, Goodhall, DA Wainwright, E Walker, Garvey, Martindale, and JL Owens.

There was one person killed on the roads in 1958, none the previous year but there was an increase in the seriously injured from six to 17 and the slightly injured increased to 32 compared with 14 in 1957.

A small Morris van, Registration No. BHF 323, was added to the fleet of vehicles and was used for many purposes.

The Annual Inspection was held on 7 August 1958 by Sir William Johnson, CMG, CBE, the HM Inspector of Constabulary.

Mr. CT Sandland

Mr Charles Thomas Sandland died on Monday 10 January 1959 aged 61. He was the former Deputy Chief Constable. He had served 38 years with the Wallasey Force, retiring on 31 July 1957. Charles Sandland was the son of Inspector Arthur Sandland and when married in 1920, had lived in the Police House in Queen's Street. They moved to the Hope Street Police house soon after and later lived in Farndon Avenue.

Mr Sandland had served in the First World War in the Royal Garrison Artillery and had been mentioned in despatches. He had joined the Wallasey Borough Police in 1919 as his father was against his first choice of the Liverpool Force. He became a Sergeant in 1929, Inspector on 1 December 1931, Chief Inspector in 1942 and Superintendent in 1949. In 1952 he became Deputy Chief Constable. He had also served in the CID as a Detective Constable.

He won the Police River Swim three times in succession and was Chairman of the Royal Life Saving Society.

One of his training swims was from Eastham to New Brighton.

He was the holder of the silver cup that had been presented by Councillor EH Backburn and won the event as a Constable in 1929, twice as Sergeant in 1930 and 1931 and as Inspector in 1932 when he won it outright. He knew the treacherous river like the back of his hand and was familiar with the paths of the currents. There was a particular point in the race where it was necessary to swim towards the shore to prevent both the swimmer and the accompanying boat being swept across the river to Crosby. During one of the River Swim Races, Dave Starkey was swimming too far

Deputy Chief Constable Charles Sandland

out and although being in the lead, he held back to allow Dave to get in which cost him the race.

At the dinner that followed, Chief Constable John Ormerod said "...his mother was on the Landing Stage calling `well done Charlie' and his wife was there looking as though she'd like to push him back in!"

He was involved with the Royal Life Saving Society and gave talks to local schools on life saving. He spent a lot of time in the Guinea Gap Baths in training and examining. He was awarded the Recognition Badge on 2 June 1951 and became Vice-President of the North West branch, received a certificate and went to London in 1952 to receive the Society's Badge from Princess Elizabeth.

Mr. Sandland was a very much respected and liked by everyone, particularly those who he worked with. He did, however, have a quick temper and was not really a 'morning person'. His office was off the General Office and there was one Constable who always slid from the door to Mr Sandland's desk on the highly-polished lino and had been doing this for a number of years. Everyone visiting him had to pass through the General Office and always asked "What mood is the Super in this morning?"

One morning Ernie Reynolds asked the usual question and was told "he's very bad, he's just told me off for sliding across his floor and told me not to do it again."

Some time later, Ernie repeated it to Mr Sandland who was highly amused and the Constable was allowed to continue sliding across the floor!

One story Mr. Sandland liked to relate was when he a Patrol Constable. A little girl came up to him with a piece of brick in one hand and a wheel from a doll's pram in the other.

She looked up at the tall Policeman and in a small voice asked, "Will you please mend my pram?" and offered him the half brick, which was to act as a hammer.

On his retirement he received a gardening book, which contained an illuminated front piece which was signed by the Mayor of Wallasey, the Chairman and Vice-Chairman of the Watch Committee, the Town Clerk and the Chief Constable.

Mr and Mrs Sandland had two daughters and one son. The latter, Mr. CB Sandland, was Chief Administrator of the Wallasey Ferries. Charles Sandland's grandson joined the Police Cadets in Liverpool but had to leave on medical grounds however, another member of the family, Barbara Sandland, was a WPC with the Liverpool Police. Truly a Police family!

There were 68 men present at his funeral who paraded through Wallasey Village to St Nicholas' Church.

He, as his father, had been a good, respected Inspector who had served the town over many years.

******

Road Accidents

A serious road accident happened at Lloyd's Corner [junction of Wheatland Lane and Poulton Road – at one time there were two shops by the name of Lloyd here, one a pawnbroker, the other a baker] involving two double decker buses. It happened at the teatime peak at 5.15pm on 23 March 1959 when two buses collided, whilst one was hurrying back to Seacombe Ferry it glanced the other, causing it to topple over on its side. A traffic sign and lamp standard helped to break the fall which prevented the windows being smashed. The No.3 bus toppled over on its side after a collision with a No.14 bus which had been coming along Wheatland Lane.

The Emergency Services were called and ambulances and Police raced to the scene. Mrs. May Elizabeth Jones of Tulip Grove was trapped under the bus and she and fourteen people were rushed to the Victoria Central Hospital. All but three went home after

Double-decker bus on its side at Lloyd's Corner following an accident on 23 March 1959

treatment. Mother of four, Mrs Jones, sadly died of her injuries a few days later.

A 90 year-old lady was killed in a road accident in Liscard Road in June 1959 and in October a 76 year-old widow was fatally injured by a bus at Seacombe Ferry. Another tragedy happened when a man and a woman were swept off Leasowe Embankment by a giant wave and were drowned on Sunday 12 July.

The Council decided that Sandon Road would partially be blocked off as two people had been drowned after their car plunged down the steep incline.

The people in Poulton were shocked to learn of the death of seven-year-old Helen Mary Doherty, of Canterbury Road, who was on her way to St Joseph's School in Seacombe with her brother, when a black Jaguar skidded in Poulton Road as the driver applied the brakes and he mounted the pavement opposite Somerville School, smashing a shop window. Mrs Elizabeth Briggs attempted to pull the child clear but was injured herself and taken to hospital.

There was also a tragic accident when my uncle, Mr Herbert Cody, was killed in Torrington Road near Marlowe Road Congregational Church whilst waiting for a bus. The driver of the motorcar took ill at the wheel, thus losing control of the vehicle.

The was also a traffic accident at the cross roads at Gorsey Lane and Poulton Road when a van collided with a Ford Popular but luckily the two girls dragged from the crash by the Ambulance men were not seriously injured.

[I would like to see all vehicles at crossroads traffic lights circle around a small island or raised centrepiece as this would make it much safer, especially when one motorist wants to turn right and the oncoming one wishes also to turn right. When I first learned to drive, I was taught to go BEHIND the other car when making this manoeuvre but, sad to say, this is no longer the case.]

******

Jaguar crash in Poulton road (see above)

New Head Quarters

It was becoming necessary to have new Police Headquarters and various sites were considered. The area bounded by Wallasey Village, Sandy Lane and Big Yard was recommended in January 1959 as a suitable site for the new Central Police Station and Magistrates' Court.

Mr. Ormerod, the Chief Constable, stated that there was a rise in crime, due to the slackening of discipline.

Superintendent WE Reynolds retired in December 1959 after being a member of the Wallasey Borough Police for 31 years.

Inspector Harry Sidney Brown was appointed Superintendent and Assistant Chief Constable. He had served as a major in the Army in the Second World War. Mr. Brown died in 1968.

In May 1959 the Watch Committee decided that Mr Walter Marshall, the Superintendent and Deputy Chief Constable, would succeed Mr John Ormerod as Chief Constable of the Wallasey Police Force. Alderman JH Wensley, JP, retired from being Chairman of the Watch Committee, a post he had held for 18 years. He was followed by Alderman JP Ashton, MC, TD who held the office until 1962. Mr. Ashton was a very popular figure in the Borough and had been a Major in the Army.

Mr. Ormerod, who made his last appearance in Court in September 1959 where he first prosecuted 33 years previously, retired from the Police Force. He was keen on sport and was Past Captain and Vice-Chairman of New Brighton Cricket and Bowling Club, also ex-President of the New Brighton Pier and Sea Angling Club and was a member of the Magazine Bowling Club (the oldest bowling club in Cheshire).

Mr Walter Marshall

Mr. Marshall was born in Samlebury near Blackburn. His father was a Police Constable in the Lancashire County Police becoming an Inspector. His younger brother also joined the Police and became Chief Detective Inspector at Seaforth. Walter Marshall became a Patrol Constable in the Wallasey Borough Police 1931, he then went into the administration department and in 1938 became a Sergeant being promoted to Inspector in 1947. He was appointed Chief Inspector in 1952 then in 1957 he became Superintendent and Deputy Chief Constable then Chief Constable in 1959 being chosen from 49 applicants. Mr Marshall served as

Chief Constable Walter Marshall

Corps President of Wallasey St John's Ambulance Brigade (1960) also Chairman of the Wallasey Centre of St John's Ambulance Association and President of the Wallasey Hospitals' League of Friends. During his service he represented the North West Region in bowls, golf, snooker and billiards. In his younger days he played cricket, football and table tennis. In 1966 he received the Queen's Police Medal for distinguished service and in the same year he was made a Brother of the Order of St John of Jerusalem for services to First Aid. He was holder of St John Ambulance Certificates and since 1961 was holder of Police Ambulance Brigade Certificate. He also had a great interest in the Sea Cadets and Cancer Research being a Founder Member of the Wallasey Boys' Club in Seacombe.

He joined the force 'because I wanted a job' said Mr Marshall. He went on to say, "Conditions were very different when I was a Constable. We only got one day off in seven. Now they get seven off every four weeks, with 50 per cent more leave. Now they have open-neck uniforms and lightweight wear for summer and radios to keep in touch with headquarters. There were no cars then, only four motor cycles. Now the force is equipped with 20 vehicles."

He also served as Assistant Chief Constable of Cheshire. He and his wife lived in Breckside Avenue and had two married children, Margaret and Ronald.

He retired from the Police Force in 1973, after 40 years' service, aged 62. He died in February, 1998 in Yorkshire.

******

Mr. John Bryan

Superintendent John Bryan was born in Stoke-on-Trent and joined the Wallasey Borough Police in November 1934. He became a Sergeant in 1948 and was promoted to Inspector in 1957. He retired from the force in 1967 when Wallasey was amalgamated with Cheshire. He was a keen bowler and lived in Glen Park Road and died in 1978, aged 64, survived by his wife, Dorothy.

Mr. Cyril Proctor was appointed Road Safety Officer for Wallasey. He did a splendid job in giving talks to schools and various clubs and to help get the message of Road Safety across to the younger children in the schools, he introduced the popular TV puppets, Sooty and Sweep. He was assisted by WPC June Evans.

WPC Violet Samson also did two tours of the schools with Mr Proctor. She would carry a suitcase full of toy rabbits, ducks and monkeys which she could use to hold the attention of the young children.

The Police took delivery of a new Humber saloon, Registration No.CHF 808.

In 1959, the Wallasey Council decided to make a film about Wallasey. Mr. Keith Medley, of Medley and Bird was the man behind the camera. It was produced and directed by Mr Cyril Proctor, the Road Safety Officer. The whole of the town is covered showing the Local Authority's many undertakings; from the Ferries to the Fire Service, dust binmen to Town Hall staff. No department seems to have been left out. The Police Force is shown covering all their aspects with several Policemen were involved.

One scene shows a man breaking into a house and a neighbour seeing him climbing over a fence and forcing an entry and she hurries to a Police Pillar Phone and calls the Police. A Ford Patrol Car (HHF 51) on patrol receives a message from HQ and speeds off to the scene where the Policeman apprehends the villain. My brother, Ron, who worked as a part-time press photographer with Medley and Bird, volunteered to act the part of the crook.

This 16 mm. film is still in existence and is shown to the public from time to time at various clubs etc. It shows how efficient and successful the town was run under the old Wallasey County Borough.

1960s

By 1960, the Wallasey Force consisted of 103 men, including six Policewomen with 22 more Officers recruited to increase numbers. Inspector Gibson was in charge of the Moreton Sub-Station with the help of four Sergeants, eight beat officers and four cyclists. Constable Douglas Knight was on patrol. The Inspector lived in the house at the side of the Station.

Sir William Johnson, HM Inspector of Police Forces, carried out the Annual Inspection at the Grosvenor Car Park.

43 year-old PC 53 Harold Kelly received a Medal for Long Service and Good Conduct. He had been a Constable for 23 years.

Mr H St CG Gasking was Magistrates' Clerk.

There were as many as 12 deaths on the roads of Wallasey in that year and 55 cases of drunkenness – 49 males and six females.

PC Dick Rhind was on duty in New Brighton when there was an incident in the river. A fishing boat had overturned and one of them who was a nonswimmer, was clinging to the craft. The Constable did not hesitate but removed his tunic etc, dived in and went to his assistance.

Constable Rhind was a good swimmer and had taken part in the four and a half mile River Swim from Woodside to New Brighton in August 1959. The event had been won by Beach Patrolman Billy Eastwood (for the second time), Constable Jeff Kehoe was second and Constable Rhind third.

Alderman E Glyn Roberts, JP, was elected Chairman of the Watch Committee in 1962. He was Mayor of Wallasey 1962/63. There were eleven Aldermen and three Councillors on the Committee.

The 1962 Annual Inspection was carried out by HM Inspector of Constabulary, Sir William Johnson and in the same year Police Cadets were introduced.

Inspectors Charles Gibson and Stan Fisher, Detective Inspector Peter Milne and Sergeant Albert Kennedy received medals for completing 22 years' service with the force.

Constable Herbert Wallace Lavery won the John Ormerod Trophy for the most outstanding work carried out by a Constable.

Mr Bert Pierpoint would come to Manor Road HQ from the Town Hall with the Policemen's pay packets. It was quite a noisy affair compared with paying out the Firemen's packets as they would they would do it in a very orderly fashion.

After working for the Local Authority, Mr Pierpoint became Pastor at Union Street (Mission) United Reformed Church, taking a keen interest in the Boys' Brigade.

Brave Wallaseyan

Another Wallasey gentleman that should be recorded is that of John William Maxwell, who was an old boy of St Anselm's College, and was a member of the old Northern Rhodesia Police. His parents lived in Wright Street, Egremont and his father, who was a Corporation employee, had completed 47 years with the Wallasey Ferries before retirement. While in Zambia, John saved the life of two African children who were stranded in the crocodile invested Kaful River in 1962. He took no thought of himself as he dived in the water and swan out to the children, fighting off a 14 foot crocodile as he did so. An African woman also assisted in the rescue. As he attempted to get out of the water, a crocodile opened its massive jaws and gripped him. He lost one leg and had the other badly mutilated. He returned to this country and the surgeons managed to save his right leg from amputation. For his act of bravery, John received the George Medal. He went to the Palace with the aid of an artificial limb to receive the decoration.

An international appeal was set which enabled him to return to Zambia where he set up his own business. This is another case where a Wallaseyan had shown great courage while serving in the Police, albeit not in his own country.

******

Brave Wallaseyan John Maxwell was awarded the George Medal for a rescue in Zambia (see this page)

Inspector Warrington

Inspector Ernest Warrington retired in 1962. He was one of the most popular members of the Wallasey Force and was known far and wide for his swimming abilities. He came from Sheffield and joined the Wallasey Borough Police on 21 May 1932 as a Probationer Constable and was made a Sergeant in 1947.

He held the Liverpool Shipwreck and Humane Society's Silver Medal for a rescue in the River Mersey, 21 awards of the Royal Life-Saving Society and seven Bars and Instructor's Certificate. He was an Official and Examiners of the ASA.

His main interest was in swimming and was one of the best known swimming officials in the North-West, being former President of the Northern Counties Amateur Swimming Association and he was the undefeated champion of the Police River Swim for 19 years, thus creating a remarkable record.

He was President of Amateur Swimming Association and officiated as an Olympic judge at the Games.

Mr Warrington received the MBE in 1971 for his services to swimming. He also had received the Liverpool Shipwreck and Humane Society's Certificate in 1938 for another river rescue.

He held the position of Honorary Secretary of the Cheshire County Polo and Swimming Association and was elected President in 1956. He had been the County Captain and played for the North of England. He also took part in the International and Olympic Water Polo Trails and was a leading ASA Official. He was the Chief Time Keeper at the National Swimming Championships on five occasions.

Inspector Warrington pictured as a member of the 1947 winning team for the Col. Hall-Walker Shield

River Rescue

During the 90 mph heavy gale of 21 January 1976 the 65 year-old ex-Inspector Warrington made a gallant attempt to rescue unemployed 23 year-old Alexander Wesley Gregson of Union Street from the River Mersey at the Egremont Slipway. It is not certain how he became to be in the water but two boys had spotted him in difficulty by the Holland Road slipway at 12.30pm. They ran and got a lifebelt and threw it to him but the waves snatched it away from him. Mr Warrington was on the promenade at the time and he said to a friend "I'm going in" as he saw the young man in distress. A light nylon line was attached to him. When Mr Warrington entered the rough seas, the waves were massive as he made a gallant effort to rescue the man. He managed to get near to him but was defeated by the sea. In the attempt, he suffered injuries to himself as he was driven against the promenade wall. When he was hauled out, he was taken to hospital. The New Brighton Inshore Lifeboat was summoned to the scene and two tugs and the Pilot launch Puffin joined in as well as an RAF Helicopter from Valley, Anglesey. The man was swept away and the waves brought him against the wall. The body was recovered at 4.45pm. He left a wife and child.

The *Daily Post* wrote in their editorial:-

"At a time when self-interest is a predominant consideration, what a splendid example has been provided by retired Wallasey Police Inspector Mr Ernest Warrington. A former swimming champion, now aged 66, he did not hesitate to plunge into gale-lashed Mersey at high tide on Wednesday when he heard that there was a man in the river. Under such appalling conditions, he was clearly risking his own life, he was dragged out bleeding and nearly unconscious. The attempt was, sadly, in vain but Mr. Warrington's example remains and must not go unrecognised."

The Wallasey Swimming Club presented him with a clock for his rescue attempt and was later presented with a pair of binoculars in recognition for his gallant attempt.

His wife, Eunice, accompanied him in an official capacity to International events throughout the world. She later became President of the Liverpool and District Swimming Association and was a member of the Wallasey Swimming Club for more than 60 years.

On retirement from the Wallasey Police, he became the Borough's Publicity and Entertainments manager. Their daughter, Sheila was the Northern Counties, Cheshire County and Liverpool District breast stroke champion. Their son, Roy, was also a good water polo player.

Mr. Warrington died on 2 November, 1979 and his wife died whilst on holiday in Blackpool in 1990s aged 77.

******

Golden Jubilee

The Wallasey Force celebrated their Golden Jubilee in 1963. An exhibition was held at the Civil Hall, a booklet about the history of the Force was printed and there were open days at the Headquarters in Manor Road. There were 205 members of the Force, including ten Policewomen and also six Police Cadets.

A Church Service was held at St Hilary's Church on Sunday 7 April 1963 to celebrate the Golden Jubilee of the Force. This was attended by the Mayor of Wallasey, Alderman Glyn Roberts, HM Inspector of Constabulary, Sir Charles Martin, CBE, members of the Watch Committee and Borough Council, Chief Officials, Magistrates and Clerk, and a number of pensioners of the Force. The service was conducted by the Rector, Canon LR Healey.

After the Service, there was a Parade and March Past in Liscard Road where the Mayor took the Salute outside the Victoria Central Hospital.

Sergeant Joseph William Barke won the 1963 John Ormerod Trophy as the most outstanding Officer in the year. A married man with a four-year-old son living in Leasowe Road. He was an old boy of the Wallasey Grammar School. His part in handling the early stages of a Moreton murder enquiry played a large part in being chosen.

Mr Macolm Scott

Malcolm Scott joined the Birkenhead Borough Police in 1963 as Constable 108. With the amalgamation with Cheshire Police he became Constable 2108 and with Liverpool and Bootle Police Forces was promoted to Sergeant 113A. He also served in Wallasey as an Inspector. He was then moved to Bromborough as Chief Inspector where he was promoted to Superintendent. He became Deputy Head of Personnel, Merseyside Police, then was appointed Acting Divisional Commander of Central Division and finally Chief Superintendent.

Death of Mr Ormerod

After retirement, Mr. Ormerod lived in Wallasey. He died at Victoria Central Hospital on Saturday 28 September 1963 aged 73 years and was buried in Rake Lane Cemetery. Seventy members of the Wallasey Police Force and 20 members of the Special Constabulary attended. Among the mourners were Mr Walter Marshall, the Chief Constable, Superintendent HS .Brown, Commandant FVW Crook, the Mayor of Wallasey, Alderman AE Martin, Mr G Harrison, the Town Clerk, Mr J Stuart Crook, the Coroner and many others. Family and friends.

The bearers were Inspectors Fisher and Gibson; Sergeants Barke and Chaddock and Constables Fidler and Walker (No.89).

His wife, Agnes Cecilia, died 25 May 1968.

In 1964 there was a record of 2,388 crimes committed in the Borough with the previous year being 1,910.

Stealing bicycles and unattended motor vehicles was common. Sgt Hugh Laughland received the Police Long Service medal and in May 1965 received a bar to his Long Service Medal which was presented to him by Sir Charles Martin, CBE, HM Inspector of Constabulary at the inspection of the Wallasey Special Constabulary Chief Constable Walter Marshall stated in his Annual Report that there was an increase in drunkenness and driving under the influence in 1965. There were 104 convictions, compared with 68 for the previous year – an increase of 53%.

The Dog Section in Wallasey was introduced about 1965 and PC Carter was one of the four handlers. He lived in Lymington Road and kept the dog at home in a kennel in his back garden.

The Wallasey Police had a van for the conveyance of personnel which had windows either side and were known as Carriers. They

Road Safety Quiz with Chief Constable John Ormerod as quizmaster

could also be used for bringing in prisoners.

There was a five-car crash outside the Victoria Central Hospital in Liscard Road in June 1965. No one was injured.

Ex-Sergeant Alfred Astbury Bebbington retired as Store Keeper at Manor Road Police Station in October 1965 having completed a record of 51 years Police service. This was his second retirement, the first having been on 30 September 1947, when the following day he joined the Police Reserve. He was holder of the King George V Silver Jubilee Medal which he had received in May 1935 and the Police Long Service and Good Conduct Medal in September 1951. He also received an illuminated address from the Chairman of the Watch Committee on 20 October 1965. He had started in the Wallasey Borough Police at the age of 19. On 5 August 1914 he joined the Royal Garrison Artillery and saw service in France and Belgium and after demobilisation re-joined the Wallasey Force in January, 1919. He was made a Sergeant in March 1928 and became Sergeant-in-Charge at Moreton until 1942 when he was placed in charge of Stores at Manor Road Police Station.

School Quiz

The Police have always kept a good relationship with the public over the years. Inspector DJC Clarke gave an enlightening talk on Police work to 125 members of the Wallasey Townswomen's Guild in 1966. The Inter-School Road Safety Quiz was very popular, having been started some years earlier when Mr Ormerod was the Question Master. Exciting finals were held in 1966 at the Wallasey Technical School in presence of the Mayor and Mayoress of Wallasey, Alderman CG Tomkins. In the Final Junior Section, Riverside Junior School retained the cup with Mount Juniors the runners-up. In the Senior Section, Oldershaw School retained the shield, which they had held for the previous three years, by defeating Gorsdale Secondary School.

Mr Walter Marshall, the Chief Constable, was the Quiz Master and the Judges were Superintendent and Deputy Chief Constable, HS Brown, Mr JC Humphrey (Asst. Director of Education), Mr LW Piper, the Divisional Organiser, Councillor TF Cavanagh, Councillor Jack Redhead and Mr. CE Proctor, the Road Safety Officer. The Rootes Shield was an annual event between Wallasey and Birkenhead for school children of all ages. The contest was held in two 'legs' – one in Wallasey and the other in Birkenhead.

Missing Schoolboy

The sad and strange case of David McCaig is still a mystery. A team of more than thirty-five detectives were engaged trying to find 13 year-old Wallasey schoolboy David. A special incident room had been set up at Headquarters. The boy had left home to return to school after a dental appointment on 9 March 1970. Later that afternoon the local newsagent rang his mother to ask why he had not come in to do his paper round After a series of telephone calls, David was reported missing. He was interested in ships and vessels, so they were searched in local docks. A boy had been seen in the area and ships were searched after they had left port. On 13 March boys found David's cycle in Rake Lane Cemetery and 40 Policemen searched the cemetery without success. Later a cape was found in Thirlmere Street and two boys admitted that was where they had discovered the cycle. Again David was said to have been seen on a Liverpool/London train and he had alighted at Crewe so the Police moved their search to the boats on the Shropshire Union Canal. After a great deal of time and work, the Police were no further. A theory was that the lad had sailed on the cruise ship, *Ocean Monarch*. David had been visiting the *HMS Eagle* on the previous Sunday and the liner had been tied up astern of the aircraft carrier. The enquiry had been led by Superintendent Stanley Fisher who confessed that it was the most baffling case in his 30 year career. In 1973 a new probe was set up headed by Detective Superintendent Des Green, Detective Inspector Bill Griffiths and Detective Inspector Alan Rimmer. Their work ended in a blank.

After all these years the file remains open.

Sea Accident

Inspector Maurice Toyn was involved in a tragic sea accident in New Brighton. A family from Huddersfield were on holiday at New Brighton in the summer of 1971. Their collie had been swept off the slipway close to the New Brighton Bathing Pool when 17 year-old Michael Shaw attempted to rescue the dog, only to get into difficulties himself and was carried out by the waves. The beach patrol men, led by Mr Joe Pringle accompanied by Michael's 39 year-old father Kenneth Shaw, launched their inflatable dingy in an attempt to reach the youth but the waves were so great, the craft overturned and the two men were cast into the water. Joe Pringle managed to hold onto the dinghy and with the help of other patrol men, managed to get to safety but their efforts to reach Mr Shaw failed. Michael, meanwhile managed to get to the slipway and was helped out. Inspector Toyn had arrived on the scene and in a last desperate attempt to save Mr Shaw, he and 25 year-old Colin Titterington from Wellington Road, dived 20 feet from the top of the sea wall with a lifebelt. Mr Shaw was some 30 yards out and they managed to get him into the lifebelt and tried to get him to the wall but he slipped through and was carried away. The next job was to get the two men out of the water. A rope ladder had been thrown into the water and Inspector Toyn believes that it was only a miracle that his leg got entangled in the rungs of the ladder that enabled the others to drag him to slipway by means of grappling irons. He later told me that it was like being inside a washing machine. Mr Titterington was also rescued from the water. The Inspector was taken to the Victoria Central Hospital where he had to remain for some days due to kidney infection.

The Lifeboat recovered the body of Mr Shaw 20 minutes later. The dog meanwhile had climbed on to the upturned dinghy and had jumped back into the water and managed to swim slowly to the slipway and safety. The men involved in this rescue attempt were commended for their bravery.

The one that got away
(But was soon apprehended!!)

There were many red faces at the Manor Road Police Station when a prisoner from Walton Gaol was being interviewed in a ground floor room at Police Headquarters. It was a nice warm late summer afternoon, when he spotted that the window behind the desk was open and, taking the Officer by surprise, leapt on the desk and through it as quick as grease lightening. A chase followed

The Mayor presenting life saving certificates

as he ran up the road and turned into Withens Lane and entered the Technical School (the old Navy League) grounds. He ran down behind the buildings that backed onto Strathcona Road followed by a neighbour in pursuit. Another Policeman climbed over the railings and followed. A Dog Handler and an Inspector then arrived. Meanwhile, the prisoner had hopped over the wall and into back gardens of a house in Penkett Road, crossed over the road and on through the back garden of one of the houses and into Seabank Road. The prisoner was apprehended in the car park of the *Pilot Boat House Hotel* and taken back to the Police Station. I often wondered who got the blame for his escape.

******

Changes

Constables were asked to hand in their whistles but some Inspectors insisted that their men kept them. One ex-Inspector told me that proved to be invaluable on at least one occasion in apprehending a villain.

When the Kingsway Tunnel and the M53 Motorway opened it became easier for a criminal to escape from the Borough by car. All the Wallasey men had First Aid Certificates and only three per cent did not have Life Saving Certificates. The Wallasey Force had one of the best swimming teams in the country.

Active Officers

Mr. Harry Lang

57 year-old Detective Chief Inspector HT Lang retired after 37 years' service in the Wallasey Borough Police. He joined as a Patrol Constable in 1928 and entered the CID in 1935. In 1940 he became Acting Sergeant and full Sergeant in 1943, being promoted to Inspector in 1949 and Chief Inspector and Superintendent in 1957.

As Head of the CID, he had been in charge of no fewer than 16 murders in the town and was commended for his part in the War Damage Trial that went on for 43 days. Following his retirement, he took up a legal appointment in Chester. Mr Lang was a sportsman and took part in the Police Annual River Swim and was Captain of the cricket and football teams and represented the force in boxing, golf and swimming. He was a married man with a son and daughter. He was President of New Brighton Cricket Club in 1975/6.

Peter Wherley joined the force whose father was the highly respected chemist in Rake Lane on the corner of Zig Zag Road. Raymond Lewis who was on Cycle Patrol for a period retired from the Force in 1968 and went into security work. His son followed his father's footsteps and became a Policeman. Ray is an active member of Christ Church and is interested in local history. Tony Weston was a well-respected Detective Inspector in the Wallasey Police who was a keen athlete and cyclist as well as a

Det. Chief Insp. Harry Lang (left) with Chief Constable Walter Marshall and Sgt. Barke at the murder scene in Moreton

rugger player. He left the Wallasey Police and joined the Port Authority force, where he rose to the rank of Deputy Chief Constable. He was the founder of the Cheshire Tope Angling Society. He died in 1999 at the age of 69.

James Leo Owens, a native of Birkenhead, who had been an Acting Sergeant and was promoted to full Sergeant, had served in the Irish Guards from 1945 until he joined the Wallasey Borough Police on 23 August 1952. As PC37, he was the first Constable to hold the John Ormerod Trophy in 1959 for the most outstanding Constable of the year. He had been commended on three occasions. He later became attached as a temporary Sergeant to the No.1 Regional Crime Squad at the Liverpool Branch.

PC Eric Lowe was made a temporary Sergeant. He had joined the Wallasey Borough Police in 1956 and was attached to the Traffic Department and Patrol Duties at Police Headquarters. He had been commended on two occasions. Mr Lowe went on to become a Superintendent and Second in Command in Wirral. He retired from the Police Force in 1993 at the age of 57. He became Chairman of New Brighton Lifeboat Committee in 1982 and held the post for several years.

During the Second World War, Samuel Rivier Foster served in the minesweepers and had become a RN Petty Officer. He joined the force and in 1952 became a Sergeant. He played cricket and football for the Police and in 1959 rescued a drowning person from the River Mersey for which he received the Royal Shipwreck and Humane Society's certificate. When he retired from the force he took up an appointment with a local firm.

John Kelly had enlisted in the Grenadier Guards in 1942 and was commissioned in the King's Regiment (Liverpool) seeing active service in Europe. He joined the Police and was in the traffic department from 1945 being promoted to Sergeant in 1956. He was interested in sport and played football, cricket and swam for the force. Sgt. Kelly rescued a person from the Mersey and was awarded the Royal Shipwreck and Humane Society's Certificate. Joseph Barke Jr. retired from the Police and took over the Post Office in Wallasey Village.

Sandy-haired William Gerrard 'Ginger' Adams at the age of 18 joined the army and became an instructor He joined the Wallasey Borough Police in 1946, and was made a Sergeant in 1959 then promoted to Inspector attached to No.1 Regional Crime Squad that was stationed in Liverpool. During the war, he served in the Queen's Own Cameron Highlanders from the outbreak of war until its end. He attended a course at the Police College at Brams Hill in Hampshire. He had been in charge of Police training at Headquarters and was transferred to the Moreton Sub-Station as Officer-in-Charge. Whilst a Patrol Constable, he was on the Wallasey Village beat. Bill, in private life, served as Vicar's Warden at the Emmanuel Church in Seabank Road. On leaving the Police Force he became attached to the Atomic Energy Department.

His brother was an Inspector in the Birkenhead Police Force.

PC Maurice Barnes was posted to No.1 District Police Training Centre at Bruche as Swimming Instructor. A position which he carried out with efficiency and marked success.

Mr Barnes was a faithful member of St Mary's Church in Liscard and served as Church Warden in 1973/74.

Harry Hesketh joined the Wallasey Force in August 1947. He was promoted to Sergeant and had been commended on two occasions. Sergeant Hesketh had served in the General Enquiry Office and the Information Room Staff at the Manor Road Head Quarters. On retiring from the force, he worked for the Local Authority in the Town Hall Annexe. His brother, Donald, was also in the Police. Their father, John, had been a Constable who returned as a reserve. The late Geoff Roberts who lived at 22 Glencoe Road was a popular Sergeant in the Wallasey Force and he is remembered with affection by a lot of residents.

John Bradbury retired from the Wallasey Borough Police in 1972, having completed 25 years service. He came from Warrington joining the force in 1947 as a Constable. He was later transferred into the CID and during his career received two Commendations and was sent to help in the Moors Murders search.

After leaving the force, he later, although being disabled, found employment with Mr. Barney Berkson the Birkenhead solicitor. The Police Life-Saving Team competed against other forces on Merseyside in the Hall-Walker Shield and met with success on several occasions. In 1958, the team were third in the event and in that year the Royal Society presented 24 awards to members of the members of the Force. Ten received Bars to their Bronze Medallions, eight received Bars to their Bronze Crosses and five received Bars to their Award of Merits. One Constable received the Award of Merit.

******

Some Early Murders

One could not write a book about a town's Police Force without including the serious crime of murder. There have been many in Wallasey over the years.

One of the earliest recorded murders was that of Peter Watts. He was a stranger in the parish and was 'done' to death in 1695. He is buried in St Hilary's Churchyard.

Another man, named Robert Benet, was killed at Salgham (Saughall Massie) by William Anyon on 20 September 1438 by striking him on the head with a 'mall'. The inquest was held at Bidston on 30 November. The Jury returned a verdict of felony. Anyone who had absconded was outlawed.

New Brighton Tragedy

In May 1890 two boys, Four-year-old Henry and his brother, 14 year-old William, were murdered at 18 Richmond Street in New Brighton. Their throats were cut with a knife by their father, 60 year-old Felix Spicer, who also attempted to murder his common law wife, Mary Palin. Superintendent Hindley was in charge of the case. Sergeant Cooper, Constables Potts and Jones were also involved. He appeared before the local Magistrates, Captain Molyneux, Mr James Smith and Mr W Heap. Mr. CW Tibbitts was Deputy Coroner and Mr Soffy was the Magistrates Clerk.

Felix had been born in London and was a ships' rigger by trade. The inquest was held at New Brighton Police Station. Mr Churton was the Coroner and the Chief Constable of Cheshire Constabulary, Colonel Hamersley attended. He was sent for trial at Chester Assizes where he was condemned to death and hanged at Knutsford Jail in August 1890. He admitted his guilt and cried for mercy at the scaffold.

Edgar S Holland

The murder case that involved a well-known Wallasey family was that of 49 year-old bachelor Edgar Samuel Holland, who was shot with five bullets from a revolver by an ex-actress, the good-looking Catherine Kempshall, in his Liverpool office. He had been involved in a case of Breach of Promise trial in London with the woman. Miss Kempshall claimed that he had been promised £10,000 upon marriage. She conducted her own case. The jury had found no case but Holland had to pay £1,000 plus costs. Miss Kempshall, who was just turned 30 years of age, was a highly emotional type of woman and had already been to see his sister and she was charged with having a loaded revolver with intent to murder and in December 1895 she had been charged with assaulting a solicitor's clerk. Mr Holland offered £900 cash and a £100 a year if she kept the peace with £50 surety.

On 31 October 1896 she was due to have a meeting with Holland and his solicitor in his Liverpool office. While they were in conversation, Miss Kempshall arose from the table and produced a revolver, and shot Holland dead. The Police were called and she was taken away. She was tried at the Liverpool Assizes on 31 March 1897 and found guilty with a recommendation for mercy. A petition was organised and 15,000 signatures were obtained, including members of the Holland family. An elderly American lady trudged around the Liverpool offices and collected 700 signatures. The forms were presented to the Home Secretary and on 9 April 1897, a day before she was due to be hanged he advised the Queen that Catherine Kempshall should be sent to Broadmoor. She denied her insanity but she remained there for 56 years and died in 1953 aged 88 years.

Massey Park Case

Detective Inspector Ennion was in charge of the Detective Force in Wallasey in the early 1900s. He was called to a house in Massey Park, Liscard in the spring of 1906 which involved the death of a woman by the name of Jessie Morgan, alias Mrs Harper. She had had an abortion which led to her death. The Inspector searched the house and found a letter and a card. Consequently, his enquiries led him to a house in Everton with DC Pierpoint of the Liverpool City Police. There he spoke to a woman named Sarah Martin who admitted having had a letter from Mrs Harper. He produced the letter and card and the woman said that she had written them. The Inspector got her to sign a statement and he could tell from her handwriting that it did not match that on the letter and card. Later, another woman named Elizabeth Blebbin was interviewed who admitted to having written the letter and card for Martin. It was later established that Martin had seen Mrs Harper on three occasions in connection with an abortion.

The evidence was contradictory and the magistrates could not bring the case for trial.

Liscard Tragedy

In 1917, Scotland Yard was called in to help to solve a murder. Margaret Alderson Hodgson, aged 37 and her four-year-old daughter, were found dead in a house in Central Park Avenue on 16 April 1917. They had been discovered by a neighbour who had heard the baby crying for a long period and went to investigate. Detective Inspector Robert Pearson carried out a search at the scene. They had been killed with an axe and blood was found on the walls and floor. A bread knife was on the floor with an empty money box and purse on the table indicating there had been a robbery. The bodies were removed to Seacombe Ferry Mortuary. The deceased lived with her husband, William, who worked for Robb Brothers in Birkenhead and when he returned home was interviewed by Chief Inspector Morris. He was taken to Police Headquarters for questioning and made a statement before being taken back to the house. On seeing the axe, he declared that it did not belong to him. At this point, no mention had been made of the killings. Back at the Police Station, spots of blood were found on his clothes. He was told of the murders, where upon he cried. Chief Inspector Morris then charged him with the murders.

Hodgson had moved to Wallasey and had left his wife living in Huddersfield while he found a suitable house. During this time he had met a young waitress named Helen Llewellyn while lunching at a cafe in Grange Road, Birkenhead. He was taken with her and they started a relationship. She became pregnant and he promised to support her.

The trial was held at Chester Assizes. Hodgson was unable to give an alibi to his whereabouts between 8 and 9am on 16 April. It took Judge, Mr Justice Avery, two hours to sum up. The jury, who were out for only 11 minutes returned a 'Guilty' verdict.

Fellowship House, near where the Leasowe Tragedy occured

Leasowe Tragedy

A father and two young sons were found gassed in a bungalow in a field off Pasture Road in 1927. William Ingham who had been separated from his wife, was secretary of the Fellowship Sports Club in Leasowe.

He met and fell in love with Sarah Rickard and his wife eventually left him. He took up with Rickard and had two children by her. His wife started divorce proceedings against him at the same time he lost his job. Ingham quarrelled with his girl friend over money matters which led to threats. She left the bungalow and went over to Liverpool leaving the children asleep. Ingham was very fond of his two boys but next day the owner called but got no reply and smelling gas, he forced the door open. Inside he found Ingham dead with his two children. A tube had been attached to a gas ring and the room had been sealed.

The Coroner returned a verdict of wilful murder against the two children and a verdict of suicide against Ingham.

Death of a Teenager

1927 was also the year that a 15 year-old girl by the name of Kathleen Lavinia Cowburn was killed. It was alleged that 54 year-old George Graham, a cabinet maker by trade, had made a suicide pact with the girl. Should one person survive in such cases, that person faces the charge of murder.

Graham had a workshop in Park Street, off Martins Lane. The girl, who was known as Vinnie and lived in Belgrave Street, was learning to be a telegraphist at Liverpool Post Office. She often called at the workshop and would help him at his work. Mrs Cowburn knew that there was something on her daughter's mind but the girl would not confide in her. She was pregnant and too frightened to tell her mother. The young lady left work and was not seen again until she was found dying at Graham's workshop. Graham went around to see Mrs. Cowburn and he told her that he had found the girl on the bench. The mother followed him to the workshop and she found her daughter. The place smelt of gas. With the help of her son, they got the girl home and an ambulance was summoned. Graham went to get the Police.

Back at the station, Mr Barry, the Chief Constable interviewed him, where he made a statement. Chief Inspector John Ormerod and Dr Martlew went to the workshop and made a number of discoveries. The post-mortem showed that the young girl had died of carbon-monoxide poisoning. She was also six months pregnant.

The trial of George Graham took place at the Liverpool assizes on 6 February 1928 with Mr Justice Rigby Swift presiding. The jury found him 'Not Guilty'. He picked up his coat and hat, left the dock and returned home.

Seacombe Tragedy

A 53 year-old widow, Mrs. Catherine Boothroyd, was found badly injured in Clarence Road, Seacombe on 11 March 1955 and later died in hospital. Constable Lee found the body and a bloodstained weapon – a marline spike. Mrs Boothroyd had gone to the aid of her daughter, Mrs. Dorothy Dearlove, who had screamed when Gowler had attacked her after breaking into the house. Constable

Adams had been called to a disturbance the previous night and he had seen the accused leave the house and walk down Borough Road in the direction of Seacombe Ferry but he to returned the following day.

As a result of Police enquiries, a description was circulated and after 25 minutes of receiving the details at the Police 'Pillar' telephone at the bottom of Magazine Lane, Constable JE Morris had arrested 43 year-old ship's rigger Richard Gowler on the promenade. At Headquarters, he was interviewed by Detective Inspector Lang and Sergeant Peter Milne and was later charged with the murder Gowler replied with the words "Yes Sir".

Gowler lodged in Sandrock Road. He was later sent to trial at the Chester Assizes where he was tried and found guilty and was sentenced to death.

Constables Morris and Ken Holliday later left the Wallasey Force and joined the Isle of Wight Police.

The Pillbox Murder

The Wallasey Police were involved to a degree in the case of the Pillbox Murder in 1955, when the body of Alice Barton was found by a schoolboy in an old wartime pillbox close to the railway line by the River Fender in Prenton, that carried the Bidston to Wrexham train. Birkenhead Police were in charge of the case and were helped by other forces. The woman had been strangled with some sort of belt. Detective Chief Inspector Harry Lang, the Head of the Wallasey CID and Detective Chief Inspector of Birkenhead CID organised house-to-house enquiries in Moreton, Upton and Woodchurch from Moreton Police Station. Scotland Yard were called in and Detective Superintendent 'Dusty' Miller and Det. Sergeant Bellany were given the task of finding the killer. The deceased was a known prostitute. On 21 September 1955 she crossed over on the ferry and went to Moreton Cross where she seems to have met up with a man. The case involved a great deal of work for the Police, interviewing a large number of people, including the crew of the *Empress of France* and following up leads. Despite several witnesses who had seen the killer, the murderer was never found.

Moreton Neighbours

A 35 year-old Moreton labourer was accused of shooting a mother of two young children on 16 March 1962. Sergeant Barke and two Policemen went to investigate after receiving a call that there had been an explosion at the rear of a shop in Hoylake Road, Moreton. On arriving, they discovered a 40 year-old housewife lying severely injured having been shot at close range. The gunshot had been heard at 2.15pm. The woman had been shot at close range. She had just finished a meal with her husband and gone into the back yard to the dustbin when she confronted with the assailant. She died in hospital. Sergeant Barke knew that the next door neighbour had been in possession of a shotgun in the past. He ensured that the area was sealed off and preserved for expert examination, then went with Constable Coles to interview the suspect who admitted having a shotgun. A search was made of the house and the Sergeant discovered the double-barrel shotgun hidden, which had very recently been fired. He arrested Clarke and took him to Moreton Police Station.

Detective Chief Inspector Harry Lang, Chief Constable Walter Marshall and other Policemen arrived at the scene.

At first the accused had nothing to say but later admitted firing at the woman whilst she was bending over the dustbin, saying "she had it coming to her". He believed that the deceased had been spreading rumours about him.

The trial was heard at Chester Assizes on 6 January 1963 where the accused was found guilty but insane.

Gorsedale Road Murder

A 38 year-old spinster was raped and murdered with a blunt instrument at Gorsedale Road in January 1973.

The woman had been an ex-Wren and her diary proved that she had men visitors. She had not been the home-loving innocent as first believed. She went to various public houses and clubs in Liverpool where she met Continental lorry drivers.

The body was discovered by her niece and the Police were called in. The case was under the direction of Det. Chief Superintendent Clifford Haigh of the Cheshire CID. Dozens of lorry drivers were questioned. Women, who lived alone, were advised to lock their doors at night. Wallasey Police records showed that there had been a pattern of vicious attacks in the last six months in the area which pointed to the work of a methodical sex maniac. An 18 year-old girl had been attacked in Matthew Street in August 1972. She had screamed and her assailant run off. Another lady had also been attacked in Clarendon Road whilst walking home. She died later in hospital. A 19 year-old was also found savagely attacked in Marsden Road. She had suffered hammer blows to the head. The weapon was found as well as a pair of bloodstained gloves. The poor girl never saw the person who attacked her however, after an operation in Walton Hospital she recovered.

Whether the spinster's killer was the same person who had committed these horrific attacks no one knows. No weapon was found at the scene of the murder. The Police questioned seamen who were in port at the time of murder and four detectives went to Scotland to interview the crew of a submarine that was in Birkenhead for repairs at the time. A folded handkerchief was found in the room where the woman had been killed. It had laundry marks, one being Chinese, detectives contacted every laundry in the country but without success. The murderer was never found.

Two Sisters

Two sisters, one aged 63 the other 54, were murdered in Greenwood Lane on 5 May 1973. They had received horrific injuries to the head and neck as well as stab wounds. One woman was nailed to the floor with a 6 in. nail through her breast. The Ambulance was called when the men found the sisters in pools of blood. A neighbour said she had noticed that one of the sisters had became withdrawn and interested in Spiritualism. The tragedy happened on the birthday of one of the ladies. Two youths, who had been kind to them when there was trouble with vandals on bon fire night had taken lodgings with them. The young men, aged 19 and 22, were apprehended by the Police and later charged with the murders. They were tried in the Liverpool Crown Court where they pleaded guilty to manslaughter on the grounds of diminished responsibility but not of murder.

They were jailed for life.

In-law Trouble

A 30 year-old Liscard man blamed his father-inlaw for the breakup of his marriage. He had suffered a series of domestic troubles resulting in his wife and two daughters leaving him. While his mind was disturbed he decided to kill his father-in-law. He got hold of a single-barrelled shotgun with cartridges and drove down to Egremont on 28 June 1974 where he persuaded two boys, giving them 50p, to take a message to his father-in-law which lured him to his death. The man was told that someone was interferring with his garage and being suspicious decided to investigate. He turned up an alleyway and was confronted by his son-in-law holding the shotgun.

"You have ruined my marriage, now you know why I am doing this to you", he said as he shot him in the head. The victim fell and as he tried to get to his feet and the assailant shot him again

through the heart from a distance of ten feet. The fellow then intended to kill himself but refrained. The Police arrived and he was taken into custody. He was later tried at the Crown Court. He pleaded not guilty to murder but guilty of manslaughter on grounds of diminished responsibility which the Court accepted. Mr. Justice Nield described as a most shocking act which was 'premedicated and deliberate'.

The 30 year-old was jailed for eight years and, I understand, was a model prisoner and released early.

Two Murder Cases

In June, 1978 the body of a 18 year-old girl was found in a shallow grave on the old gun site in Leasowe. She had been strangled and had suffered blows to the head. A youth had been seen running away from the site. 80 Officers were engaged on the case. Detective Superintendent Bob French led the enquiries with the help of Wallasey CID and Detective Superintendent Mike Southwell.

Another horrible murder was when a skittle and a fisherman's knife was used to bludgeon to death the manager of a New Brighton bowling alley. The 54 year-old man was left with a fractured skull and 46 knife wounds to his neck and body. The murder took place in the early hours of 7 September 1979.

Lorry Driver

Two men, a 43 year-old Wallasey man and a 27 year-old from Eastham pleaded not guilty when accused of stabbing a lorry driver in a an old unused Police Hut on the Birkenhead Dock Estate, he died from 13 stab wounds to his chest and side. He had 'grassed' to the Police about one of them concerning the theft of plastic pellets. Their palm prints were found inside the hut. They were tried at the Liverpool Crown Court in March 1980. Each blamed the other. The Jury found them guilty and were jailed for life. Another lorry driver received four years for trying to help them to cover up their tracks. The Judge commended Det. Chief Inspector Roger Corker and his team in the conviction of the two men. He also commended a Driving Instructor Bob Whittaker who had followed up his suspicions and discovered the body.

******

Toxteth Riots

The Wallasey and other local forces assisted with the Toxteth Riots on 4-6 July 1981 when rioters took to the streets and caused mayhem. Arson, petrol bombing and looting went on with battles

HM Inspector of Police Forces with Chief Constable John Ormerod inspect Mounted Policeman George Walker on "King Kong"

between youths and the Police resulting in many injuries. There were 781 Officers in hospital and there was £3,314,285 damage to property. with £525,858 worth of property being looted. It cost the Police Authority £4,403,000 to conduct the operation.

Mounted Police

The Mounted Section go back on Merseyside to 1885 when the Chief Constable, Captain William Nott-Bower, submitted a report to the Watch Committee which resulted in the formation of the Mounted Police with Troop Sergeant Major Stephen Sales of the 7th Hussars becoming the Inspector in charge. He purchased eight horses in 1886 and Liverpool was the first force outside the Capital to have a prominent Mounted section. They were also responsible for fire engines and ambulances in the city. A decade later, the section could boast 36 horses.

Captain Nott-Bower resigned as Head Constable at Liverpool to become a Commissioner of the City of London and Mr Leonard Dunning became his successor on 24 March 1902. The Mounted Police were in action against the rioters in 1909 and again in the riots following the transport strike of 1911. They also escorted the food wagons through the streets of Liverpool and the Mounted Police took part in the Royal Lancashire Show at Preston in 1912 and won awards in the show ring with their skill. The following year the section had 97 horses. A large amount of the men were primarily drawn from cavalry regiments and this can be seen in the fact that the ceremonial dress still worn by the Mounted Officers was modelled on that of the 4th Dragoon Guards. With the arrival of motor vehicles, there were less transport duties, such as prisoner transport, so that the number of horses began to fall, and when the First World War started, many of the young Officers joined up and by 1924 they were down to 44 horses.

The Mounted Head Quarters in Allerton was opened in 1938 where

Wallasey Mounted Policeman, George Walker

they trained and the Second World War again interfered with the Department with 27 horses being stabled at Lord Derby's Knowsley Hall as a precaution against enemy air attacks. They later returned to Allerton and the number of horses has remained at 27. There were 36 Officers at the Head Quarters and some men who entered the department had little riding experience and they had to be trained from scratch in four months. The horses were usually four years of age when purchased and were all geldings 16 hands high. They were retired after 14 years service. It was some years before a Mounted Policeman was seen again in Wallasey but as now they are part of the Merseyside Police it is quite a common sight to see the Mounted Section particularly in the summer or when a special occasion arises where they are more suited to handle the crowds. In the 1970s one would see a couple of Mounted Policemen on patrol at the weekends in Wallasey. The horses were usually Athos and Van Dyck that came over from Liverpool, ridden by Constables William Thompson and Philip Letford. The present day duties of the Mounted Officers involve crowd control in such places as football matches, demonstrations and where there are large crowds. A horse-box can take them to various places where they are required. It is said that one Mounted Police Officer on a trained horse can do the work of over 12 foot patrol men. They have the advantage of height.

They were represented at a Gymkhana in the Tower Grounds Stadium in the 1950s. In the musical event, a white horse was ridden down two columns of Mounted Police while the band played 'Here comes the Bride'.

The horses are trained to cope with noise of the traffic and large gathering of people. They are able to push crowds without fear of injuring them. Sergeant Phil Smith came from Wallasey and was one of the men to be on patrol in Wirral. Where there are crowds, the Mounted Police do a splendid job, and they always lead the winner of the Grand National Steeplechase to the saddling enclosure at Aintree. The Department holds an annual show over a two day period in June where they do Sword Dance Displays and Show Jumping.

******

The Dog Section

Most Forces had a dogs' section from the early 1950s but the Merseyside Police Dog section was formed on 1 April 1947. In 2001 the section had one Inspector, nine Sergeants and 53 Constables. There were in the 1990s 53 male Alsatians (German Shepherd). They were trained for street patrols, and all manner of criminal work. There are ten drug dogs and eight explosives dogs both sections use Labradors and Springer Spaniels (male and

An early Wallasey Mounted Policeman

Chief Inspector Walter Marshall presents cup to dog handler

female) as they are smaller than the Alsatians and more suited to the work. All the dogs have been donated by the public. One Officer will train the animal for between eight and 13 weeks and it will have a working life of about eight years. The dogs are specially trained to deal with chasing an armed villain and to grip the arm and bring him to the ground. The dogs must be friendly as children stop and stroke them.

The department have 25 dog vans that can take them to wherever they are needed. The Dog Sections are based at Bromborough, Crosby, Knowsley and Wirral. The larger kennels are at Mather Avenue in Liverpool. Inspector Tony Dean has now taken over from Bob Coote as Head of Merseyside's Dog Section.

Cheshire Police have 36 dogs, which include seven drugs dogs. They are on the look-out for new recruitments for their training section at Nantwich especially unwanted spaniels (springer and cocker), labradors and pointers. Sergeant Neil Brown became in charge of the Cheshire Police Dog Unit.

******

Merseyside Police Band

Loudly let the trumpet bray!
Tantanara!
Proudly bang the sounding brasses!
Tzing! Boom!"
As upon its lordly way
This unique procession passes

WS Gilbert

The Liverpool City Police Band, now known as the Meseyside Police Band was formed way back in 1858 which consisted of buglers whose job was to sound the alarm and call the Officers to their duties.

Major Grieg who was Head Constable at Liverpool, submitted a report to the Watch Committee proposing the formation of a Band

for the Borough Police Force. Following the Fenian Alarm where the Buglers had played an important role, their numbers increased, which led to a number of musicians practicing. The Committee discussed the matter and the Liverpool City Police Band was formed consisting of a number of brass players and percussionists under the baton of Inspector Francis Beardhall who had been a Bandmaster in the Army. He was appointed in 1867. There were a dozen members (all Constables) of the Band who played at various local events. By 1869, the band was made up to 20 players on a military style, having woodwind added to the brass.

Arthur Crawley, who succeeded Mr. Beardhall as Bandmaster in 1887, received a salary of £150 a year for the position and that of being a Constable. The Band rose in fame and gave concerts all over the City including St George's Hall. To maintain the Band it proved to be costly and was threatened with disbandment In 1905, the Band played before King Edward VII at Knowsley Hall. Charles Bricks became Bandmaster in 1912 and introduced concerts on the LLandudno boat. After the First World War, Mr Bricks served as a Captain in a Battalion and on his return to the Band in 1919 was made a Chief Inspector and after they had re-formed with 45 members, they were giving as many as a dozen concerts a week in addition to daily performances in St John's Gardens.

The Second World War caused the Band to cease in 1939 and one of their members, Constable Black, died as a result of injuries received from an enemy bomb whilst on duty on 19 September 1940. Mr Bricks died on 20 October 1941 and Charles Marriott became Conductor and the Band was again re-formed with12 members. The Watch Committee had hoped for five times that figure. By 1946, the number had risen to 16 and they played at the Passing Out Parade at Bruche Training Centre.

Eventually it was made into a proper band of 64 members who played in the parks in the summer and at other events in the area under the direction of ex-Marine Band Director, Captain Albert Pottle.

On one occasion they played at a special service at Egremont Presbyterian Church (now Manor Church Centre) in Seabank Road. The Band had many important engagements, including performing in the presence of Queen Elizabeth II in 1973 and again in 1978 when the Liverpool Cathedral was officially opened.

Captain Trevor Platts succeeded Mr Pottle, who had to retire on health grounds.

With the shortage of finance, the Police Authority in 1985 decided that the Band would have to be given up and they gave their last performance before the Prince and Princess of Wales at the famous Grand National Steeplechase at Aintree.

However, this was not the end of the famous Police Band. There was an outcry from the public and Chief Constable Kenneth Oxford helped to reform the Band once more with Sergeant Kenneth Pollitt who was appointed in 1989. He had been with the Lancashire County Police before joining the Merseyside Force. Today, the band consists 15 members who play at various functions on Merseyside and when the occasion requires a larger band, they can call on the services of retired members of the force and that of the Special Constabulary.

******

Private Detective

Wallasey has had a few private detectives over the years, including Alfred Davies who lived at 22 Upper Rice Lane and Charles Fredrick Williams of Parkside.

One of the best known was Zena Phillipa Scott-Archer. It was in 1946, at the age of 17, that she joined the Liverpool Detective Bureau which had been founded in 1937 by her father, ex-Detective Sergeant Sydney James Scott of the Flying Squad. The agency was originally known as Scott's Detective Bureau. She must have been one of the youngest private detectives in the country as she began to learn the trade from her father. Her first assignment was to serve divorce papers on a cheating wife of a client. She took over the business when her father died in 1953.

"I apply the little grey cells to a problem", she would say. "Mine is an imaginative, intuitive mind. I don't know how I'm going to invest a case until I start. That's why you can't instruct someone else. It's an art form. Women are very good at it."

In 1968, she was elected the first woman president of the Association of British Detectives. There were 350 male detectives in the Association and only 12 females. She also served a term as President of the World Association of Detectives in 1982.

She has been called Mrs Sherlock Holmes on a number of occasions. Zena was often seen in disguise as she went off on a case. There was one time when she was outside her house when a neighbour failed to recognise her and when they later met up, the neighbour told her that there had been a stranger looking for her! Her work took her far and wide. She has tracked down witnesses for Court cases, chased suspects and trailed cheating husbands. What she found difficult was to follow a person by car. There was one occasion when she had to serve a man with certain documents. He denied that he was the man concerned in the matter and was determined not to have them. She thrust them into his hands and hurried off and got into her car. He jumped into his own car and chased after her in the hope of giving them back to her. A chase followed through the streets of Liverpool. He tried to ram her car as she pressed her foot down on the accelerator. It was exciting and dangerous and she thought it best to stop before there was an accident. Zena got out and he walked over to her and stuffed the documents down the front of her dress whereupon, she slapped his face and he hers as he yelled out for the Police. When they arrived the first thing they asked him was his name and before he knew it, she had served him with the documents.

She was successful in her career due to the fact that she was a woman and had an array of disguises and was able to impersonate such characters as a bingo player, model, a foreign student, a South African journalist and that of a nurse. Her husband was David Archer, a pharmacist at Manley's chemist, Lycett Road, Wallasey Village. Most of her work involved civil actions and she enjoyed her career which continued until 1999. Surely, she must have also been the country's oldest working private detectives, reminding one of Agatha Christie's Miss Marple.

But at the age of 79, she had not finished, as she landed a TV role when she presented a series, which began in June 1999 called *The Crime Squad* She gave practical advice on how to tackle crime at the grass-root level. She went onto the streets with a hidden camera in her handbag to demonstrate the major issues of the day.

In the summer of 1999, the Scott Detective Agency joined forces with Ellison Gough in Manchester and Hooker's in Wirral to form the largest private detective agency in the North West with all the latest devices. Michael Wright is one of the unknown faces of the agency which is based in Dale Street in Liverpool who carry out a wide variety of detective work.

Sherlock Holmes

The world famous fictional consulting detective, Sherlock Holmes who was created by Conan Doyle has a connection with the town. In the case of he Cardboard Box, New Brighton is featured. The case involved two human freshly severed ears covered in salt that were sent in a cardboard box to a Miss Susan Cushing of Croydon.

Inspector Lestrade of the Yard asks Holmes to help. By studying the label and string, the famous sleuth deduces that they were

sent by a sailor. He tracks down a ship's steward named, James Browner. Browner had murdered his wife and her lover, Alec Fairbairn, off the coast of New Brighton whilst they had gone out in a hired rowing boat. Miss Cushing had two sisters, Sarah Cushing and Mary Browner. After Mary had married, Sarah went to live with the couple in Liverpool but this proved to be disastrous and she left and went to live with her other sister, Susan, before going to live in Wallington. Susan received the cardboard box that was intended for Sarah. Holmes told Inspector Lestrade the name of the murderer and the Police arrested Browner, who confessed to the crime.

"PC49" & Co

Wallasey's actor Brian Reece, who was a member of the well-known local family – owners of a milk and confectionery company who, will always be remembered for his role as PC Archibald Berkley-Willloughby in "The Adventures of PC 49" on the radio. The show started on 24 October 1947 and continued for ten series, the final episode being 'The case of the Small Boy' which was broadcast 26 May 1953.

Another well-known local actor, who played the part of PC Corky Turnbull in the Eric Sykes shows on television, was Derek Guyler who was born in Wallasey on 29 April 1914. Among the many roles he played over the years was that of Inspector Scott in "Inspector Scott Investigates" on radio. It ran for seven series from July 1957 until 1963.

******

Reorganisation

Reorganisation of the Police took place in 1967. The Liverpool City Police merged with the Bootle Borough Police.

The Police Forces of Birkenhead, Cheshire, Stockport and Wallasey were amalgamated to form the new Cheshire Constabulary and came into being from 1 July 1967. Mr H Watson, FCA was the Chief Constable with Mr. SJ Harvet, OBE as his Deputy. Mr Walter Marshall was the assistant Chief Constable in the West District. Inspector Robert Hughes was promoted to Chief Inspector.

Manor Road Police Station became Divisional Headquarters for the Wallasey Division which comprised the Wallasey County Borough (excluding that part of the Mersey Docks and Harbour area), Hoylake and Wirral Urban Districts areas with the Headquarters at Hoylake with Sections at Heswall and Moreton. The changes in Divisional boundaries meant that Officers serving in Sub-Divisions and Sections transferred from one division to another became new members of the District and Division to which their Sub-Division or Section had been transferred 1 August 1967. There were Divisional Superintendents. Alderman John P Ashton

Inspector Leslie Whitfield discusses the new 'Panda' patrol cars with Ald. John Ashton and AG Harrison, Town Clerk

was the Wallasey representative on the Cheshire Police Authority. Mr. Cliff Halsall became Chief Superintendent at Wallasey. He was followed by Mr W Beesley.

The Breathalayser test came into force in 1967 under the Road Safety Act. The Police were able to stop motorists and ask them to breathe into the gadget which analysed the amount of alcohol in their body. The first test was made on 8 October 1967 in Somerset.

Long Service

Long Service and Good Conduct medals for 22 years in the Wallasey Division were presented at the Cheshire Constabulary Head Quarters in Chester by Mr CLS Cornwall-Leigh, JP, Chairman of the Police Authority to Superintendent William Beesley, Sergeant Ronald Squires of the Motor Control, Alan Rimmer (who later was transferred to Birkenhead), PC Robert Anderson (Motor Control) and PC Leslie Fisher. Wing Commander KM Stoddart the High Sheriff of Merseyside presented long service medals to Chief Superintendent Cliff Halsall, Constable Physick and Constable Watson.

Mr Halsall was Chairman of the New Brighton Lifeboat Committee. Mr Robert Hughes came out of the County and became Chief Superintendent at Wallasey. Badges were changed and Officers' coat buttons were decorated with Prince of Wales' feathers. Wallasey had had its own Police Force for 54 years.

The Home Secretary called for a 10% cut in men and the 'Panda' Patrol Cars were introduced. The Patrol Cars were fitted with flashing blue lamps, radios and sirens. There were two to begin with and others followed later, thus doing away with Constables' beats. Looking back in hindsight, one wonders whether this was for the better as the familiar Bobby on the Beat was no longer seen. Contact with the public was lost and Police Forces have not been the same since, albeit, there are now a number of Patrol Policeman. Foot and Cycle Patrols were discontinued. Some years later, certain Officers were seen about the town on a bicycle.

The 'Lollypop' (School Crossing Patrol) men and women were introduced for stopping traffic so children could cross roads safely especially near their school. They wore a peak black cap and white overall and were employed by the Police. Several years later, they were taken over by the Local Authority.

The CID was brought up to date with the latest equipment available. Fingerprints were found by dusting areas, such as glass, with aluminium powder and these were transferred onto specially made sticky tape. Plaster casts were made of footprints and many other advanced methods introduced in the fight against crime.

With the takeover, things were not the same as the town had, to some degree, lost control. It was no longer a 'Local Force'. Changes are not always for the better.

The Manor Road Station proved to be inadequate and a new Police Headquarters was badly needed. It was about 14 years previously that it was decided that the existing building was no longer suitable for the ever-growing force but for various reasons the proposal was delayed. The original site in Wallasey Village was abandoned as it was to be used for the new St Mary's College. The plans for the new building would include the Magistrates' Courts. Eventually, the Authorities decided that the new Police Station would be built on a new site the other side of Wimbledon Street in Manor Road. Plans were drawn and accepted. The old building would continue to be used as a Court House. The new Police Head Quarters was opened in 1973

The commemorative plate reads:

Cheshire Police Authority. Divisional Police Headquarters. Opened 28th November 1973 by Sir Arthur Peterson, KCB, MVO, Permanent Under Secretary of State Home Office.

The following year saw more changes. With the reorganisation of Local Government throughout Britain providing a Police Force remained the responsibility of Local Authorities. New Counties and districts were set up 'Merseyside' became a Metropolitan County. The Wallasey Division of the Cheshire Constabulary became part of the new Merseyside Police Force in 1974. The area was broken up into divisions. Wirral became 'G' Division and on the Liverpool side there were six Divisions, 'A', 'B', 'C', 'D', 'E' and 'F'.

Mr Bruce Humphries was the Wallasey Coroner in the 1970s.

The Sex Discrimination Act of 1975 saw a change in the selection of women in the Police Forces in Great Britain. Policewomen were be called Women Police Constables with the same rights as their male counterparts. They used to work a half hour less each day. Received 9/10ths of the male pay. After the Act was passed, WPCs were treated the same as the men. The new Headquarters were opened in 1981 at Canning Place in Liverpool.

The Control Room received the 999 calls and were in direct contact with patrol cars and the personnel. There was also a large Computer Unit. Messages could be relayed from Liverpool and appear on the screens. An Officer could decide what action to take. It was manned 24 hours a day. Sergeant Mal Hopewell was in charge in the 1980s. Each district was divided into divisions which were run by Superintendents or Chief Inspectors. There was also a Traffic Division.

The Constable's uniform of today retains the familiar helmet that has been worn by Officers in Wallasey since the time that the town took over the Police in 1913. The single-breasted tunic has an open-neck front with lapels, four silver buttons, two breast pockets and two lower pockets. The pockets have a flap which is held down with smaller silver button. The colour of the uniform is black and Officers wear a short-sleeved white shirt instead of the pale blue that was in use a few years ago. The black tie is attached to the shirt collar to avoid any ruffian grabbing it in an attempt to make it to tighten around the Officer's throat. They are also issued with a long-sleeved open-necked navy blue woollen jersey, which reminds one of the colour of the old uniform. The new baton and modern handcuffs, are attached to the belt and clipped to the shoulder is the two-way radio.

Police Constables today have two straps to their helmet, one the chin strap and the other a shorter one that is used in the case of riots. Police Constables on the beat are allowed to wear shirt sleeves and shoulder epaulettes were introduced.

One seldom sees the Policeman wearing a cape nowadays. However, a short black nylon waterproof jacket is worn instead.

They have reintroduced the whistle, although it is now largely decorative. Some of the patrol men wore white tops to their peak caps. Inspectors and Sergeants, have the chequered band around their caps. Originally, this was only used by Scottish Police.

The WPC wear a bowler-style hat which has a chequered band and the same design is taken up in a form of a cravat. They have the choice of wearing a skirt or trousers with the latter more suitable, especially when chasing a suspect.

The Police use modern white motorcycles which are equipped with radio, 'stop' signs, sirens and panniers for special equipment. The radio originally had a traditional type receiver which was above the rear wheel or attached to the petrol tank.

The white Patrol Cars that are used on motorways had a red band and are nicknamed by some as a 'Jam Sandwich'. Other white Patrol Cars have two green lines down the sides and a multicoloured rear. The latest colours at the rear of most emergency vehicles are yellow and red diagonal stripes.

Police throughout the country use the Truvelo meter for motorists exceeding the speed limit. The meter records the time that a vehicle travels between two wires that have been laid across the road with a known distance between them. The instrument indicates the speed of the vehicle. Special cameras are also used to catch speeding motorists.

The Police can call on the help of the frogmen of the Underwater Unit or the Helicopter Unit when the occasion arises.

Headquarters are now equipped with the latest technology and the National Computer is a great asset to the force.

Constables can do 25 or more years but they have to retire at the age of 55 however, Inspectors and other senior ranks may go on to 60.

Chief Superintendent Bill Beesley retired from the Police on 28 February 1984 after serving in the Police for 44 years. He started his career as a messenger in the Cheshire Force in 1940 working from Northwich, then as a Patrol Constable and then served in 20 different areas in the country before coming to Wirral in 1968 and until 1974 served as Deputy Division Commander. He joined 'D' Division in Liverpool, returning to Wirral the following year to work on the new divisions. Mr Beesley has served as Chairman of the New Brighton Lifeboat Committee, President of the New Brighton Sea Cadets and Chairman of the local St John's Ambulance Centre.

Mr Rex Taylor was Coroner for Wirral. Councillor Dave Jackson and Councillor Kate Wood from Wirral Council served on the Merseyside Police Authority and Ronald Beech transferred from the Cheshire Force as Superintendent in the Wallasey Division and remained in that position until retirement in 1969.

Superintendent Steven Cahill was appointed Area Commander in April 1997 with Ronnie Garnett as Chief Inspector.

The Merseyside Police had four areas: 'A' - Wirral, 'B' - Sefton, 'C' - Liverpool and 'D' - St Helens & Knowsley. A1 district covers Wallasey and Hoylake Division with Head Quarters at Manor Road. A2 District covers the Central Wirral area. Liverpool has five districts, Sefton and St Helens each have two. Chief Constable of Merseyside Police, Sir James Sharples was succeeded by Mr Norman Bettison in 1998 and Superintendent Beech died in the same year.

Mr Bernard Hogan-Howe became Assistant Chief Constable. The cost of maintaining the Fire, Police and Probation at the new Millennium was two million pounds which represented 2% of the Council Tax.

'Swasie' Turner

No book about the local Police should fail to mention Ronald 'Swasie' Turner. He was born on 13 April 1940. The ex-Sergeant served in the Police for more that 30 years, starting his Police career as a Special Constable, then as a Park Constable before being accepted into the regular Force. During his career in the Police, he suffered a number of injuries in the course of duty. One accident left him with a damaged wrist which meant wearing a metal brace. This was not the end of his misfortune.

Poor Swasie was knocked down by a hit and run motorcyclist while on duty at New Brighton in 1987. Eventually his leg had to be amputated which forced his retirement. He took to writing and in 1994 he saw the publication of his book, "Off the Cuff" and he followed this up with two more books.

He now uses a wheelchair to get around but it did not stop him from scaling the 130 cast-iron steps inside Leasowe Lighthouse to the top in the aid of charity and then the ex-Officer went on to do the same at Perch Rock Lighthouse in New Brighton with his wheelchair in tow. He was covered in cuts and bruises from the climb as he carried his wheelchair in his left hand. "I didn't think I'd manage it", he confessed, "As well as the stairwell there were a couple of sets of steps that were vertical and it was very difficult. I was relieved when I finally got to the top." He sat on the top and waved to the people below.

He has also climbed Talacre Lighthouse and the Liver Buildings and has made the 41 mile journey from Talacre to Upton, around the Chester City Walls, the 72 mile coastline journey of Anglesey and has covered the 38 mile Isle of Man Motorcycle Racing Course. A documentary film has been made about his work for charity. He was filmed by Ally Boxie competing in Newcastle's Great Run North in 1997. Devastated by the loss of his wife, Marjorie in 1997, Swasie has fought back to raise funds for the Clatterbridge Cancer Gene Appeal in her memory. In the spring of 1998 when he tackled the ascent of Blackpool Tower, climbing steps to the lift as far as 380 feet, then climbing 120 feet to the top, including two metal vertical iron ladders to reach the base of the flag pole. The event was recorded on video. To crown off the day, he came through the Birkenhead Tunnel in his wheelchair! He also took part in the 15 mile walk for Charity from Seacombe Ferry via the promenades to West Kirby and the Wirral Way to the Thurstaston Visitor Centre, albeit in his wheelchair.

A book was published in 1999 about his achievements, entitled "Wheelchair Pilot". One of his latest exploits was the of crossing over the soft sands from West Kirby to Hilbre Island in his wheelchair. This enabled him to add to the £12,000 he has already raised for Cancer Gene Appeal. Swasie still uses the same wheelchair that he received in February, 1997!

In May 2000 he travelled from John O'Groats to Land's End, covering 897.3 miles in 44 days and raised over £10,000 for the Clattterbridge Appeal and the Fire Brigade Benevolent Fund. Swasie stayed at several Fire Stations en route. He has also been to the Falkland Islands where he retraced the steps of the British Paras during the 1982 war.

******

Special Duties and Reorganisation

Wallasey Policemen patrolled the docks in Liverpool during the disputes between the dockers and management and also when the farmers protested at the imported beef from Ireland. Between two and 12 foot patrols were used.

The Merseyside Police Force was reorganised being implemented on 4 April 1994 when the new Wirral District, with the District Control Room and Coordinator, Chief Superintendent Peter Davenport, based at Manor Road, Wallasey, replaced the Wirral

Community Constables PC George Thomas (left) and PC Ian Thornton with the Mayor's Attendant

Chief Constable of Merseyside Police, Norman Bettison, who was also honoured, said that he was delighted to receive his award but was "more proud that a Constable involved in community work had been similarly honoured".

George is a bobby in the old mould and many folk would love see more of this kind of Constable patrolling the streets of Wallasey. He is grand fellow and greatly respected by his fellow Constables and public alike.

Constable Ian Thornton is the Community Constable in New Brighton. He is well-known in the district both as a Constable and friend. He lives in the resort, takes an active part in events in the area and is also a member of the Lifeboat crew and is involved in their fund rasing activities. Ian was on long duty hours recently when the film crews came to New Brighton making a film about the early life of John Lennon. One lady who visiting the resort came up to him and wanted to know if he were a real Policeman or an actor!

Blonde-haired WPC Michelle Hogg used to be seen in the Liscard Shopping Centre where she became well-known to the shop workers and public.

Helicopter

Advancement meant that the Merseyside Police took charge of a helicopter in 1990s. Contact could be made with the force on the ground and a searchlight could pan the area where a crime had taken place as the aircraft hovered above. Body-heat scanners were used to pick up a person hiding out of view. Sgt. Ian Howe and PC Stuart Knowles made up the helicopter's crew.

Division. The three areas which replaced the former four divisions with a Commander in charge of each were, superintendent Bernie Holmes at Wallasey and Hoylake Area (Wallasey, Moreton Leasowe, Meols, Greasby, Hoylake West Kirby and Caldy), Superintendent Steve Lowe at the Birkenhead and Upton Area (Birkenhead, Rock Ferry, Tranmere, Bidston, Noctorum, Oxton, Beechwood, Woodchurch, Upton, Overchurch and Prenton) and Superintendent Vic Swift at Bromborough and Heswall Area (Bromborough, Heswall, Pensby, Irby, Bebington, Eastham and New Ferry). The Merseyside Police Badge consists of a Crown and the words Merseyside Police encircling E II R.

Gordon Reid became the Community Safety Co-ordinator for Wirral.

Community Constables

Constable George Thomas used to be the Community Constable for the Seacombe Area. He patrolled the beat in his own inimitable way and saw that the Peace was kept. He knew all the shopkeepers in the area, chatted to the locals and was loved by young and old alike. George became a School Governor and worked in close connection with the youth activities in Seacombe, becoming the Chairman of the Allandale Centre (formerly the old Wallasey Boys' Club). At a later date he was transferred to Hoylake being based at Moreton Police Station. Fifty year-old George received the Queen's Police Medal in the Queen's Birthday Honours in June 2000. This top honour is given to Police Officers who have made a significant contribution to Policing. An award justly deserved for his work in the community. George said "I could not have carried on this important work with the young people without the help of the volunteers and staff at the Allandale Youth Centre and I have received tremendous support from the people of Seacombe. It is a tribute to them as much as me and I will be delighted to accept it."

A protective nylon coat for Police Dogs has been tried and may come into general use before long.

CS sprays were introduced as an effective tool for self-defence as there were many assaults on officers over a 12 month period on Merseyside.

People were surprised to see armed Police on duty at the Mersey Tunnel entrances a little while ago.

Sergeant Kehoe said "It is a pro-active exercise; week by week we stand at various places throughout Merseyside to act as an overt deterrent".

Wallasey and Hoylake Police Officers, Deborah Kerr and Det. Constable Simon Fitzpatrick from the Family Support Unit were commended in 1997 by the Chief Constable of Merseyside Police, Sir James Sharples, in recognition of their work during a two year investigation into child abuse.

In October 1997 nine Officers received commendations for outstanding action in the course of their duty. Two Officers from the Operation Support Division were given commendations for arresting three violent men. One of them was wielding a knife. Two Constables received awards for their part in rescuing seven people from a burning house. Councillor Kate Wood of the Merseyside Police Authority made the presentations. Superintendent Steve Cahill said that he was very proud of the award winners.

In 1997, a Control Room was set up at Manor Road Police Station to deal with the 999 calls with Constable Jim Edwards as one of the trained team taking the calls. They had ten seconds to respond to a call and then had to decide whether a Patrol Car was needed. Sport is still encouraged in the Police and the Merseyside Police Football Team play in Division One of the Carlsberg West Cheshire League Division One.

The Police encourage Home Watch groups whose meetings are held throughout Wallasey. They give advice on making homes secure by fitting locks, security chains to front doors and seeing that windows have proper catches fitted. Garden tools must be locked away as these can be used by thieves to force an entry.

"Change Again"

From 1 April 2001 the structure of the Merseyside Police was changed. The two separate areas in Wirral became one Division with Superintendent Val Barker as Area Commander.

The Borough was split into eight neighbourhoods with its own Police Station, Inspector, two Sergeants and eleven Constables. The North Neighbourhood consists of Moreton, Leasowe and Wallasey with Inspector Veeves and the North East Neighbourhood consisting of New Brighton, Liscard and Seacombe with Inspector Bart in charge. Some Constables go out on foot patrol.

British Transport Police

Regarding the British Transport Police, there are 115 based at Lime Street Station and five at Southport Station. The men and women of the BTP are kept busy as railway stations attract people with all sorts of problems. Loneliness, homelessness, drug and alcohol abuse, runaways and others.

The Policemen have their problems too, just like any one else. Stress and worry is high on the list and recently, two serving Officers have committed suicide by throwing themselves under trains.

Chaplain Paul Holloway of the Liverpool City Mission makes regular visits and help is on hand when needed.

The BTP Headquarters are at Rail House where Chief Inspector John Smith is the Commanding Officer.

Best in the World

In the past, sad to relate, there has been the odd member of the Wallasey Force who has committed an offence but by and large they, over the years, have been a fine bunch of dedicated men and women who have served Wallasey over a long period, proving that the British Police are the best in the world.

Postscript

The present-day Police do a very good job considering the financial position. The people of Wallasey would like to see more Policemen on the Beat, rather than in Patrol Cars. Police presence would give more confidence in the neighbourhood. Vandalism costs the Council and other authorities umpteen thousands of pounds annually. The glass in telephone kiosks and bus shelters are smashed for no apparent reason.

Revellers leaving night clubs in New Brighton in the small hours of the morning do not help. In addition to the licenced premises there are so many shops now selling alcohol which creates a growing drink problem.

Measures are being taken to ban all drinking of alcohol in the town's streets. Wirral also has a drug problem among young people and there is a lack of good youth clubs in Wallasey.

Youths gather and do damage in the parks and other public places. Grave stones in cemeteries are pushed over or smashed. People are attacked as they attend graves and these places are not safe to enter. I am sure the situation will improve when we see an increased Police presence.

****

END OF PART ONE

A COMPREHENSIVE LIST OF PERSONEL OF BOTH WALLASEY POLICE AND WALLASEY FIRE BRIGADE APPEARS AT THE BACK OF PART 2: –
THE WALLASEY FIRE BRIGADE

PC Bill Woolley congratulates PC Ernest Warrington on winning one of the Annual Police River Swims in the 1930s